SATYAJIT RAY

Ray at work in his study.

SATYAJIT RAY

A Study of His Films

Ben Nyce

PRAEGER

New York
Westport, Connecticut
London

Library of Congress Cataloging-in-Publication Data

Nyce, Ben.
  Satyajit Ray : a study of his films / Ben Nyce.
    p.   cm.
  Bibliography: p.
  Includes index.
  ISBN 0-275-92666-4 (alk. paper)
  1. Ray, Satyajit, 1922–   . —Criticism and interpretation.
I. Title.
PN1998.3.R4N93   1988
791.43'0233'0924—dc19   88-6620

Library of Congress Catalog Card Number: 88-6620
ISBN: 0-275-92666-4

First published in 1988

Praeger Publishers, One Madison Avenue, New York, NY 10010
A division of Greenwood Press, Inc.

Printed in the United States of America

The paper used in this book complies with the
Permanent Paper Standard issued by the National
Information Standards Organization (Z39.48-1984).

10 9 8 7 6 5 4 3 2 1

For Katy and Chris
—and for Ann

CONTENTS

PREFACE

Satyajit Ray is regarded as one of the world's leading film directors. For the past 25 years or more, his films have enjoyed wide attention around the world and won many international prizes, and yet no detailed study of his films has been published in English in the West. This book is an attempt to fill that gap. As usual, the French have paid consistent attention to his work. One or more of his films is usually on an extended run in Paris at any given time. Henri Micciollo's *Satyajit Ray*, written in French and published in 1983, is the first good comprehensive study of Ray's films published in the West. A careful study of all of Ray's films in English is long overdue. Since several of the films cannot be seen in the West, except at retrospectives and other special showings, this book attempts to describe them in ways which will allow a student of Ray's work to get a visual sense of them without having viewed them. In the discussion of all the films, I've tried to put special emphasis on Ray's cinematic procedures, his way of arranging the flow of images to present his meanings and implications. As a non-Bengali speaker, I've had to rely on subtitles for the verbal dimensions of the films. I've undoubtedly missed some of the subtlety of language as a result. I can only hope my attention to the visuals makes up for this. Ray's gifts as a portrayer of the commonality which underlies human behavior in different cultures have been a great help to me here. Needless to say, any errors of fact or interpretation are entirely my own.

I'd like to add that an international project such as this has affirmed for me, once again, the pleasure and value of cross-cultural effort.

Del Mar, California
1988

ACKNOWLEDGMENTS

During the seven years this book has been in preparation, I have received the help of many people. Above all, I'd like to thank Satyajit Ray for his generosity and support. Also in India, thanks go to Soumitra Chatterjee, Sharmila Tagore, Chidananda Das Gupta, Nemai Ghosh, Soumendu Roy, Ramesh Sen, Manisha Vardhan, Shankar Basu, Malthi Sahai, Subhash Desai, Mangla Chandran, Manji Pendakur, P. K. Nair, Satish Bahadur, Amaresh Chakraburtty, Lall Jaswaney, Vinod and Hira Desai, Mushtaque Ahmed, Sidharta Dutta, T. G. Vaidyanathan, and Dr. R. S. Murthy. In England, thanks to Andrew Robinson and Nici Nelson; in France, Rene Lichtig. In the United States, my gratitude to Zette Emmons, Lee Amazonas, Joan Erdman, Somi Roy, and Barbara Winard; at the University of San Diego, my colleagues Irene Williams, Mary Quinn, Bart Thurber, and Lee Gerlach—and those excellent typists Monica Wagner, Michelle Barlow, and Collette Russell. The staff of the media center at USD was very helpful, as well. Thanks, also, to the University of San Diego for research grants and grants in released time and to the Indo-American Friendship Society for its generous assistance. I'd like to thank the students in my film courses at USD for their insights into Ray's films and for their support. Finally, I'd like to thank Ann Gardner for the encouragement and help she gave me in so many ways.

All photographs used in this book, including the jacket cover, have been taken by Ray's eminent still photographer, Nemai Ghosh.

1
THE WAY TO *PATHER PANCHALI*

Satyajit Ray is one of the best examples in world cinema of the complete director. He writes the script and the music as well as directs. He also does the casting and has a great deal to say about the art direction. Recently, he has even taken on the camera work. Total control of the film medium has enabled him to put a personal stamp on each of his films, even though there is a large variety of subject matter and style in his films. The reason he performs so many tasks of filmmaking is not only that he is multitalented, but that he works generally from small budgets (minuscule by Hollywood standards!). He doesn't have the large budgets given to directors of commercial Hindi films either, because he works outside the commercial system in India. His work can be seen as a consciously created antidote to the formulaic escapism of the Hindi film with its melodramatic plot, improbable settings, and contrived songs and dances. Indeed, it is not an exaggeration to say that the artistically serious film in India finds its early maturity in the work of Ray, Ghatak, Sen, and others—all of them Bengali directors, working in the restricted marketplace of a Bengali-speaking audience. With a gifted director such as Ray, such limitations of marketplace and budget take on the appearance of a positive advantage and point up the problems inherent in our own North American film culture in which so many films seem overbudgeted in terms of special effects, huge salaries for major stars, and a generally dispersed production scheme, with half a dozen script writers, a casting director or two, several editors, and perhaps one director who may be in charge of the project—if the producers don't interfere too much. In order to maintain his creative independence, Ray has avoided such big-budget films as the sweeping historical epic (though *The Chess Players* is a smaller scale effort in the genre) or the science-fiction fantasy loaded with special effects (though his script for *The Alien* would have entailed a large budget).[1] On the whole, he has made what Wim Wenders has called "little films"—those less grandiose efforts which are increasingly absent from our film culture in the United States. His films may be small in scale but they are true, and the best will last a long time.

Another characteristic of Ray's film work is its variety. Like most truly creative artists, Ray likes to try something new rather than repeat past successes. As a result, when one looks over his total film production, one sees an astonishing variety of subject matter and mode of expression. The early mode of poetic realism of *Pather Panchali* (influenced by the neorealism of DeSica and Rosselini) leads to comedy and social satire (*The Philosopher's*

Stone), which gives way to straight documentary (*Tagore*), which is followed by a pure fantasy film replete with songs and dances (*The Adventures of Goopy and Bagha*). Ray's meditative inquiries into the historical past give us such period films as *The Music Room* and *Charulata*, but this distanced perspective is gradually replaced by the harsher political and social urgencies of present-day India in *Pratidwandi* and *The Middleman*. The conventional genres of the horror film (*Monihara*) and the detective film (*The Golden Fortress* and *The Elephant God*) are treated, as is the historical epic (*The Chess Players*). The wide focus in subject matter shifts from rural poverty (*Pather Panchali*) to the upwardly mobile urban middle class (*Company Limited*), or from the life of a famous commercial film star (*Nayak*) to the decline of the zamindar class of landowners at the turn of the nineteenth century (*The Music Room*). Each film, for Ray, is a new project demanding new modes of expression. As a result, though one can arrange some of his films into groups (the social/political films, the historical films, the entertainment films), such an approach conceals a sense of his development as a filmmaker that a chronological approach can best provide. With the exception of the Apu trilogy, I have followed this approach.

Among the many interesting turning points in this development, the most important, it seems to me, involves the period from 1962–70 in which we see Ray moving circuitously, but inevitably, toward an examination of the social/political tensions of Indian urban life. In 1962, Ray makes *Kanchanjungha*, his first close look at contemporary Indian life. Here, he safely and wisely chooses the middle class—the class he knows best because it is his own. In *Abhijan* (1962) and in *Mahangar* (1963) he examines contemporary India as well. There is a sense of experimentation and growth in these films, though they aren't always successful, as in *Abhijan*. With *Charulata* in 1964, he returns to Tagore and to the distant past and accomplishes a masterpiece. The three films following *Charulata*, *The Coward and The Holy Man* (1965), *The Hero* (1966) and *The Zoo* (1967), are well beneath Ray's usual standard of quality. There's a sense of aimlessness and uncertainty in the period immediately following *Charulata* which is quickly redeemed by two superb efforts: *The Adventures of Goopy and Bagha* (1968) and *Days and Nights in the Forest* (1970). It's as if the return to Tagore and the past acts as a kind of touchstone after which, momentarily, there is nothing to say. After having found himself again, Ray is then able to turn to the wrenching problems of contemporary urban life in *The Adversary* (1970) and *Company Limited* (1971).

Ray's great theme is change. Marie Seton says that Ray pointed out to her that all his films are "concerned with the new versus the old."[2] The most obvious manifestation here is the monumental process of change which has taken place in India since the turn of the century—a period during which the country has struggled to move from the feudal past into the twentieth century. Bengal has been the leader in this process of change, particularly that middle-class group of reformers known as the Brahmo Samaj, to which Satyajit Ray is a direct heir, from both his father and from Rabindranath Tagore, the central influence in Ray's intellectual and artistic development. The influence of Brahmoism in Ray's worldview can hardly be overestimated. It accounts for that particular spirit of universality which animates many of his films and makes them so accessible to Western viewers. It also accounts for Ray's humanism—an attitude that seems to say that all human beings have something of value within them, no matter how confused or troubled they may be. Ray's great master, Jean Renoir, expressed this humanism when he said, "everyone has his reasons," but Ray's humanism has its origin not in Renoir, but in his Brahmo heritage. This heritage, particularly from Tagore (who was himself poet, novelist, musician, artist, social reformer, and Indian nationalist), accounts, in part, for Ray's interest in so many aspects of art and his ability to practice them at a high level of skill in his films. Brahmos were often *bhadralok*, a collective term referring to a class of wealthy Hindu traders and businessmen who had a yearning for the best of European learning. As Ian Buruma points out, "they organized reading societies, established English-language schools, stocked libraries, started printing presses, and published newspapers. [They] were the first Indian urban middle class: modern men who sought a spiritual answer to modernization in a fusion of European liberalism and enlightened Hinduism."[3]

The historical aspect of change is, as I've suggested, the most prominent of Ray's concerns. He has remarked that his "overall aim is to depict different facets of Bengal's history."[4] In *The Chess Players*, *The Music Room*, *Charulata*, *Distant Thunder*, and *The Home and the World*, Ray looks at central moments in the development of modern India, using Bengal as his focus. The main emphasis in these films is upon the growth of the movement for independence from England, a major Brahmo interest. There are other Brahmo concerns as well, both in the historical and other films. Most prominent is the emphasis on greater equality for women. This idea is manifest in Ray's films, not as a program of social reform, but as a demonstration in dramatic form of the power and strength of the Indian woman. Indeed, this idea is the most pervasive in all of Ray's work. Another Brahmo concern involves a demonstration of the vicious inequalities of the caste system. As David Kopf has pointed out, Brahmoism, like so many aspects of modern India, had its origins in the West—specifically in the rational faith and social gospel of nineteenth-century American Unitarianism.[5] Influenced deeply by the West, Tagore and other reformers nevertheless struggled to preserve the national character of their movement. Seen in this context, Ray's films are an attempt to establish, in Bengali terms, a national imprint on a cinema largely given over to cheap (but expensive!) adaptations of Hollywood formulas. His history films are attempts to remind his Bengali audiences of the glories of the Bengali past; their goal is to establish a sense of national identity in the face of the enormous influence of the West—an influence which has been welcomed nevertheless in its capacity to exert reform. His nonhistorical films are attempts to depict Bengali life the way it really is (as opposed to the escapist fantasies of the Hindi cinema) and to celebrate the glory of the commonplace. They, too, are attempts to preserve and enhance a sense of national identity. A discussion of Tagore's and Brahmoism's influence occurs in somewhat lengthier form in Chapter 8, the examination of Ray's documentary on Tagore.

Ray presents the theme of change on an intimate, internal level as well as on a large, historical scale. He's especially concerned about internal growth. The growth of Apu from babyhood to mature fatherhood is the best example. On a smaller but no less exquisite scale, there's the awakening of young Pikoo to the problematic nature of existence in the short film, *Pikoo's Day*. When internal change takes place within one of his male characters, a strong woman usually takes the role of helping agent.

This study of Ray's films will attempt to chart his stylistic development and to define that particular quality of rhythm and mood which characterizes his work. For many North American viewers, used to the fast pace of television and our action-oriented films, Ray's films are too slow and, what is more, nothing happens in them. In a typical Ray scene, two characters chat in a desultory fashion with longish pauses during which nothing is said, or they move in a seemingly random way about a room, speaking from time to time in a kind of shorthand. An attentive viewer will see that something is happening beneath the randomness. Ray has the ability to catch the essential in the ordinary, the sense of the large and imminent in the small and supposedly inconsequential. His style tends to avoid big, dramatic scenes in which the director shamelessly manipulates the feelings of the audience. Such keyed-up, melodramatic procedure is foreign to him and when he attempts it, as in *The Hero* (*Nayak*) or *Abhijan* (*The Expedition*), the result is predictably unfortunate. He doesn't want his audience to languish in the total relaxation of melodrama, observing without effort every blatant emotional signpost. He wants his audience to participate actively and attentively in the subtleties and halftones of human behavior. As a result, his films are almost totally lacking in the two main ingredients of Western film fare: sex and violence. Though his scripts are written with great care, with a Flaubertian precision of language, they are essentially nonverbal. They are, as many have noticed, closer to music than to fiction; their structure is as much musical as narrative—or rather, his narratives proceed with an inner musical rhythm. "I feel crucial moments in a film should be wordless, if possible," he has said.[6] The way his characters speak is often more important than what they say. The rhythmic pacing of the cutting strongly suggests a keen musical intelligence. In this regard, two great Western artists are often mentioned when attempting to define the exact flavor of Ray's work: Chekhov and Mozart. Needless to say, Ray is deeply familiar with the work of each.

Ray's attitude is essentially meditative and distanced. He can depict the mythical and the timeless in the ordinary. Such a vantage point is useful in treating subject matter which is distanced in time and place: the rural poverty of the 1920s of *Pather Panchali*, for instance, or the decline of the feudal landlord of the same period in *The Music Room*. One of Ray's greatest challenges as an artist has been to find an attitude and a style which would enable him to depict the strains and difficulties of contemporary India. It hasn't been an easy process for him, but he has managed successfully, particularly in the *The Adversary* and *The Middleman*. The charting of his progress is one of the main endeavors of this study.

How did Ray become a filmmaker? He was born in 1921 into a family of artists/intellectuals. His grandfather, Upendra Kishore, was a writer, artist, scientist, and storyteller for children. His father, Sukumar, was an accomplished illustrator and writer of children's books—many of whose nonsense verses are still read and recited today in Bengal. Sukumar died when Satyajit was only two years old, leaving the family saddled with heavy debts. The family assets had to be sold and Ray and his mother, Suprabha, an accomplished singer and artist, went to live with an uncle. After graduating from Calcutta University in economics, Ray decided to go to Santiniketan, the university founded by Rabindranath Tagore, a close friend of his family, particularly of the grandfather. During his two and a half years at Santiniketan, Ray came alive as a creative intelligence, studying with painters, musicians, and writers. Terminating his education when the Japanese bombed Calcutta, he decided to become a commercial artist. After searching for work in Calcutta for six months, he found a job in a British-owned advertising firm as a layout man and advanced to the position of art director in six years. During this period, he wrote film scripts (one was a Bengali version of *The Prisoner of Zenda* (!), another, an adaptation of Tagore's, *The Home and the World*) and founded, with others, the Calcutta Film Society, where they were able to see Western films unavailable in the commercial cinemas. As he was influenced by Western classical music (Bach, Vivaldi, Mozart), so his early passion was for Western film directors: Capra, Ford, McCary, the American Renoir, Lang, and Lubitch. In 1950, soon after his marriage, he was sent by his advertising agency to London for six months, during which time he managed to see 99 films, often taking detailed notes on matters such as cutting, lighting, and use of music. When he saw DeSica's *Bicycle Thief*, he was convinced that his idea of using nonprofessional actors and shooting mainly outside the artificial studio settings in natural light was entirely feasible. These ideas, which he had entertained well before his encounter with Italian neorealism, were to revolutionize serious filmmaking in India. On the voyage home, he wrote a script for Bibhuti Bhusan's *Pather Panchali*, a novel he had earlier illustrated for a Calcutta publisher. Now began a five-year struggle to turn his script into a film. A search of several months for a producer was unproductive, so Ray decided to put up his own money and shoot a single scene, the marvelous sequence where Apu and Durga go through the field of white flax flowers to see the train. The crew had to catch the flowers before they died or they would have to wait a year; little did they imagine that they would still be unfinished more than two years later. It is mind-boggling to realize that Ray's crew for *Pather Panchali* had almost no experience in filmmaking. Ray himself had none, of course, and his cameraman, Subrata Mitra, had only worked as a still photographer. Only the art director, Bansi Chandragupta, had professional film experience. They learned as they went along—and produced a masterpiece. Ray's wife, Bijoya, pawned her bangles so they could shoot more footage, some daytime scenes at the family house. After another eight months of frustration, during which Ray pawned his treasured books and records and then was cheated three times by middlemen who promised to put him in touch with producers, Ray managed to edit the 4,000 feet of footage he had already shot. This was shown to John Huston who had come to India to scout locations in an early attempt to make *The Man Who Would Be King*. Huston offered to promote the finished product and spoke to his friend, Monroe Wheeler of the Museum of Modern Art, about the high quality of what he had seen. Meanwhile, Ray's mother had managed to approach the chief minister of Bengal, B. C. Roy, who agreed to have the government fund the film in return for sole ownership. The money for *Pather Panchali* (*Song of the Little Road*) came from the West Bengal government agency for road improvement!

Ray now proceeded to push hard for completion, having received an invitation from Wheeler to have the film shown at MOMA. The final ten days before their deadline, the crew worked without sleep. When the completed reels were finally mailed off, Ray fell asleep standing up at the airline counter. The success of *Pather Panchali* at MOMA provided a chance for the film to be shown at Cannes the following year. At Cannes, the film was first shown in a small hall at a decidedly off-hour to a small but influential audience. Directly, it made its presence felt, so that the third showing was made to a large audience in a big hall, and the film went on to win a major award as Best Human Document. It would be pleasant to add that from this point on Ray's reputation was secured, but *Pather Panchali* was given commercial release in London and New York only after its sequel, *Aparajito*, won the Golden Lion award at the Venice film festival in 1957. *Pather Panchali*'s immediate popularity in Bengal did establish Ray as a successful director in the Bengali film industry and enabled him to obtain funding for his subsequent efforts. The days of pawning his books and records and his wife's jewelry were over.

NOTES

1. *The Alien* script (1968) was idiosyncratic for Ray. A science-fiction fantasy which would require a large budget for special effects, the film was promoted in Hollywood but never funded. With the appearance of *E.T.* some years later, Ray accused Steven Spielberg of stealing his idea (from sketches he had done) for the three-fingered visitor from space. Ray's Hollywood venture was, perhaps predictably, a disaster.

2. Marie Seton, *Portrait of a Director* (Bloomington: University of Indiana Press, 1971), p. 143.

3. Ian Burma, "The Last Bengali Renaissance Man," *New York Review of Books*, 38 (November 19, 1987): 12.

4. *Portrait of a Director*, p. 114.

5. David Kopf, *The Brahmo Samaj* (Princeton, N.J.: Princeton University Press, 1979), p. xv.

6. Interview with Satyajit Ray, Calcutta, January 4, 1988.

2

PATHER PANCHALI:
Apu's Childhood

I wish to discuss *Pather Panchali* in relationship to the other films which make up the Apu trilogy, *Aparajito* and *The World of Apu*. Two other films, *The Philosopher's Stone* and *Jalsaghar*, were made between *Aparajito* and *The World of Apu*, but the Apu films are best considered as a whole. Their unity derives, first of all, from the narrative unity of the story of Apu's growth from childhood to manhood. The trilogy also offers a marvelous semi-documentary study of Bengali life in both the rural areas as well as the cities of Benares and Calcutta. The deepest power and unity of the trilogy comes from a different source, however. In its depiction of loss, regeneration, and renewal, the trilogy gives life to an enduring pattern of human existence. How else to explain the strange reaction of refreshment and renewal many viewers have experienced after having seen all three films in a single viewing (the best way to see the trilogy, by the way). Six hours of straight viewing would normally leave any viewer exhausted. The power of Ray's depiction of the pattern of regeneration in Apu's life is the binding force of the trilogy.

The central sequence to *Pather Panchali* ("Song of the little road, or path") involves a seemingly circuitous preparation for young Apu's discovery of death. Apu, about six years old, has witnessed the melodramatic performance of a traveling group of actors. He steals some silver leaf from his older sister, Durga, and makes a small crown for himself and a mustache and sees himself in a mirror, grimacing like the actors. Durga chases Apu into the forest near their home (the path-filled forest in *Pather Panchali* is always a place of mystery and discovery—a fascinating playground for a child, but also a dark and disturbing place, much like the dark, subconscious side of life). While Apu and Durga run through the forest into the open countryside, the film cuts to the old auntie's return to the family home. She has been kicked out by Apu's mother, Sarbojaya, mainly because she is viewed as a parasite and dishonest. She is ill and knows that she hasn't long to live. In a moving close-up, she gives a pleading smile to Sarbojaya, only to be sent away again. Durga has now led Apu to a power pole carrying high voltage electricity through their poor rural area. In this sequence we watch both of them listen to the vibration in the pole, but the camera places us particularly close to Apu in his discovery of this wonderful and strange manifestation of power sent from distant other regions. The pole and the train are Durga's gift to Apu and contribute to his eventual encounter with the larger world. The pole sequence prepares us for the important sequences of discovery that follow. A short passage in which Apu momentarily loses Durga in a field of white-plumed pampas grass intensifies the feeling of uneasiness and mystery. Their discovery of the train introduces one of the major visual symbols of the trilogy and is filmed with particular vividness. This sequence is the first one Ray shot and one of the ones he showed to John Huston. In a medium close-up of Apu and Durga, we first see the train's smoke behind them in the far distance. A shot of the train moving swiftly at a diagonal shows Apu running toward the tracks. We then see him run up to the tracks in a shot in which the fast train separates him and the camera. The final shot shows Apu standing at the tracks in a swirl of smoke. Did the train really exist or was it an illusion? The whole sequence is filmed with the freshness and surprise of childhood. As Apu and Durga return through the forest, playing and chatting, the camera pans ahead to show old auntie dying. Durga sneaks up to her and gives her a playful push; she falls over heavily and her head makes a hollow thump when it hits the ground. Once again the camera focuses on Apu's first sight of death. Significantly, the camera lingers on the dead auntie longer after Durga and Apu have left. We hear her songs, just as we hear them in the funeral procession that follows. Her spirit lives in us and in Apu and Durga. It is a spirit of regeneration and creative play. Her repeated acts of watering the small plant in the dry courtyard, of singing and telling stories, and of maintaining her vitality well into old age make her one of the most influential characters in *Pather Panchali*. Her regenerative powers are very strong. Apu incorporates them in his own growth, for, like her, he will become a survivor.

As I've tried to suggest in my description of the above sequences, *Pather Panchali* is very artfully made, though it has the look and feel of extreme simplicity. This is all the more remarkable when we learn that the film was essentially shot by a group of amateur filmmakers. Only the art director, Bansi Chandragupta, had prior filmmaking experience (his expertise was needed to reconstruct the family home for the large number of studio shots Ray used for sequences in the house and on the porch). The cameraman, Subrata Mitra, had never shot a moving picture before nor, of course, had Ray. They learned as they went along. How does one account, then, for the sophistication of so many of the scenes? The answer would appear to lie in Ray's careful planning; he knew what he wanted to do in each shot, often sketching the precise form of the shot, indicating the lighting and camera movement and so on. Often likened to the documentary simplicity of such studies of folk customs as *Nanook of the North*, *Pather Panchali* has a great deal more artifice than *Nanook*, but it is concealed artifice.

The lyrical rhythms Ray achieves in *Pather Panchali* give a tender and nostalgic feeling to his depiction of childhood. Childhood is vivid and engrossing, he seems to say, but it is also evanescent, sliding into the past even in its most highly charged moments in the present. Often we see Apu alone or with Durga moving along a path in the forest or in the open country. They are walking away from the camera while the *Pather Panchali* theme is played on the flute. The effect is decidedly wistful. They don't know what sorrows are to come. A good example of Ray's manner here can be seen in his depiction of the whole family before the father's departure. Though we don't know it, it is the last time we will see them together. This sequence is a good example of Ray's artfulness. It is prepared for by a fine bridge passage linking it and the episode of the candyman, in which Durga and Apu are unable to buy candy for lack of money. The bridge passage depicts the close of the day and is made up of four shots linked by dissolves. There's a shot of Durga and Apu moving through a large field as they bring the family cow home under a lowering sky. The *Pather Panchali* theme is played on the flute. In the second shot they put the cow in its crude shed. The third shot shows the courtyard in deep dusk as Sarbojaya makes her religious observances at the tulsi plant pedestal; auntie enters the frame and does the same. In the fourth shot we see the silhouettes of the palm trees over the calm, windless water of the pond. The *Pather Panchali* theme is replaced by the sound of someone far off blowing a conch shell. A mood of deep calm has been established.

The family sequence is made up of 18 shots, only a few of which will be described. The family is sitting at night on the little covered porch of their simple house. The camera moves forward and to the left showing Hari doing his accounts, while Apu sits next to him practicing his school work. Auntie comes out of the house and sits down, complaining to herself about not having a proper shawl to protect her from the cold. Sarbojaya, after slapping Durga gently and reprimanding her about not taking care of her hair, sits down with Durga and begins to comb and braid her hair. Durga puts her tongue out at Apu. Auntie tries hard to thread a needle with which to repair her old shawl. Durga asks her mother to give her four braids like her friend, Ranu, who is about to get married. There's a calm, desultory rhythm to the scene. It is quiet; everyone is at peace, comfortable being herself. The camera selects each character for notice, and then pans slowly along the porch before it moves, in the final shot, gradually away into middle distance, showing them all together. In the eleventh shot, the sound of a far-off train is heard and the camera moves to a medium close-up of Apu. It is he who will experience the oncoming changes most fully. When he asks Durga if they can visit the train, there are a brief series of medium close-ups of each one as Durga gives her noncommital response ("mmm"). The cuts in this passage are placed rhythmically so as to enhance the feeling of calm and peacefulness. There is no music. We hear Hari's soft mumblings as he tallies his figures, auntie's grumbling, Durga's and Apu's brief exchange about the train, and the sound of the chirring crickets as the camera pulls away and pans to the right in the final shot, which again shows us Hari and Apu sitting together—a reverse of the camera movement in the opening shot, which gives the sequence a feeling of precise symmetry. The seeming simplicity of this scene is very artfully achieved.

It is hard to describe precisely, but this scene and others like it have a musical structure in the rhythm with which the images come to our eye. We see this musicality in its most literal form when, in several scenes, the speaking characters' words are unheard while the music of the sitar or tabla registers the emotion (the drums accompanying auntie's angry reaction to Sarbojaya's criticism early in the film or, most notably, the use of the wailing dilruba, a cousin to the sitar, to articulate Sarbojaya's grief when she breaks down over Durga's death upon Hari's return). A better example of such musicality can be seen in a brief passage in which auntie rocks baby Apu and sings to him while Durga softly counts some beads. The rocking motion of the cradle and the overlapping sounds of auntie's and Durga's voices are presented in a series of shots, the careful rhythm of which can only be described as musical. Indeed, it is not farfetched to say that the structure of the film as a whole is as much musical as episodic. The repeated references to empty pots and to Sarbojaya's bruised pride have a refrainlike reference to the family's poverty. After auntie's and Durga's deaths, there are a series of refrainlike references to the one gone, the best example of which is the necklace which Apu finds and throws in the pond. Each incident—the train scene, the deaths of auntie and Durga, the candyman, the public performance of the melodrama—leaves an echo of images as a stone dropped in still water produces ripples. The structure of the film is the structure of memory—of a vivid presentation of a present incident (the awakening child) and an echo of the incident in the remembering mind (the mature adult who looks back). For example, directly after Durga and Apu encounter the candyman, there is a lengthy pan shot of them reflected in the water of the pond as they follow along behind him. The use of the reflection in the water and the sitar music which accompanies this shot suggests both activity in the present and a memory of that activity. When Apu discovers, late in the film, the necklace Durga has hidden, the shot of him reaching high up on the shelf is a nearly identical repeat (an echo) of his stretching to reach up to the same shelf to get Durga an ingredient for the mango treat they enjoy so much together in an early episode. The film catches precisely in its images the partially elegiac tone of the novel by Bibhuti Bhusan, on which it is based. Moreover, the film establishes a characteristic tone for Ray—the note of distance, of reality perceived through the lens of time.

From the opening shots of the film Durga is connected closely to auntie, and it is Durga's death which affects Apu the most. The opening sequences show this connection when Durga steals a guava from her neighbor's yard and hides it in a pot, only to have auntie find it and "appropriate" it. They are identified chiefly in the playful attention they give one another. Auntie is most like Durga in her childlike dependency and play. When Durga falls ill, water images are associated with her oncoming death. The pond near the forest and its water bugs and lily pads are used to suggest the idyllic calm as well as the coming storm which accompanies her death. When she bathes in the first rains of the monsoon, while little Apu watches and waits under a tree, we are reminded that she is on the verge of womanhood. After she dies and Apu discovers among her possessions the necklace she denied she had stolen, he throws it into the algae-covered pond. The opening in the algae seems about to close completely, but stops with an inch or two to spare; like auntie's, Durga's spirit lives and will continue to nourish Apu. This process of regeneration is beautifully promised when, shortly after, Sarbojaya draws a bucket of water slowly out of the dark well into the sunlight. Accompanying all of these important images, Ravi Shankar's sitar rhythmically speaks of the strong pulse of renewed life.

The basic pattern of Apu's growth involves passages in which he sees (and we see) the beauty and cruelty of life. Our first view of him, at about six years of age, underlines the double nature of this seeing process. Apu is asleep under a blanket and Durga lifts up a fold and reveals a hole directly over his eye. The eye opens and sees, and then Apu sits up fully exposed to our sight. We see him seeing. Again, during his earliest schooling, Apu witnesses the beating of another student. This scene is a preview of his witness to the violent beating given Durga by her mother after a neighbor has accused Durga of stealing the necklace. In both sequences, the camera looks mainly at Apu's sensitive reaction. Finally, Apu witnesses his father's intense grief when he learns of Durga's death after returning from months of job seeking. Significantly, Apu is wearing a shawl and holding an umbrella in this sequence. He is no longer wearing his childhood clothes; he is growing up.

The depiction of Sarbojaya and Hari is important to our understanding of Apu's growth. Hari is essentially an absent father. True, he loves his wife and children, but he's off in a different world. He's a dreamer, who's somehow absent even when he's present. He loves writing plays, but he doesn't seem to have any sense of the danger of his family's poverty. He believes that things will always work out for the better, that money he is owed will come in eventually and that they will survive. He's a sweet, kindly, loving, and unworldly man who always has a few pennies for his kids when they want candy or want to go to a fair. He goes away from the family, on the promise of work, and stays away about six or seven months and never seems to be worried (if his two postcards are any indication) that his family may be starving. Only a kindly neighbor's gifts of food and money preserve them. When he returns to discover the house in a state of wreckage after the terrible storm during which Durga dies, he is not immediately aware from Sarbojaya's manner that something is radically wrong. He starts pulling out the gifts he's brought, only to be interrupted with the news of his daughter's death. He lives in his own head more than in the real world.

As a result, the stress of the family's survival devolves upon Sarbojaya. If she often seems petulant and even mean (particularly in her treatment of old auntie), it is because she's in the difficult position of doing all the worrying about the family without being able to do anything about their situation (she's not a wage earner). The opening scenes of the film show her scalded pride as she hears the neighbors criticizing Durga for stealing fruit from their forest—the forest she and Hari used to own before they had to sell it to pay for his father's debts. She is terribly sensitive to the family's standing in the community; she kicks auntie out for "ruining" Durga by encouraging her to steal fruit. When Durga is accused of stealing the necklace, she's so humiliated she attacks Durga in a rage. She says she won't accept any help from her neighbor, even when the neighbor discovers that the family has less than a handful of rice left (empty pots are as prevalent an image in the film as paths and trains). Her devotion to Apu and Durga (particularly Apu) sustains her and enables Apu to have a nourishing childhood. He knows that he is loved. He'll have a struggle separating from his mother (in *Aparajito*), but essentially he is given the power to follow his own path. As for his father's absence, it is worth pointing out that Apu follows the same pattern even more severely after the death of his wife in the birth of his son (in *The World of Apu*). It takes the mediation of a close friend to bring him back into a close friendship with his son. It is at this point, in breaking the pattern of his father, that he enters full manhood.

The film suggests the intimate relationship between loss and growth, or between destruction and creation. This can be seen clearly in Ray's depiction of Durga's oncoming death, a sequence worth looking at in some detail. The preparatory sequence to Durga's death scene, in which she bathes in the heavy monsoon rain and catches a chill—her destruction, in short—is linked to her growth into puberty and to entry into marriageable age. The sequence is introduced by two fine shots of water lilies on the pond, lifting their edges or swaying as the freshening wind catches them. Durga puts *kajal* on her eyes and *bindi* on her forehead, and then plants a sapling in a ritual act of worship in which young girls pray for a good husband. Sarbojaya lies relaxed, for a change, on the porch; she's just heard that Hari is returning. As the storm approaches, Durga quickly winds up her ritual and runs off into the fields with Apu, who has just returned from school. There's a quickened beat to the rhythm of the shots here, as the first rains of the monsoon approach and new life is promised. A humorous shot shows the first drop of rain striking the bald pate of a fisherman. As the downpour begins, Apu runs under a tree to the accompaniment of a lively sitar, flute, and drums. The heart of the 23-shot sequence now begins with a shot of Apu watching Durga, who is standing near the pond (shot 8). Shot 9 is a fine, medium-long shot of Durga in the rain as she bends forward, her long, heavy hair hanging down. In shot 14 she turns round and round, her hair swinging beneath her. There's a feeling here of her emerging womanliness, even though two shots earlier she childishly puts her tongue out at Apu in response to his call. When she puts her shawl around the shivering Apu as they sit under the tree, she's once again his loving, adored sister. The final shot of the sequence shows Durga chanting "Rain, rain, go away!" as she sneezes twice. The opening shot of her death sequence follows immediately—a close-up of the doctor listening to his stethoscope. She's been suffering from fever in recent weeks, and her death is near. The death sequence (at night during a storm) is dramatic, even melodramatic, and not nearly as subtle or as powerful as the sequence of Apu and Durga at the pond.

Pather Panchali remains in the eye's memory as a film of startlingly fresh visual perception. This poem of childhood has, in so many of its images, childhood's feelings of first sight: the train; the field of pampas grass; the shadow-filled forest; the dry, dusty courtyard; the military band playing "Tipperary"; the paths leading out into the wider world; Durga bathing in the rain; the wind blowing the lily pads on the pond. The film has a lyrical flow unmatched by its two companions. It is a superb opening to the story of Apu's growth and regeneration. Like the few other first films worthy of the term "great," the film has the feel of a director already at home in his new medium (*Citizen Kane* is the best example). There is no sense of awkwardness or uneasiness. Indeed, after several viewings, one is struck by the mastery of Ray's essentially musical approach to his visual procedure. The rhythmic linking of the shots reveals a sense of timing which is rare in a first film.

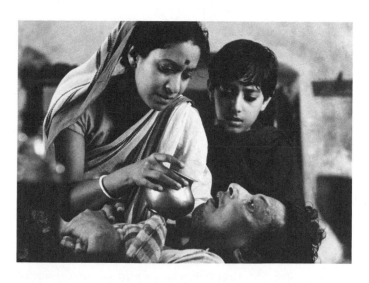

3

APARAJITO
(THE UNVANQUISHED):
Apu's Youth

Aparajito dramatizes the deaths of Apu's father and mother and Apu's growth into young manhood and independence. The film covers a lot of ground. It shows us young Apu, still a child of his family, and Apu as a young man at the university. These roles are played by different actors. The film also moves from Benares to the village, and then to Calcutta. Though there's a lot of movement in time and place, the film isn't rambling, as some have suggested,[1] but basically sound in its structure. It is divided into three nearly equal parts, the first of which deals with the family's life in the city and the father's sickness and death. The second part shows Apu's rejection of the priesthood, his early education in secondary school, and his determination to go to the university in Calcutta. The third part dramatizes Apu's life in the university and his mother's gradual weakening and death. The end of each part shows Apu's growth through loss: of his father; of a close, dependent relationship with his mother in part two; and finally of his mother herself. The pattern of regeneration begun in *Pather Panchali* is continued.

The opening shots of the film present us with a vastly different environment than the rural village setting of *Pather Panchali*. The family has moved to Benares, where the father has found work as a priest and as a seller of medicinal herbs. The camera observes Apu as he strolls along the Ganges, watching the worshipers, bathers, exercisers and, most particularly, Harihar as he conducts his services at the edge of the holy river. As in *Pather Panchali*, we watch Apu as he sees this new world for the first time. Ray's use of bird images is especially striking here. The pigeons which live along the river seem constantly to be spinning and wheeling in the air. In part they represent the aspiring human spirit and their movement complements the rituals of the worshipers. These early images also build toward the brilliant use of bird flight at the moment of Harihar's death.

The family's situation in Benares is both better and worse. It is better because they have money to buy food and sundries. Sarbojaya has a rare, pleased look on her face when she gives Hari a list of things to buy at the market, and he replies by saying, with his usual optimism, that if they don't have money, their credit is at least good. On the other hand, they have little privacy in their small apartment. As Sarbojaya washes dishes, there's a steady traffic of neighbors in the common courtyard. Later she's nearly attacked by a monkey in the courtyard. The sense of crowded living is inescapable in the opening sequences. This is fine for Apu; he enjoys scampering around the mazelike streets and alleys with his friends, discovering surprising new things every day. But the city is also a strange and even threatening place to Apu and his family. For instance, when Apu's mother sends him to borrow some matches from a neighbor, the camera, shooting from behind Apu, shows us his approach to the neighbor's door, his sight through a crack in the door of the man's thick back, the sound of his singing, and then the encounter with the neighbor, in which the man attempts to conceal a bottle of liquor he is holding only to assure Apu that it's medicine he needs for his health. Not much later this man makes a sexual approach to Apu's mother, and after that he seems to lurk at the fringe of their lives. In another instance, Apu's father brings home a fellow priest who shows inordinate interest in Apu and who makes a series of ingratiating comments about Harihar's chanting and then indirectly asks for money.

The Benares section is the finest part of the film. Harihar's death, which culminates it, is worth looking at in close detail. The death is presented in religious terms, quite suitable to his sweet and loving nature and to his priestly vocation. This extended sequence is made up of 41 shots. In the first three shots, we see Harihar struggling up the long flight of stairs from the Ganges. He has gone down to bathe much too soon after an episode of fever. A woman in an alley sees him stagger at the top of the stairs, and we have a shot from her viewpoint down the dark alley as he collapses in the sunlit entrance to the alley (it's like a telescopic view). In the background of the first shot, as Harihar staggers on the stairs, we see the whirling, spinning flight of pigeons. While Harihar is being examined by a doctor at home, Apu is watching water being pulled up in a large leather sack from a deep well by two cows. This is an echo of the water-drawing images in *Pather Panchali* and is a meaningful visual reference to processes of regeneration and renewal. The film then cuts back to Sarbojaya as she is nearly molested by the upstairs neighbor. I don't think this brief seven-shot episode is unnecessary, as Chidananda Das Gupta has suggested.[2] It reinforces our awareness of Sarbojaya's (and Apu's) vulnerability as they live in this strange, new city without the help of extended family. In the light of early morning, Harihar's face is more drawn (shot 25). He moans for a drink of sacred water from the river and Apu is sent, rubbing sleep from his eyes, to get it. He runs down the steep steps of the ghat, pausing with the water to notice the exercise clubs belonging to the bodybuilder he had watched earlier in the film and also to glance at a man doing knee bends in the distance (shots 32 and 33). This pause seems to me to be the only false note in the sequence. Apu knows his father is dying and that he must hurry with the water, but Ray wants to remind us of the presence of rude physical vigor in the midst of death (everything is mixed). Apu's pause is not from within him but is a thematic gesture by Ray. When Sarbojaya gives her husband the water, Apu has been positioned by Ray so that he witnesses his father's death agony at close hand. The shot of Harihar's quivering mouth and bulging eyes as he struggles to receive the water (shot 37) is from the wife's position's, not from Apu's, for it is she who will experience the greatest loss. As Harihar's head falls back, there is an abrupt cut to the pigeons bursting into flight from one of the stone parapets over the river (shot 38)—a magnificent image of the soul's departure from the body. This shot has been carefully prepared by the other bird shots earlier in the film; in fact, we've seen the pigeons on top of this same parapet in four of the first dozen shots of the film. The explosive sound of the birds' wings is replaced by a mournful, grieving melody on the flute. There is another shot of the birds flying off the parapet by the hundreds—this time, a low shot showing the parapets in silhouette—as the flute melody continues. The final two shots of the sequence show Apu being dressed for the funeral, then walking slowly in the processional along the river.

The sequences which open part two show Sarbojaya's grief and uneasiness as she and Apu are forced to take a job cooking and helping with a wealthy family in a large house in the countryside. Like his mother, Apu is now a servant. He scratches the head of a dozing man and is given a coin and then waved off imperiously. But he manages to find many things to interest him, particularly the monkeys who inhabit a nearby temple and ring the temple bells. Sarbojaya is deep in a mourning which is moving toward melancholia. Asked if she would like to move with the family to another location, she assents with no enthusiasm, no affect. Her mistress tells her that she's concerned that Sarbojaya has not been eating. In a particularly evocative sequence, we see her slowly descend the stairs toward the camera as she observes Apu lighting a pipe for his master. Her face is tragic and fretful. Apu is the sole subject of her concern now. As she moves her head abruptly to one side, the camera follows this movement and we hear a train whistle. The film then cuts to a shot of a fast-moving train going over a bridge, within which Sarbojaya and Apu are riding. In this brief transition Ray dramatizes, wordlessly and with both smoothness and economy, Sarbojaya's decision to accept the offer of an uncle to use a small house in the country. It is worth pointing out here that the brilliant economy of this kind of transition is a measure of the greater cinematic sophistication Ray brought to *Aparajito*, when compared with *Pather Panchali*. As the landscape flows by the window of the train, we hear the *Pather Panchali* theme played on a flute, and Sarbojaya's face softens. The setting of the uncle's house is particularly telling, with its pond, paths, and forest. The house itself is very like the one in *Pather Panchali*. Apu has returned to the setting of his childhood. He can remain here if he chooses, or he can grow into his own manhood and independence. Significantly, there is a train Apu and Sarbojaya can see from the house (it is nearer than the one in *Pather Panchali*); the potential for change and growth is always present—and in fact, for Apu, more possible than before. This is the setting for the struggle between Sarbojaya and Apu which follows.

The pull of the past is especially strong upon Apu. The uncle wants him to be a priest like himself (and like his father), and Apu begins his training. But he is drawn to a local school and does so well there that, at 16 or 17 (in a nicely managed foreshortening), he's chosen to go to the university in Calcutta. Sarbojaya resists this idea. The first stage of Apu's separation from his mother is accomplished after they have a fight in which she strikes him and then lovingly gives him the money she saved from her earnings as a cook. In the sequence that closes part two, Apu walks away from the house toward the train station carrying a globe of the world the principal has given him. The world is before him. Sarbojaya stands smiling in the doorway, then she looks aside and down, her face turning to deep grief. By this time in the film we know that she is severely depressed and, without Apu, likely to get worse.

Part three involves a good deal of cross-cutting between Sarbojaya and Apu. As his world expands, hers shrinks to the point of nothingness. Her decline emphasizes his growth and regeneration. His growth isn't achieved without a struggle and without guilt. When he dozes in class we're given to understand, in a subtle way, that it's not only because he is tired from his work at the printing press but also because he's homesick. At the same time, however, he's learning a lot and finding the experience exciting (Ray uses the same quick montage he used in the secondary school sequence to show the learning process). When Apu and his friend, Pulu, take a break from classes (they've actually been kicked out for not paying attention), Ray has their conversation occur on a grassy area overlooking the harbor, with boats from all over the world plying back and forth.

Though he doesn't know it, Apu's first visit to his mother during school holidays will be the last time he sees her. Characteristically, she sits outside the house waiting to see the train which will bring him, and Ray uses a nice shot of the tightening rope of the bucket she's using to draw water to suggest her excitement when she hears his voice (this shot echoes two similar shots of the bucket and rope in *Pather Panchali*). Her continuing anxiety is shown when Apu bathes in the pond and she worries that he'll catch cold. She's remembering Durga's death from fever after becoming chilled in a rainstorm. Later that night she tries to tell Apu about her poor health, her lack of appetite and anxiety, and her hope to come to Calcutta eventually and live with him, but he has fallen asleep. It is clear from this scene that Sarbojaya is failing. She seems totally unable to move out of the tight enclosure of her depression. Nothing in the world is able to call her out of herself. Apu, on the other hand, has had a glimpse of the larger world. He is bored with the kind of amusements which used to excite him and Durga: the candyman, a drummer, and acrobat. He wanders around the village as if it has nothing to offer him. Having looked forward to his return, he now finds that he can hardly wait to leave. At the deepest level, as in the scene when he falls asleep, he is resisting his mother's signal that he must help to rescue her. Unconsciously he knows that if he is to survive, he must move in a different direction than his mother. Her decision not to awaken him at sunrise so that he can return to Calcutta on the train is a sign of her desperation. She reacts to her behavior as if she's committed a kind of crime. Apu leaves without saying goodbye. At this point Ray provides an incident which will spare Apu in the future. While waiting at the station Apu decides to return home. The visuals here do the work. He is sitting by a post, as is his mother at home. They are in the same place, regretful of the harshness of their parting and wanting to make it up. His 24-hour visit allows them to part on good terms and prevents him from experiencing severe guilt at her death.

Apu is neglectful of his mother, however. He writes her that he can't come home when the next holidays occur because of pressing university work. His friend, Pulu, doesn't seem entirely convinced when Apu cheerfully tells him that his mother won't mind if he doesn't go home. This scene occurs on a lawn at the university, with Apu lying near a young tree. The cross-cut to Sarbojaya shows her sitting against an old tree near the house. Here, they are not in the same place. Apu is full of youthful good spirits and self-concern, while Sarbojaya is in extreme decline. Her hair is disheveled. There are dark circles under her eyes. She deflects the aid offered to her by a couple of neighbors. She has given up.

The depiction of her death is one of the finest cinematic renderings of natural death I know of. It is introduced by a shot of the darkening face of the sundial Apu made. This shot gives the basic strategy of Ray's depiction of her death: diminishing light. The camera pans down the great, old tree to show her looking out to the train in the distance. She tries to rise but has difficulty (low tremolo on the sitar). There's a shot of a burning candle in a niche by the front steps on which she waits. She thinks she hears Apu call and moves to see him coming along the path, but her eyes are held by reflections of light which are coming through the trees from the darkening pond; then she sees the dimming paths of light cast by fireflies against the dark water. Finally, the screen becomes completely dark, with only the diminishing sound of the crickets. The effect is powerful and extraordinary. It was not achieved without effort, for Ray found that the faint light of actual fireflies could not be recorded on film. He resorted to the studio, where he had his actors and assistants dance around holding flashlights in front of a black background. This shot was then superimposed upon the shot of the pond.[3]

Apu's struggle for freedom has exerted deteriorating pressures upon his mother. As Robin Wood points out in his extensive study of the trilogy,[4] the process of creation also involves destruction and loss—that, one might add, the two processes are inseparable if there is true regeneration. It should be added, however, that Sarbojaya is more the cause of her own decline than Apu.

Upon his return to discover his mother dead, Apu is again presented with choice. His uncle tells him to return to the priesthood, that it was good enough for his father. But Apu has already made his choice. The final shot shows him walking away from the village, down the path to the train station. The camera makes a subtle movement downward to show the immense sky above Apu as he walks into space. The final image is not visual. A good ten to fifteen seconds after the screen has darkened, the grieving melody of Shankar's sitar turns into joyous and promising rhythms.

If Sarbojaya's death is, in a partial sense, the price Apu pays for his growth, it is also the measure of that growth. Sarbojaya is totally unable to experience regeneration. From Durga's death onward, she is in irreversible decline. She is the weakest woman character in all of Ray's films. In part this may be due to the fact that she's a simple countrywoman, untrained to support herself. She doesn't have the sustenance of the extended family, either. As a woman of limited internal resources, living alone is terribly hard for her. She doesn't seem to make friendships easily or want them. She is essentially a depressive, the primary cause of which we do not know. The dark spot within her, which begins to enlarge itself at Durga's death, finally consumes her. In the face of her decline and death, Apu's obedience to the life force within him seems all the stronger.

The main unifying device in *Aparajito* is not its three-part structure but a pattern of visual repetitions which Ray employs throughout the film. I've pointed out the echoes of *Pather Panchali;* a similar system of cross-reference or repetitions is present within the film itself. The repeated shots involve the same setting presented from the same camera position, but with different lighting and, of course, different actions taking place within the setting. *Pather Panchali* utilizes this pattern as well, but it is most noticeable in *Aparajito* and indicates a simple, subtle strategy which Ray employs in all his films. For example, Ray focuses upon two or three elements of the simple house in the country, where Sarbojaya and Apu move from Benares. One element is the doorway to the house. In the first shot in which we see the doorway used, Sarbojaya enters the house slowly for the first time. The camera moves behind her, then stops at a medium distance and observes her entrance to the dusty courtyard. Because the set is designed to be like the house in *Pather Panchali* (and yet different from it), we know that Sarbojaya is thinking of her former home. In the second doorway shot Apu calls his mother to notice the train in the distance, and she comes up behind him, putting her hands on his shoulders and slowly lowering her head so that it touches his. In the third shot, Sarbojaya stands in the doorway as she says good-bye to Apu as he leaves for the university, her face turning to sadness and abandonment. The fourth doorway shot shows Sarbojaya waiting to greet the imagined Apu, her eyes hollow, her hair down. It is from this doorway that she sees the darkening pond. The fifth shot is a repetition of the first doorway shot in which the camera, from a middle distance outside the house, shows the grieving uncle standing in the court-yard. Another example has to do with Apu's leavetakings. Directly after the third doorway shot, in which Sarbojaya looks forlorn, there's a shot of Apu walking away down the path. He is part-way along when he turns to look back. The second time he leaves, after his mother has failed to wake him up, the camera catches him at the same place in the path, but he doesn't turn to look back. Both of these shots are taken from the same camera position, Sarbojaya's point of view. Still another example involves two arrivals at the village house. In the first, Sarbojaya, Apu, and their porters come along the path near the pond and then enter the house for the first time. In the second, Apu returns home from the university. In each shot the camera starts at a high angle, picking up the character(s) at the same place on the path and then panning to the right as they move toward the house. It is the same time of day in each shot; the light is the same. In fact, these two shots were undoubtedly shot at the same time, not only for reasons of economy but because Ray wished to use their repetition. If I am correct about the time the shots were made, we have a good example here of how a fine artist uses the economic constraints of a tight budget for creative purposes. Many directors shoot a number of shots in a given setting at one time, but it is Ray's particular purpose to make these shots slight variations of each other. The rhythms of life are constant, he seems to say, beneath the turbulence and seeming variety.

One effect of such repetitions—and I've focused only on the village epi-sodes—is to give the viewer a firm sense of the place within which repeated acts occur. This full, three-dimensional sense of place is a cardinal charac-teristic of Ray's work. We feel we, too, have lived in this particular space, with its familiar objects, its familiar slant of light. But the main effect of the repetitions is to suggest continuity within change. There aren't any jagged, fragmented happenings which seem unrelated to what has gone be-fore, as in many action-oriented Western films, or films which leave it up to the viewer to put the pieces together, or films dealing with disturbed or dissociated personalities. The painful episodes of loss and violence (the at-tempted sexual attack) are all parts of a larger pattern, like the great flow of the Ganges itself. This cosmic view of humanity is both unfamiliar to West-ern eyes and comforting at the same time. If it has the slight chill of a distant perspective, it also promises peacefulness and resolution, could we but attain it.

Ray's own attitude to the suffering of his characters, it should be added, is by no means distant and unfeeling. He clearly loves his characters and sympathizes with them. Their pain and joy is, nevertheless, presented in the context of the infinite and the cosmic.

NOTES

1. Chidananda Das Gupta, *The Cinema of Satyajit Ray* (New Delhi: Vikas, 1980), p. 23.

2. Ibid., p. 24.

3. Marie Seton, *Portrait of a Director* (Bloomington: Indiana University Press, 1971), p. 130.

4. Robin Wood, *The Apu Trilogy* (New York: Praeger, 1971).

4

APUR SANSAR
(THE WORLD OF APU):
Apu's Maturity

The World of Apu (*Apur Sansar*, 1959) describes Apu's marriage, the loss of his beloved wife, his prolonged melancholy, his eventual regeneration through the love of his son and his friend Pulu. It is the final film of the Apu trilogy and the finest. Oddly enough, it is the shortest of the three films (*Pather Panchali* and *Aparajito* are the other two), and yet it has the feeling of the greatest density and weight. Only in the later *Charulata* does Ray equal the supreme achievement of *The World of Apu*.

Perhaps one reason Ray was able to function at the top of his powers in the film is that he didn't undertake the project directly after *Aparajito*. Instead, he turned his energies to a comedy/satire in *The Philosopher's Stone*, and then to an elegy on the end of the feudal era in *The Music Room*. Having "taken a break" from the Apu story and stretched his creative interest in other directions, he was then able to turn to the completion of the trilogy with newly enlarged and refreshed powers. As a result, *The World of Apu* has an overflowing abundance of superb sequences. Even the less important sequences are superb and the minor roles excellently cast (the landlord's visit to Apu; the neighbor lady's concern for Apu and Aparna, and later for Apu alone; the conversation with Mr. Roy, who reads Apu's mail; the interview with the manager of the labeling factory; and the conversation with the fellow typist who's bored with his wife and goes to prostitutes). Before I discuss Ray's cinematic procedure in seven of the major sequences, I would like to offer a rather lengthy examination of the thematic implications of the plot of the film.

The opening sequences present us with Apu at age 25 or so. He has graduated from the university and is leading the life of a poor, unemployed artist and writer. We can be sure he is going to go through many changes when we see that he is living in a run-down room next to the train tracks. Those agents and symbols of change, the trains have moved from the background of *Pather Panchali* to the foreground of *The World of Apu*. He owes three month's rent and his landlord is about to throw him out. After looking briefly for work as a teacher and in a labeling factory, he decides he must sell his precious books. At this point, his old friend from university days, Pulu, shows up and asks Apu to go with him to his sister's wedding in a countryside he describes in very romantic and exotic terms. Pulu counsels Apu to get a job, settle down, and stop wasting life in dreaming and flute playing. In response Apu tells Pulu that he has just had a story called "A Man of the Soil" accepted for publication. He then tells Pulu the story of the novel he is writing. It is about the growth of a boy into manhood. The boy has talent but he doesn't really succeed. The important thing, says Apu, is that the young man never turns his back on life; he continues to live and to grow even though life is always difficult for him. At this point the theme from *Pather Panchali* returns on the flute. Apu's words are defenses against Pulu's criticisms, and they also indicate that *The World of Apu* is about the two films which precede it in the sense that Apu has grown now to the point where he can look back on his earlier life and begin to offer, in the form of a novel, some understanding of himself. The Apu we see here is very much the young romantic idealist, confident of his own powers, absorbed in his own visions and unaffected by poverty. He is like his father.

The section dealing with Apu's unexpected marriage is presented with great warmth and humor, as is all of the first part of *The World of Apu*. As Apu lies napping in the shade of a tree, the bridegroom is found to be deranged and Apu is quickly enlisted as a substitute groom, for the bride must marry at the appropriate time or become a pariah, along with her family. In many of these shots, the river flows steadily behind the foreground action, like the trains and paths of the earlier films. Apu's decision to marry, partly based on Pulu's chiding, is most fortunate. The sequences of his and Aparna's married life in his room in Calcutta are full of domestic pleasure and tranquility. We are further reminded of Apu's father when we see him playing the flute while Aparna scrubs and cleans the apartment. But their love for each other is cruelly short-lived. Aparna leaves to visit her family, where she plans to have their child. After a brief exchange of letters, Apu learns that she has died in childbirth but that the child lived. Having lost auntie, sister, father, and mother, this death is almost too much to bear. After lying for days in his room, he goes down to the train tracks and nearly commits suicide.

The scenes of Apu's emergence from the initial trauma are the most problematic in the film for a Western viewer. He goes to the ocean and watches the waves breaking on rock and sand. His face is bearded, grieving. He walks in a forest, listening to birdsong, looking about him in awe and wonder. Now heavily bearded, he stands on a hilltop and watches the sun rise. These three short sequences, connected by slow dissolves, are full of a renewed sense of first sight and first sound. Apu's grief has opened him to the wonder of the simplest elements of nature. It is as if he has returned to the freshness and newness of his childhood—but only "as if," for these sequences have a different tonality than the awakening scenes in *Pather Panchali*. After looking at the sunrise, he sits down on the hilltop and slowly takes up the pages of his novel and lets them fall into the valley. He is abandoning some central part of his creative self to his grief. A sweetly lyrical flute song accompanies the act. The screen becomes dark for several frames.

Certain details of Apu's posture are worth noting here. After he has gently released the last page, his arms are bent at the elbow, hands raised to chest height, with palms up. There is a sense of completion and calmness to his posture which is echoed by the flute. The effect is decidedly iconographic. Robin Wood is correct when he says that the camera gives him "an almost saint- or prophet-like stature."[1] But Wood goes on to say that the ocean, forest, mountaintop sequence is the most unsatisfactory of the film. I agree that the sequence is not one of the best in the film (it is out of key with the poetic realism of the other scenes), but it does have an important function in our understanding of Apu. Perhaps it is helpful to consider this sequence in religious terms. Apu is seen in a posture of calm transcendence, above and unconnected to other human beings. This transcendence is the second stage of his grief and leads into the prolonged, subterranean depression of his work in the mine, which is the third stage (the first is his angry, death-seeking stage). Chidananda Das Gupta helps us understand this sequence by observing that "Apu has become a *sannyasi* [a seeker of the truth who has rejected the world]; he has given up all claims to life and he no longer needs his novel."[2] The important aspect here is the religious. Apu has earlier been likened to the god Krishna by Aparna's mother. Krishna is an incarnation of Vishnu, and he is also a flute player. It doesn't seem too farfetched to suggest that Apu himself has elements of the god Krishna within him and that he himself is going through stages of regeneration which can be likened to incarnations. Ray's need to use different actors to play the growing Apu even makes a contribution here. As Apu's spirit moves through its various growths, his body takes different forms. He is both single and multiple; he is the same Apu throughout the trilogy, and yet he is in the process of becoming different from his prior selves—or, more accurately, of becoming more and more himself.

The film now turns to observe the development of Apu's son, Kajal, who is now five years old and has been left in the care of his grandparents. We observe him wearing a mask as he hunts with a slingshot in a palm forest. Though we can't see his face, we sense at once that he is very much like the young Apu of *Pather Panchali*. When he finally removes the mask, our anticipation to see his face uncovered is the same as when the young Apu emerged from under the blanket in *Pather Panchali* or peeked out from behind the corner in *Aparajito*. Though Apu has not been near him for five years, Kajal informs a servant that his father will break his neck if the servant punishes him. Kajal's energetic and inquisitive spirit, so like the young Apu's, is regarded in this household of older folks as merely rebellious. He is seen as a ne'er-do-well and rather harshly punished, and he responds accordingly. When Pulu looks at Kajal, standing alone at the gate, he sees Apu and resolves to make contact with him to attempt to bring him and Kajal together. Pulu's agency is once again crucial to Apu's fate.

The scene between Pulu and Apu is shot, not surprisingly, on a road near the mine where Apu has been working for over a year (the mine is a fitting indicator of Apu's profound depression). Apu tells Pulu that he just happened to stop off at the mine. When Pulu brings up Kajal, Apu says that the child killed Aparna and that he has no love for him. He walks away, but Pulu pursues him and begs him to see Kajal and tells him that the boy needs him. Apu again rejects Pulu by walking away. One has the feeling that he could continue walking away from Pulu, the mine, everything; but he searches for Pulu after he has gone away.

The last section of the film describes Apu's return to health through the growth of his love for his son. At first Apu tries to bribe Kajal with gifts and stories, but Kajal is suspicious and angry at this "father" who has stayed away so long. Apu begins to form a connection with Kajal when he prevents the grandfather from beating Kajal after he has thrown a stone at them. But Apu's persistent attempts seem finally to fail and he sets off on foot, only to discover Kajal tentatively following. Apu stops and Kajal questions him at a distance: "Will you take me to my father? Will he be angry with me? Will he ever leave me? Who are you?" Apu says, "I am your friend," and in saying this, he smiles for what seems like the first time. They set off together.

One of the great pleasures of watching *The World of Apu* lies in our observation of two of Ray's finest actors at work. Soumitra Chatterjee as Apu and Sharmila Tagore (at age 13) as Aparna are wonderfully cast. In the beginning of the film, we are drawn to this poor but handsome writer who laughs so easily despite all the hardship we know he has suffered in the two earlier films. We wish him well and are buoyed by his good fortune in being matched with the exquisite Sharmila Tagore. The growth of their love is so movingly presented that her death is hard to take. It is a *Love Story* without the syrup, false sentiment, and elitist social setting. A detailed examination of several of the most potent sequences in the film reveals that Ray's procedure was as fine as the performances of his leading actors.

The lyrical flow that characterized *Pather Panchali* is recaptured in *Apur Sansar* in such sequences as Apu's and Pulu's river journey to Pulu's home and the wedding. This sequence has been introduced by Pulu's humorously romantic description of his home region in the restaurant. It is old Mother India, he says: rice paddies, rivers, forests, and peasants living as they have for centuries. The river sequence itself renders the return to Mother India in lyric images. Pulu and Apu are being rowed along in a large wooden boat. Scenes of peasants and animals at the water's edge flow by as Pulu reads Apu's novel, and Apu plays the flute or chants some poetry celebrating the virtues of Bengal (like the poetry he recited in school in *Aparajito*). Shots of the oar dipping into the water are intercut with scenes on the riverbank and shots of the sinewy oarsman as he moves rhythmically, smiling at Apu's poetry. The sequence closes with Pulu's ecstatic reaction to the novel. The emotional surge of this scene carries over into the setting of the marriage episode that follows—a setting nearly as lyrical as the journey, with the great ancestral house by the river and the boats plying up and down.

A far different sequence occurs in the marriage bedroom directly after the ceremony. Here, Apu is in a state of remorse and agitation about how Aparna will react to his poverty and lack of social station. This four-and-one-half-minute sequence is restricted to the confined space of the bedroom, in the center of which stands the great ancestral bed with its carved spiral bedposts (a recurrent image in several of Ray's films), the whole bed decorated with flowers. Aparna stands motionless by the right front bedpost, while Apu paces back and forth behind the bed. They are both in wedding costume. There are three shots, each nearly one minute long, of Apu as he blurts out his misgivings: "You don't know me; I'm a poor writer who lives in a dingy apartment in Calcutta." The camera, at middle distance, follows Apu as he paces, sometimes picking up Aparna in the right side of the frame, but more often leaving her offscreen entirely. These three shots are separated by brief cuts to Aparna, her head bowed. From time to time she answers his questions; her answers are always short, calm, and to the point. Though the camera notices Apu mainly in this scene, it is Aparna's meekness and calm strength that emerges as the salient factor. In other words, what is occurring on the screen (Apu's agitation) isn't the most important element. Apu is revealed here as naturally upset. He is more concerned with his own turbulent emotions; he hasn't begun to look closely at Aparna. Our awareness of her strength occurs before his does. Toward the end of the sequence, he has begun to slow his pacing; he is beginning to feel the effect of her presence.

Another fine sequence involves Aparna's first entry to the apartment. According to Sharmila Tagore, this scene was the first one in which Ray used her as an actress. Ray was aware how nervous she would be in her first film role and wanted her to be comfortable in the presence of the camera. He had her merely walk into the room without speaking any lines.[3] The sequence as a whole is done entirely in pantomine. Still wearing her marriage costume and carrying Apu's marriage headdress, Aparna walks slowly into the room. Her motion is so slow that it appears as if the film is momentarily running in slow motion. She moves across the room to the window, where she stops. Her apparent calmness now gives way as the camera, shooting from behind her, shows her leaning against the window, sobbing and trembling softly. There is a tear in the window curtain, which we've seen in the first shot of the film when the camera pans down to reveal the sleeping Apu. As she glances through the tear, tears still running down her cheeks, she hears the cry of a baby and looks down to see a toddler teetering toward its mother on the ground below. There is a shot from outside the window of part of Aparna's face through the tear. Slowly she begins to calm down. The baby's cry is, of course, a promise of good things to come. Just before he learns of Aparna's death, Apu, in a hopeful and loving mood, will pick up a baby sitting unattended near the railroad tracks.

The fourth sequence I want to cite deserves a very close examination. It is the sequence when Apu and Aparna awake in the apartment, and it is one of the glories of the film. The waking-up sequence is composed of 13 shots and feeds into a passage which might be called Apu's sulk, which then flows into a fine resolution of the problems between them. The whole extended passage is one of the finest evocations of domestic love in all of film. It functions to answer the questions Apu was nervously posing in the marriage bedroom scene.

The waking-up sequence begins with a shot which duplicates the first shot in the film. The camera first notices a fresh, new curtain in the window, then pans down to the sleeping lovers in bed. An alarm clock goes off and Aparna rises, only to find (in shot two) that her shawl has been tied to Apu's (shot three is a close-up of the knot). In shot four, she unties the knot and gives Apu a playful slap with the end of her shawl. Shot five is the longest and most important in the sequence. In it Apu slowly awakens, raises his head from the pillow and looks fondly at Aparna, his hand meanwhile having dropped into the crack between the pillows, evidently in search of his cigarettes. Soon he withdraws his hand, which has discovered a hairpin. The shot ends as he yawns and smiles at Aparna. Soumitra Chatterjee's use of his eyes in this shot is very evocative. At first he gazes dreamily and unfocusedly at his wife; then, as he wakes further, he hears the sound of water dripping and then the sound of birds outside and his eyes flicker toward the window. His eyes then drop down near the pillow, and only then do we see his hand emerge from the crack with the hairpin. In this shot we see his consciousness emerge from sleep like the hairpin from the pillow—a sleep, moreover, in which he has been in intimate dreaming relationship with his beloved. Shots six through eight give us Aparna lighting the charcoal stove while Apu continues to stare at her, even though she asks him if he can't stop. In shot nine, his eyes still upon her, he pulls out his cigarettes from under the pillow, only to find (in shot ten) that Aparna has written a note to him on the package reminding him to have one only after each meal. Aparna notices Apu's discovery of the note and smiles at him as a train whistle sounds nearby. The sequence closes as Apu smilingly puts the cigarettes back and turns over and yawns. Brief though it is, the sequence captures perfectly the contentedness of the young couple as they discover their married roles. There is a warmth and humor between them that tells us all is well.

Immediately after, however, Apu goes into a sulk. Aparna has discovered a beetle or cockroach as she cooks, and she's upset. Apu, who has been playing the flute while she cooks, flings the flute away and tells her he is going out to find another servant to help keep the apartment cleaner. As in the marriage bedroom scene, he is once again unhappy about the conditions he's brought her into. He is willing to do more tutoring, he says, to pay for the additional servant. His face is full of momentary suffering and unhappiness. At this point, Aparna demonstrates for us why she is the perfect mate for Apu. As she moves toward the bed to sit next to him, the camera, shooting from a low angle, shows the tenderness and wit and practicality in her face. "Get rid of the servant we have now," she says, "and then you'll be near me more and I won't repine" (he's just taught her the meaning of the word "repine"). Her comforting (in a mothering way) of Apu here reveals all her womanly strength and power. He will be stronger with her than he was without her, we now know. As in the marriage bedroom scene, Apu is more absorbed with his own emotions than he is aware of Aparna's responses. Her calmness, matter-of-factness, and strength is the perfect balance to his artist's emotionalism. The whole extended sequence closes with a series of marvelous two-shots in which we see Apu in profile, his face gradually becoming calmer, and Aparna in all her beauty, her chin resting on his shoulder.

The fifth sequence that deserves notice includes a fine visual transition from the frame of the movie screen (Apu and Aparna have gone to the movies) to the rear window of the carriage in which they ride home. The carriage ride has the same feeling of mutual love as the waking-up scene. When Aparna lights a cigarette Apu has inadvertently produced, she holds the burning match for a long time, softly illuminating their two faces before she blows it out. This poignant scene, in which Apu tells her he is going to dedicate his novel to her, is a subtle foreshadowing of her death.

Apu's devastation at her death calls forth Ray's finest efforts. As he lies endlessly in his room, Ray uses two magnificent slow dissolves of his grieving face. The first shot of his face shows his pain and torment, mainly in his eyes. In the third shot his face has softened; it is smoother and calmer. Each slow dissolve superimposes the former face upon the "new" face, giving a strange visual sense of inward change. It is strange because the composite face in the middle of the dissolve, particularly the first dissolve, is grotesque and misshapen as the new face grows out of it. It is the perfect image of extreme pain. Each shot is held a long time; there is no music, only the overlapping voice (in the third shot) of the chatty neighbor lady who brings him food. After she leaves, the camera moves slowly to the right, showing us the vacant spaces of the room as the sound of a ticking clock grows louder and louder. Apu rises with difficulty, and we are given (in the next shot) a close-up profile of his stubbled face as he stands by the wall, a small mirror in the background. The loud ticking of the clock suddenly stops, and the camera moves to show us Apu's tormented eyes reflected in the mirror. A train whistle interrupts the stillness, its shrillness increasing like the sound of the clock, as Apu's eyes close in pain and then open. Ray's use of sound and silence here is as powerful as the visual images. When he opens his eyes into the mirror, Apu seems to have thought of something. The next sequence bears out this supposition. There is a low shot of the train tracks as a train approaches from the far distance. We then see a chest-high shot of Apu's grieving face. The camera moves down and left to the vacant sky and holds on the sky for four full seconds. The vacancy is Apu's inner void. The sound of the train grows louder and louder during the shot as the camera moves back to Apu's face and closes in on it as he bows his head. A shrill screeching sound occurs as Ray gives us three very fast shots of (1) Apu turning his head quickly to locate the sound, (2) a crowd of men running toward the tracks, and (3) a dead pig twitching near the tracks as the men scoop it up. In the last shot of the sequence the camera, from behind and to the side, shows Apu standing close to the moving boxcars. He turns slowly, head down, and walks out of the frame. Before this last shot, we haven't known precisely where Apu is standing. Finally we know that, but for the pig, Apu would have gone under the train. It is a very skillful withholding of exact spatial relationships.

The seventh and final sequence to which I want to pay brief attention involves the reunion with Kajal. Apu has given up his strenuous efforts to reestablish a loving relationship with his son. He decides to go to Calcutta alone. As he walks away, we're given a very painterly, long shot of the ancestral mansion by the river (it is like a fine nineteenth-century landscape). When he turns to look back at the house, Kajal has appeared. Apu's approach to Kajal here is different than his first attempts at reunion, in which he pressed his role as "father." Now, as he questions Kajal, he speaks to him out of a full awareness of Kajal's separateness. Ray uses a series of cuts back and forth between the two as the space narrows between them (Apu is moving slowly forward). When he tells Kajal that his grandfather won't beat him for leaving because "I won't tell him," Kajal is completely won over and runs to Apu's open arms. The final shot of the film shows Kajal on Apu's shoulders as they walk off together. It is a very moving ending.

Where is Apu going? We know that he has returned to life after the profoundest despair. We also know that he did not cancel his essential self, even though he scattered the pages of his novel years ago. His return to life through Pulu and Kajal involves the rebirth and regeneration of the creative man. He will write another novel or make a film. He will tell the story of his life in words and images and, in so doing, he will reaffirm his connection with human beings. He has returned to the world and, at the same time, he remains distant from it. His spiritual attitude (for, after all, his story is about the growth of the soul as much as anything else) involves both passionate involvement in temporal existence and a detached sense of living in a continuum of eternity. It is the kind of finely balanced attitude I try to describe in the end of the previous chapter on *Aparajito*. He isn't a holy man, but he comes close to it. It doesn't seem a total fantasy to imag-

ine that the Apu we see at the end is on the verge of creating *The Apu Trilogy*. He has gone farther in life than his father. He has found his essential creative self and his life will continue to grow and deepen.

But he has not been able to do this alone. He has needed Pulu. Pulu is, in many ways, an alter-ego to Apu. He is sensible, solid, kindly—the active man in the so-called real world. Apu is dreamy, idealistic, prone to excess, like most artists. It takes nothing away from Apu to note the importance of Pulu's active agency. Indeed, it suggests a strength in Apu: that he is able to let another human being help him.

NOTES

1. Robin Wood, *The Apu Trilogy* (New York: Praeger, 1971), p. 87.

2. Chidananda Das Gupta, *The Cinema of Satyajit Ray* (New Delhi: Vikas, 1980), p. 25.

3. Interview with Sharmila Tagore, New Delhi, August 6, 1985.

5

PARASH PATHER (THE PHILOSOPHER'S STONE): A Turn to Comedy and Satire

*P*arash Pather (*The Philosopher's Stone*, 1957), based on a short story by Parashuram, was made while Ray was encountering some difficulties in bringing *Jalsaghar* to completion. It's a moral fable done in a comic style. In only his third effort, Ray revealed his range as a filmmaker by staging a successful social satire. Ray undertook the project not only as a change of pace, but because *Aparajito*, unaccountably, was initially a flop at the box office. Perhaps *The Philosopher's Stone* is a bit too long for its substance, but its comedy is undeniably funny and its gallery of broadly caricatured social types is a pleasure to observe. The story of the man who finds a stone which turns base metal to gold and who becomes rich is shopworn and banal, but Ray gives it freshness and new life. It's a very different film for Ray, relying as it does on word play and wit and lacking those extended nonverbal passages for which he'd already become famous.

The opening scenes, which show us Paresh Dutta finding the stone, are full of wonderfully observed life. Paresh, a bank clerk, has just been sacked from his job. We watch him leave his office building and, in a long tracking shot, walk along the crowded street. He's in late middle age, his body sagging and heavy. He gets caught in a downpour and seeks shelter. As he sits out the rain, his body relaxes, he yawns and falls asleep. His human comfortableness and weakness are perfectly evoked here. As the rain drums on the steps beneath his feet, the little stone appears. After the close-ups and medium shots of Paresh hiding from the rain, there's a long shot of the road, the park, and the shelter. It's a minor but telling detail, typical of Ray, in that it establishes the central character in deep space, distancing him from us and momentarily slowing down the action.

Paresh returns to his neighborhood and gives the "marble" to a small boy who, in turn, presents him with an amusing nonsense rhyme, which pleases Paresh immensely. As played by Tulsi Chakravarty, Paresh is the perfect evocation of the average, sensual, cheerful, and greedy man. Chakravarty's extremely mobile face is a superb register of a variety of emotions acted out with comic exaggeration: from bug-eyed surprise and joy to uneasiness and sadness. When he discovers that the stone turns metal to gold, he goes on a buying spree at the local store. The broad comic effects of the early part of the film are displayed when Paresh's laughter turns to lugubrious tears and a neighborhood gentleman also joins in with his own tears. Paresh instinctively knows that sorrow must follow joy at finding the stone. He wants to throw it away, but his practical wife suggests that they sell the gold instead.

Paresh's taxi ride to "take the air" is one of the high points of the film. The camera shoots his face in close-up as the breeze through the taxi windows cools and soothes him. His face suggests both anxiety and dreaminess, joy and pathos. He has a fantasy of reviewing troops like a great political leader. Shots of imposing government buildings in the imperial style are mixed in with shots of his face. He sees his own statue in the center of a city square. He commands the cab driver to stop near a junkyard (all that metal!). The landscape of twisted metal he walks into momentarily suggests a world in devastation. He buys some cannonballs and returns to the cab and his fantasy of being honored at a political celebration in which he gives a speech and hands out gold medals.

Four years later Paresh and his wife are rich beyond their dreams. Paresh now has a private secretary to whom Ray puzzlingly gives a lot of attention. Priyatosh Henry Biswas is charming and attentive to Paresh, but he's also a hustler (in attempting to make time with his girlfriend, he tells her he has her picture on his desk—he does not—and that he'll become a Hindu to please her). Though Biswas plays an important role in the story later on, his function at this point is unclear (particularly the function of his long telephone call with his girlfriend, whom we never see) as is the function of the speeded up shots of Paresh's servant getting dressed. Our glimpses of Paresh and his wife suggest that they have not suffered from their new wealth; his wife sings a beautiful song for him, and he gives her an expensive necklace and then lies down, his face radiating happiness. His plans to go into politics are not used by Ray for any forays into political satire—a significant omission, and one suggesting Ray's basic disinterest in politics.

The satirical center of the film is the cocktail party which Paresh attends. A Western writer probably can't precisely locate all the exact types caricatured in this scene, but it's not hard to place wealthy businessmen, military leaders, and decadent aristocrats. At first these people laugh at Paresh and freeze him out for he is, of course, a newcomer. He gets drunk, and his basic geniality unfreezes the situation. Most of the men are at least partly drunk by now, and they join Paresh in laughter, dance, and song (the women remain sober and irritated at Paresh's antics). When two men try to throw him out, Paresh, in a last effort to impress "his betters," pulls out the stone and puts it to work. The result of his foolishness is that two men at the party alert the police about Paresh, and his wife says that she is leaving him. The mildly slapstick nature of this comedy is reminiscent of Frank Capra, one of Ray's favorite directors. Paresh manages to maintain his humor the next day (perhaps he's still drunk). When the decadent aristocrat visits him to get the magic formula for using the stone, Paresh gives him the same kind of nonsense rhyme the little boy gave him earlier ("yellow and gold orangutan") and sends him off, telling him it's from the old Sanskrit.

The film now moves furiously to its conclusion with fast cross-cutting between the police, who burst into the house; Paresh and his wife, who are fleeing (in lovely early-morning long shots in the classic Ray style); the aristocrat, who takes the formula to a Sanskrit scholar; the secretary, who has been given the stone and swallows it. Paresh is brought before the police inspector for a lengthy interrogation and makes a pitiful statement denying that he has been smuggling gold ("I'm just a simple man, and I haven't hurt anybody"). The police inspector, dressed in white, looks significantly like one of the two men who are cold and suspicious to Paresh at the cocktail party. Is Ray using these authority figures to suggest the guilt and uneasiness that Paresh instinctively feels as he uses his stone? In any case, the narrator who opened the film returns to tell us that in 1958 in Calcutta a financial panic occurred because of the abundance of gold. There are speeded-up shots of turbulent crowds (like those which opened the film) and shots of frantic financial traders. This brief segment of the film is not very convincing.

Paresh and his wife are finally relieved of their distress when the secretary's powerful gastric juices dissolve the stone (such is his most important function). We see gold objects returning to their original form; Paresh laughs weepingly as he and his wife ride off in a simple horse-drawn carriage.

The Philosopher's Stone is an enjoyable and amusing entertainment. As such, it probably shouldn't be judged by the same standards as its great companions, the Apu trilogy and *Jalsaghar*. It served as a useful interruption for Ray from his more intense efforts. I suspect that Ray had a good time making this film; and though it is nearly 30 years old, it is still enjoyable to see today.

6

JALSAGHAR (THE MUSIC ROOM):
The Passing of the Old Order

Jalsaghar (The Music Room) was made in 1958, directly after *The Philosopher's Stone* and before *The World of Apu*. It is one of Ray's finest films. Its topical subject is the decline of the old feudal order and its replacement by the merchant middle class. Its real subject is music—classical Indian music, to be more exact—and it is one of the great treatments of music in film. The slow, meditative rhythms of *The Music Room* are perfectly suited to an elegiac treatment of time's passage. The film is a modern elegy, however, in its ironic treatment of its central character. Biswambhar Roy, a "zamindar" or feudal landlord, is the last of his line of landed aristocrats in British India. He is both a practitioner of classical Indian music as well as a tasteful patron of the finest musicians. He is also a vain and reckless fool, squandering the meager remains of his wealth on musical evenings in the name of family pride, as well as for the music itself. The film consists of a brief prologue and two parts, the first of which is an extended flashback. Three superb concerts form the focal points. Each concert is carefully placed in the dramatic context of the film, and each captures the magnificence of the fading tradition of classical Indian music.

The prologue consists of a brief sequence of shots which present Biswambhar Roy in decline. The first shot gives us a close-up of his frozen, expressionless face (Biswambhar is played by Chhabi Biswas). He seems lifeless, depressed. The image seems like a still shot until, in a characteristic movement for this film, the camera then backs away to show us Biswambhar sitting in a cushioned chair on the terracelike roof of his mansion. The last light of day illumines the empty landscape. One of his two remaining servants brings him his hookah and Biswambhar asks him, "What month is it?" He has been attempting to live outside of time, even as time presses down upon him. He hears the distant sounds of music from his neighbor's house, the rich merchant, Ganguli, and is told that Ganguli's son is celebrating his young manhood in the sacred thread ceremony. This information prompts him to recall the splendor of his own son's sacred thread ceremony.

The flashback that dramatizes this nostalgic recollection lasts approximately 55 minutes, or nearly half of the film, and contains the first two musical concerts. The first three scenes of the flashback establish the causes of Biswambhar's decline with precise clarity and help to account for the curious emptiness we feel from him in the prologue. In scene one, he returns from a brisk ride on his beautiful white horse, Toofan ("Storm"), to be informed by his servant that the bank refuses to loan him more money. Biswambhar dismisses this news and, a bit later, treats his neighbor, Mahim Ganguli, with contempt when he offers to lease some of Biswambhar's land. For him, Ganguli's money is unclean because his father was a money lender. He'll use the money, but not for fine things like the sacred thread ceremony. We have our first glimpse of the music room when Biswambhar walks upstairs and inspects the preparations being made for the ceremony. The columned room is handsomely proportioned, its walls filled with large oil portraits of Biswambhar's ancestors. At one end of the room, under a couple of portraits, stands a large mirror. The camera watches Biswambhar approach the mirror in his riding costume and posture in front of it. He then takes a seat facing the mirror and barely notices Ganguli, who has come to lease the land and whom Biswambhar leaves standing. Biswambhar's vanity and self-absorption are total. Ray makes skillful use of the mirror throughout the film in this regard. We see the performers and audience reflected in it during the concerts as the camera moves about. It adds depth and luster to the handsome but decaying room. Most of all, the mirror evokes our sense of Biswambhar Roy. As an important visual object, it is second only to the beautiful, ornate chandelier which hangs in the center of the room and to which Ray makes repeated reference.

Scene two presents us with the ceremony itself. After some exterior shots of the mansion and a fireworks display, a shot of the brilliantly lit chandelier introduces the music. Shots of the performers alternate with shots of the audience. The camera moves slowly around the columned space as if in calm attention to the music. Ray has designed the scene so that we have the illusion that we are hearing and seeing the whole concert. In a typical shot, the audience is shown by the camera, which is positioned behind the performers; as a generously long musical passage is performed, the camera moves to the side in a slow, sweeping, and rising movement and comes to rest behind the audience, showing that Biswambhar and his friends are held in rapt attention by the music—all save Ganguli, whose nervousness plainly shows (too heavy-handedly) that he has no taste or understanding of the finer things in life. Ray's treatment of Ganguli amounts to caricature—he gives him no depth, no sympathy. Ganguli is crass and twitchy, without redeeming features. Insofar as he represents the new age, Ganguli promises a bleak future. Ray's fondness for the distant past may be at work here; nevertheless, it is an odd portrayal for a director who invariably gives his less appealing characters a strong, even warm, human dimension. Ganguli is the contrast figure to Biswambhar Roy; it would throw the elegiac treatment of Roy out of key if Ganguli were presented sympathetically.

The third scene of part one consists entirely of a conversation between Biswambhar and his wife, Mahamaya, in which she accuses him of careless squandering of what little remains of their wealth for musical concerts. Her jewelry has been sold to pay the musicians and she's unhappy about it, but

Biswambhar is half drunk on brandy and full of elation at the success of his concert. (Ray subtly gives the impression that Biswambhar is as much pleased by the social impression he has made on his guests as by the music itself.) His wife tells him "Music is an obsession with you," and advises him to close the music room. She is also worried that their son, Khoka, is too much influenced by his father's wastefulness. The whole scene is shot in their darkly lit bedroom, very much in the manner of the scenes between husband and wife in Ray's later film, *Charulata*. As in those later scenes, the husband does not understand what the wife is saying. The atmosphere is deeply shadowed and foreboding.

The end of part one gives us the culmination of Biswambhar's tragedy and, significantly, couples it with his craving for music. The second concert is hastily arranged in response to Ganguli's invitation to come to a concert of his own. Biswambhar cannot allow Ganguli to upstage him, so he tells Ganguli, in the presence of his astonished servant who knows how nearly destitute they are, that he happens to be giving a concert and forces Ganguli to defer to his aristocratic precedence. His wife and son are away visiting her parents, so he evidently feels free to disregard her desires and sells the remainder of her jewelry while imperiously informing his servant, who says that the remaining jewelry is the last, that "there's no such thing as last." The concert itself occurs in the midst of a storm so violent that the chandelier sways from the ceiling of the music room (the swaying chandelier is used as the backdrop shot for the titles which open the film). Biswambhar paces about nervously as a supple-voiced male singer performs. An insect falls into his glass of liquor and drowns (earlier, a decorative wooden boat was blown over by a gust of wind entering his bedroom). After several extended passages of magnificent music, Biswambhar is summoned outside and told that the boat carrying his wife and son home has capsized and that they have drowned. The body of his son is brought to him. In the aftermath of this tragedy, he retreats to his darkened upstairs bedroom where he sits immobilized in his chair, vowing never to listen to music again and never to descend to the ground floor of his mansion. He also refuses to witness the forced auction of his remaining land to pay his huge debts. His retirement from the world is total. This is the situation in which we encounter him in the opening shots of the film.

The second part of *The Music Room* is really an extended denouement dramatizing Biswambhar's downward spiral to his death. We are back in the present time of the prologue. Roused by the music from Ganguli's house, Biswambhar descends to the ground floor for the first time in four years and goes to visit his horse, Toofan, and his elephant, Moti. Once again, a personal invitation from Ganguli causes him to arrange for another concert. The effect of Ganguli's invitation, and the concert itself, gives us the finest extended passages in *The Music Room*. I would like to examine them in some detail.

Ganguli's effect on Biswambhar is presented in 16 shots, many of them slow and all without dialogue. As Ganguli prepares to leave, the camera slowly moves in on Biswambhar. He hasn't been listening at all; his face turns solemn, frozen, as in the opening shot of the film. In the next shot, we find him sitting in the dark on the same couch in which he received Ganguli. He hasn't moved in several hours. There is a shot of the lights from the cars going past his mansion to the concert at Ganguli's. There are brief shots of the moon and of the mansion in the moonlight. The fifth shot is a variation of the second, in which we see Biswambhar sitting in the dark, the camera moving slowly into a medium close-up. It is a lengthy shot, deepening our sense of his detachment from life. A servant emerges in deep focus, and Biswambhar asks him if the music room is still closed and if he knows where the key is. There's a fine, low shot of Biswambhar's fingers excitedly drumming on the head of his cane as he enters the room, bats flying around in the distance. A high shot from one of the columns shows him moving into the room, the camera traveling to the right and down, noticing the chandelier as a low tremolo begins on the sitar. Biswambhar looks up at the cobwebbed chandelier, smiling, and touches it with his cane. The camera slowly pans the ancestral portraits in the room, and then moves down one of the columns to reveal that the room is exactly as it was on the night of his wife's and son's deaths—pillows strewn on the rugs, the master's hookah slightly tilted. As he sits forlornly on the rug, we hear snatches of music from the first and second concerts. He rises, as his servant watches him, and goes to the dirty mirror, wiping it with his sleeve and gazing into his haggard face. This shot is a repetition of the earlier one in which he postures in front of the mirror. The sequence ends with his question to the servant about how much the famous dancer hired by Ganguli might cost him. The servant is horrified at the implication. The sequence is a masterful evocation of Biswambhar's gradual return to life. The two servants, it might be added, are like the two sides of Biswambhar. The stern, clean-shaven one is the voice of caution and moral responsibility—which he ignores; the smaller, bearded servant is the reckless, joyful voice—which he pursues to the end. Both grieve over his dead body in one of the last shots, but it is the impish one, of course, who grieves the most.

The third concert is introduced by a brief transition sequence in which the music room is prepared. We see the bearded servant joyfully unroll the big carpet in a low shot in which the carpet travels directly at the camera, to the accompaniment of a lively melody on the sitar. The dark, slow-rhythmed mood of the previous sequence is broken. There are several shots of the chandelier being cleaned (and the mirror, as well). The last shot is the lighting of the chandelier. In its glistening and shimmering surfaces, it is like a visual embodiment of the music which is to come. The concert itself lasts nearly ten minutes and is centered on a wonderful performance by a young Kathak dancer. Unlike the first concert, there isn't as much poetic camera movement as we might wish. Ray wants us to see the dance. The camera is thus not freed as it was in the purely musical concerts. Once again, Ganguli is defeated when, after a sensational climax to the dance, he is prevented from showering the dancer with coins by a firmly placed cane put down on his wrist by Biswambhar, who then offers his last gold coins. After the guests have left, Biswambhar drunkenly drags his servant around the music room, showing him the portraits of his ancestors and expounding upon the glories of his family's history. He even drinks to his own portrait, only to discover a large black spider crouching on the painting (this heavy-handed touch—from Ingmar Bergman—is really the only jarringly discordant note in the whole film). The candles in the chandelier are burning out. At one point he glances down into his glass of dark liquor and sees the swaying chandelier reflected there (this shot is an echo of the one in which an insect drowns in his glass at the second concert). Reminded of his son's and wife's deaths, he insists on riding his horse. After a frenzied gallop, he is thrown to his death near the ominous black hull of a beached boat. The last shot of the film is of the swaying chandelier.

The structure of the film is simplicity itself. Each concert is longer (and better) than the one which precedes it. We thus move toward the celestial concert in the music room of the gods, about which Biswambhar speaks in the middle of the film. Biswambhar's return from limbo in the final concert is made up, in part, of a series of sequences that echo earlier material: the preparation of the music room, the concerts themselves, Ganguli's invitations, the triumph over Ganguli, the absorbed attention of the listeners, and the brilliant surfaces of the mirror and chandelier. As in *Aparajito*, Ray uses the simplest elements of repetition to suggest continuity and change through time.

Though both Biswambhar and Ganguli are fools in their own ways, it is obvious that Ray has more sympathy for Biswambhar's aesthetic passion than for Ganguli's crudity. Biswambhar's love of music is deep and genuine, but so also is his snobbish belief that he is superior to upstarts like Ganguli and that his aristocratic blood will prevail. The music room itself is an excellent visual embodiment of his psyche. It is both tasteful and grandiose; it exists in a state of torpor and decay, like Biswambhar himself after his son's and wife's deaths, and then it achieves (in the last concert) a kind of glorious, incandescent life just before the end. Indeed, the film as a whole comes close to dramatizing a fairly common idea: that often the greatest art is created in that space of time just before the processes of disintegration take over. Other visual elements evoke the atmosphere of passing grandeur: the magnificent decaying mansion itself, set as it is in the vast, vacant, and treeless spaces of the dusty plain; the crumbling river bank, moving closer and closer to the mansion as the river eats away the land; the forlorn elephant, Moti, lumbering solitarily on the plain. But what remains most strongly in the eye and ear is the music. Ray's handling of the three concert sequences is masterful, and the performances themselves are superb. Vilayat Kahn's incidental music perfectly evokes the nobility of the classical tradition at its best. *The Music Room* is, thus, like the later *The Chess Players*, both a dramatization of a fading culture and a permanent record of some of the finest artistic achievements of that culture.

7

DEVI (THE GODDESS):
The Tragedy of Incarnation

Devi (The Goddess) was made in 1960, immediately following *Apur Sansar*. Because the film lies so close in time to the Apu trilogy, many commentators have seen similarities between them, but *Devi* is really a very different film from the trilogy. It's not surprising that *Devi* is associated with the trilogy, since Ray decided to use Sharmila Tagore and Soumitra Chatterjee once again, following their wonderful performances in *Apur Sansar*. We also see Chhabi Biswas in the second of a series of roles he played for Ray as a representative of the vanishing old order (his first is the feudal landlord in *The Music Room*). Set in the middle of the nineteenth century, *Devi* is a study in religious superstition and upper-class decadence. Like *The Music Room*, it's a study of the historical past and a comment on the present. In the conflict between Uma and his father Kalikinkar, we see the struggle of modern India to escape the suffocating traditions of the past. Uma is part of the Bengali renaissance.

The story may be summarized fairly easily. Seventeen-year-old Daya is married to Uma, the younger son of the rich feudal landlord Kalikinkar Roy (servant of Kali), who has recently lost his wife. A deeply devout man, the elderly Kalikinkar is devoted to Daya, who comforts him by rubbing his aching legs and participating in his religious observances. Kalikinkar represents the conservative Hindu orthodoxy which Brahmoism had arisen to modify. After Kalikinkar has a dream in which he sees Daya as the goddess Kali, he proclaims Daya as a true goddess, to the horror of the larger family. Enshrined in one of the devotional rooms of the mansion, Daya actually seems to perform a cure on a dying child whom Kalikinkar has arranged to be brought to her. Uma now persuades Daya to flee on foot with him to Calcutta but as they begin their journey, Daya has second thoughts and they return (she is partially convinced that she is actually a goddess). Uma dejectedly leaves once more to continue his studies in Calcutta and while he is away, Daya's beloved little nephew Khoka falls ill and she is unable to cure him. He dies in her lap. When Uma returns he finds that Daya has gone mad.

Even though a belief in the incarnation of a god or gods has been fairly common in India, as an explanatory note tells us just after the credits, *Devi* caused a strong reaction among certain conservative Hindus and the film was denied an export license on the grounds that it portrayed Indians as backward and superstitious. Only the intervention of Nehru himself removed the ban.

As a study in one of the varieties of religious experience, *Devi* is an interesting and powerful film. Kalikinkar is never merely an old fool but rather a lonely, suffering old man used to absolute authority. In an early sequence he kneels on the floor before Daya, her toes curling under in anguish, as he proclaims her godhead. His older son Tarapada uncertainly joins him in prostration before Daya. Tarapada is a weak, cynical drunkard. He has always conformed to his father's autocratic ways and it has cost him. He loses his son Khoka because, along with Kalikinkar, he refuses to let a doctor examine the boy until Daya has had a chance to cure him. Corrupted from within by his response to his father, he endures an unhappy marriage to Harisundari, who is deeply jealous of Khoka's love for Daya and for her power over Kalikinkar. Tarapada is clearly a contrast figure to Uma, the strong son. The second sequence of the film, in which Uma and Daya are lying on their bed, suggests their love for each other as well as Uma's desire to pursue a kind of learning different from his father's. Uma identifies with Rammohun Roy, the founder of the Brahmo movement in India, which stressed the need for India to enter the modern age. He's learning English in Calcutta; he wants to find a job in the wider world and not remain in the orbit of his father's power like his disgruntled brother.

The religious experience that *Devi* examines plays itself out as a family tragedy in which father-son relationships are at the center. "To please the father is to please the gods," as the drunken Tarapada mockingly tells his wife. This injunction is later repeated at length by Kalikinkar as he lectures Uma. When we observe Uma and a friend at a comic play in Calcutta, the scene we have a glimpse of involves a series of accusations among the entirely male cast that each is illegitimate (not true sons). Later that evening Uma's friend confesses that he's worried his father will disapprove that he's fallen in love with a widow and Uma suggests that he help him present the case to the father. When Uma consults Professor Sarkar, one of his former teachers, he hears of the professor's conflict with his own father when he decided to change his religion as a young man. "Stand up for your rights," the professor advises him. The professor represents the new, rationalist emphasis in Indian education. He's a Brahmo. Finally, discovering his wife mad, Uma accuses his father of killing Khoka and nearly killing his wife. Kalikinkar is, at this point, hardly capable of understanding the accusation. The film endorses Uma's views, however, even as it demonstrates the logic of Kalikinkar's actions. As Kali-Durga is the goddess of both creation and destruction, so Uma's accusations at the end serve to destroy the old and enable the new. Ray isn't merely dramatizing the process of change in the historical past but advocating it in the present.

Visually, the latter part of the film tends to move from dark to light, with Ray's use of overexposed light particularly effective in the last sequences. Two scenes illustrate this movement very well. The first is an eleven shot sequence in which Uma attempts to persuade Daya to leave with him. It's essentially a dark sequence, with Daya sitting forlornly on her netted bed in the early morning as Uma comes slowly into the room. He's been out by the river, agonizing over their predicament. As the camera slowly swings to the left, we see, in shot four, Uma push aside the netting and tenderly embrace his wife. The camera keeps a discreet distance from the embracing lovers until they begin their dialogue since the convention of not showing any kissing on the screen was in effect when *Devi* was made. In shot five, Uma urgently poses a series of questions to Daya about whether she believes she's a goddess. Though she is unable to reply, all her responses here suggest her confusion; she keeps her eyes lowered, her breathing is rapid. There's a noticeable look of relief on her face when Uma says he's taking her away. In the next sequence, however, the darkness intensifies. They're walking in the dark paths, nearly engulfed by tall grass, hearing scary night sounds. Suddenly they come upon an image of Kali washed up at the edge of the river, and Daya decides she can't leave ("What if I'm really a goddess?"). Her motivation here isn't entirely clear though it's fully convincing. She feels she can't desert her devoted father-in-law, nor can she abdicate what may be a role as one of Kali's agents. She feels she must return to her fate. The ambiguity of her position is further illustrated when she sits with her sister's sick child Khoka on her lap. Her lips seem to be moving in prayer, though it's hard to tell because of the shadow of a fan moving across her face. In the next shot the camera moves gradually upward over smooth, windless water until we see a boat far off in the distance and we cut to a shot of the brooding Uma returning home on the boat. The shot of the water is a transition to Uma, and yet in its vacancy and stillness it also evokes Daya's inertness. It's an interior shot of Daya as well as a shot moving us to Uma. The emptiness of the water is accentuated by a series of fairly quick shots of the vacant courtyard of the mansion, of an empty devotional room with a bare altar. Daya has failed to revive Khoka; her potency as a goddess is nonexistent.

The images of blindingly diffuse light Ray uses in the final shots of the film are carefully prepared for by earlier shots. There's a shot of Uma sitting pensive and depressed near a bright window as he listens to his brother's wife tell him of the growing worship of his wife as a goddess. We also see a flashback in which Daya remembers the aftermath of her wedding and we see a bright, blurred shot of the lovers still in wedding costume as we hear Uma tell Daya she looks like a goddess. Part of the flashback sequence involves a blurred, overexposed shot of Uma laughingly struggling to get out of his shirt with Daya's help, a note of domestic tranquility. In the aftermath of Khoka's death, the blinding light seems to have invaded all the rooms of the mansion. There's a kind of bright mist in the room when Uma confronts his grieving father and tells him he has killed Khoka. We can barely see Khoka's mother as she lies by the bed screaming at Uma that Daya has killed her son. And when Uma finally locates Daya, she is lost to our sight in the blinding light which fills her room. As she emerges from the light, walking toward Uma, her disheveled appearance and abrupt, jerky movements suggest that she has gone over the edge. The blinding light also suggests a kind of electrical overload. She's like an incandescent wire. The next to the last shot shows her running across a field of flowers as a bright mist sweeps across the screen. According to Marie Seton, Ray had actually shot a sequence in which Daya drowns, like the drowning of the images of Kali earlier in the film. The sequence was damaged somehow and could not be reshot for some reason, probably budgetary. Ray then substituted a shot of Daya dying on the bank of the river but removed the shot prior to sending the film to Cannes, leaving our final view of Daya in the field of flowers, presumably running to the river.[1] Whatever changes were made to the ending, this shot perfectly evokes a sense of her tragic ending.

The final shot of the film is a pure white image of the goddess Kali. It's unpainted, unlike the image which opens the film, or the black, threatening image of Kali which appears at the time of Khoka's death. In its half-smiling serenity, the blank whiteness of its visage perfectly evokes the enigmatic power of the gods.

NOTE

1. Marie Seton, *Portrait of a Director* (Bloomington: Indiana University Press, 1971), p. 154.

8

RABINDRANATH TAGORE:
The Brahmo Heritage

Ray made the documentary *Tagore* in 1961 to commemorate the one-hundredth anniversary of the leader of the Bengali renaissance. The importance of Rabindranath Tagore in Ray's creative life, however, even outweighs his importance for Ray in the history of Bengal. It is no exaggeration to say that Tagore was, and is, by far the most important influence upon Ray. Chidananda Das Gupta, in many ways the most perceptive of Ray's critics, has even gone so far as to say that Ray is trapped in the Tagore mythos and therefore is unable to deal with the issues of his own day. Suffice it to say that *Tagore* is a fine documentary, balanced in its approach, lacking in any worshipful genuflection. Ray narrates the film in his own voice.

The opening shots of the film show documentary footage of a huge crowd following Tagore's bier, then shots of flames from a fire like that which consumed his body, and finally shots of the setting sun. Ray's voice tells us that Tagore's "mortal remains perished." The rest of the film goes on to show what he accomplished in his life and to demonstrate that his spirit lives on.

The documentary gives details of Tagore's grandfather, Dwarkanath, a wealthy merchant and one of the first Bengalis to visit England. In a dramatic recreation, we see Dwarkanath having his portrait painted. The film mentions Dwarkanath's passionate interest in the ideas of Raja Rammohun Roy, who advocated the incorporation of the social gospel of American Unitarianism and the best of Hinduism and Indian culture—the movement known as Brahmoism—which he and Roy founded together. Brahmoism is to become a major influence in Rabindranath's life and on Ray himself. Dwarkanath's son, Devendranath, is shown, as are several of Devendranath's 14 children, almost all of whom became writers and artists, Rabindranath (the last child) chief among them. The palatial family residence at Jorosanko is shown as the camera moves down its hallways, and we see a young Rabindranath listening to the sounds of plays being read and music performed by his brothers and sisters as he moves along. There are a number of still photographs showing him as he grows into an extremely handsome youth whose first volume of poetry is published at age 13. He visits England but doesn't complete his studies at London University. Instead, he returns home and writes operas which incorporate English music of the Gilbert and Sullivan variety and Indian classical music. This mixture of

Western and Eastern cultures is a central trademark of Tagore's work and, one might add, of Ray's as well.

Tagore's spiritual development is presented, first in reaction to the death of his grandmother (which produces in him a spirit of renunciation), and later, at 20, when he experiences a religious awakening through watching the light of the rising sun as it filters through the leaves of a tree (seeing behind the facade of reality). Images of sunlight and firelight are central to the visual evocation of Tagore's life. His experience of nature, when he's sent by his father to manage the family's rural estates, is presented by a long, fine pan shot of a heavy sky lowering over a river and of birds wheeling overhead. Tagore's profound interest in education is chronicled as he founds Santiniketan (where Ray went to school) by selling the copyrights to all his published work and his wife's jewelry as well. Soon thereafter his wife dies, as do two of his children.

Up to this point in the film, Ray has used dramatic recreations of many of the most important incidents in Tagore's life. As Tagore becomes more and more a public figure, with his role as a leading demonstrator against the partition of Bengal, he is able to use documentary footage. There is, however, a recreation of Tagore leading a demonstration. He's shot from above and behind as he raises his arms in exhortation of the crowd. The man playing Tagore here looks very much like Ray himself, and though he isn't Ray, perhaps it is significant that Ray chose a look-alike to play Tagore at this moment. Tagore's emphasis upon nonviolent resistance is strongly emphasized here. His importance as a poet is presented with the publication of "Gitanjali," which the Irish poet Yeats praises as "the finest lyrics of his time," and with his award of the Nobel Prize for Literature in 1913.

Increasingly we see Tagore forced to leave Santiniketan, "the abode of peace and contemplation," to travel around the world bringing his message of universal brotherhood and raising money for his school. In one of the most visually interesting sequences of the documentary, Ray gives us Tagore's evolution as a painter when he is nearly 70. The odd, abstract forms he first makes seem to be the result of the patterns made by words blocked out by him in textual revision. Gradually these shapes take on a life of their own as they assume a more figurative quality, culminating in some extraordinary depictions of women's sorrowing faces. Tagore is now presented as a world leader, honored on his seventieth birthday by such people as Einstein and Gandhi. He turns to publishing textbooks and nonsense rhymes for children. We see him, bent and white-headed, sitting on the ground while children dance around him. The growth of Santiniketan into a full-fledged university emphasizing painting, music, and literature is presented.

The final shots of Tagore show him in a wheelchair, publishing *The Crisis of Civilization* in the early months of World War II, and raising his arms in prayer. As grisly images of the holocaust change to images of the sun rising over the ocean, Ray voices Tagore's prophetic (and optimistic) words about a "new dawn, a new chapter in history when chaos will end and all will be rendered clean in a spirit of service and sacrifice."

Tagore is a moving biography of a great man. As a documentary, it manages to compress a large amount of factual material into the short space of 55 minutes. We feel we have been able to look into a rich and eventful life. The inner spiritual development of Tagore is presented as well as the more public aspect of awards and relationships with other famous men. Ray's own personal relationship to Tagore through his grandfather, father, and his own early youth, is omitted. We have the shot of the actor who looks like Ray as Tagore leading the demonstration against partition, and that is all.

As I've said, the influence of Brahmoism and Tagore are central to any understanding of Ray's basic attitudes. It is not the purpose of this study of Ray's films to go into this influence at any length; Andrew Robinson's forthcoming study of Ray's work will undoubtedly do that. Nevertheless, Ray's films reflect Brahmo values and can even be seen as a continuing effort to carry out Brahmo objectives.

Brahmoism began as an attempt to move India into the modern world. Centered in Calcutta, the focus of British influence, the Brahmo movement attempted to revive a Hinduism encrusted with centuries-old customs and superstitions which seemed, to thoughtful, progressive Bengalis to be blocking progress. Brahmos thus addressed the excessive worship of images, the abject status of women, the retrograde condition of Indian education, and many other problems. Oddly enough, Brahmoism took its inspiration not from England but from North American Unitarianism. William Ellery Channing's idea that Christianity was a spirit rather than a fixed creed or dogma, an utterance of love rather than an institution or theological system, was appealing to the Indian mind. This "rational religion," with its emphasis on "universal humanism," allowed for Western influence in ways congenial to Hinduism. Rammohun Roy, the founder of Brahmoism and, for virtually all historians, the founder of modern India, was particularly attracted to Unitarianism's social gospel. He wanted to change the excesses of the caste system and to improve the status of women. In his study of the Brahmo Samaj, which has been of particular help to me, David Kopf says the following about Rammohun Roy's interest in the woman question:

If Unitarians increasingly worked to alleviate the sufferings of the industrial proletariat, Rammohun chose the Bengali Hindu woman as his "proletariat." With extremely important implications for his successors, he saw in her depressed condition the root cause of social immobility in India. The new social conscience and consciousness of Unitarianism was in Rammohun almost entirely directed to the miserable state of Hindu women. He found them uneducated and illiterate, deprived of property rights, married before puberty, imprisoned in purdah, and murdered at widow-hood by a barbaric custom of immolation known as sati. One has only to read Rammohun's works on social reform to realize that most of it deals with one aspect or another of man's inhumanity to women in Bengal. The conclusion is that only by freeing women and by treating them as human beings could Indian society free itself from social stagnation.[1]

This is an important source of Ray's own interest in the status of women in his films. True, he doesn't dramatize particular examples of the suppression of women (with the exception of the depiction of the Anglo-Indian Edith in *Mahanagar* or *The Big City*); that isn't his way. Instead, in film after film, he dramatizes the great strength of the Indian woman, often exhibited in adverse circumstances. His women are often stronger than his men. They are the source of India's power as a nation.

The "universal humanism" of Ray's films may have its source in Brahmoism as well. His ability to give a Westerner a sense that a Bengali character in one of his films is like a spiritual brother is his greatest achievement, when all the discussion of his cinematic artistry is over. Ray's highmindedness may be essentially Brahmo as well. He goes beyond Renoir in his depiction of the essential human goodness of his characters. There is no Battala *(The Crime of Monsieur Lange)* in his cast of characters—no single figure of pure evil, of cold malice. Bhupati's brother-in-law, Umapada, who luxuriously contemplates stealing from Bhupati, doesn't even come close. This absence of a sense of evil may be the price one pays for the gift of a sense of universal humanism, of spiritual brotherhood.

Brahmoism's attempt to balance the conflicting demands of universal humanism and Hindu nationalism can be seen most clearly in the figure of Rabindranath Tagore. The Brahmo movement wished to use Western influences in the modernizing of India, but it wanted to maintain a proud spirit of nationalism, as well, in resistance to British colonial domination. Raised in a sophisticated, upper-class family, and deeply influenced by Western art and literature, Tagore constantly sought to return to the roots of Bengali culture. His novel *Gora* tells of the difficult, painful conflict between the desire to encourage beneficial Western influence and to maintain indigenous national character at the same time. It is a working out of the struggle going on within Tagore himself.

In the same way, Ray's films can be seen as an attempt to reaffirm a sense of national identity, to show Bengalis and other Indians what their lives are really like, as opposed to the Hollywood fantasies purveyed by the Bombay producers. The Apu trilogy is, in this sense, a return to the roots of Bengali culture—the way life has gone on in the countryside for years and years. It is a return to simple folk customs by a deeply Westernized, sophisticated filmmaker. The pull of rural settings is so strong for Ray, a city man, because it is there, away from the media-saturated urban setting, that one can find the roots in the purest form. To an extent, Ray's rural films are quiet celebrations of national pride, like Tagore's *Gitanjali*. They are also a fantasy of a rural simplicity he can never know, except as an observer. Like the great Russian writers (also uneasily influenced by the West) who idealized the peasants in their time—Tolstoy and Turgenev come to mind—Ray longs for a clear, simple resolution of the conflict between his dual heritages. Anyone would. The difference is that, in the Apu trilogy and elsewhere, Ray's peasant villagers seem truer than Tolstoy's or Turgenev's. This is no mean accomplishment.

Perhaps the influence of Tagore can be seen best in Ray the multimedia creator. Sukumar, Ray's father, was both a painter and writer of children's stories, but his son's manifold artistic gifts are closer in variety and strength to Tagore's. Tagore produced many forms of literature as well as painting, music, political tracts, and essays on education. Ray's production, besides film, involves stories, novels, poetry (of the nonsense variety for children), film scripts, essays, painting, and music. Like Tagore, he is a renaissance man. He has said that he discovered his creative self at Santiniketan, the school of the creative arts which Tagore founded.

Ray has been drawn again and again to Tagore's writings as subjects for his films. From *Two Daughters (Postmaster* and *Samapti)* to *Charulata* to *The Home and the World*, Tagore's fiction has provided consistent inspiration (*Postmaster* and *Charulata* are two of his finest films). Ray's historical imagination has been attracted to Tagore's depiction of the birth of modern India—or, more accurately, the rebirth of Bengal. Like any great artist with a sense of the past, he is interested in what forces made India what she is today. He is interested in depicting his own Brahmo heritage and dramatizing his own prehistory. Chidananda Das Gupta's charge that Ray is trapped in the Tagore ethos needs to be addressed here.[2] Das Gupta criticizes Ray not merely for returning to Tagore's fiction as subject matter for his films, but for bringing the Brahmo values of Tagore's world into his depiction of contemporary life. As a result, he claims, Ray's contemporary films have a distinctly literary quality. In an eloquent sentence, Das Gupta puts it this way: "In Ray's work, drawn more from literary than personal experience, the local truth is at times in doubt; the universal, almost never."[3] This comment seems to me both telling and not wholly accurate. It doesn't account for the sharply observed social detail and the sense of Ray's comfortableness in the first half of *The Middleman (Jana Aranya)* or the marvelous subtlety and realism of *Days and Nights in the Forest (Aranyer Din Ratri)*, a study of momentarily displaced urbanites. Still, Das Gupta is right in suggesting Ray's uneasiness with contemporary urban Indian problems. Tagore's world *is*, in many ways, more congenial to him. It has called forth one undisputable masterpiece of world cinema in *Charulata*. How can one quarrel with that?

There *is* a difference between Ray and Tagore—and it is the overriding difference. Tagore believed it was possible for a politically active writer and artist to bring about social change. Ray emphatically rejects this role for himself. Tagore's writings, even his poetry, often have a rational program built into them. Ray's creations almost never do. He remains an inventor of stories, of situations, of atmospheres—in which a presentation of complex, breathing life is essential. As fictions, his recreations of Tagore's stories and novels are often better than the originals. Perhaps this is because he has worked in a less politically turbulent time than Tagore. In any case, he finds a character who is politically active to be of decidedly less interest than one who is not.

NOTES

1. David Kopf, *The Brahmo Samaj* (Princeton: Princeton University Press, 1981), pp. 14-15.

2. Chidananda, Das Gupta, "Ray and Tagore," *Sight and Sound* 36, (Winter, 1966-67); 30-35. This article appeared before Ray's examination of contemporary urban problems in *The Adversary, Company Limited*, and *The Middleman*.

3. Chidananda, Das Gupta, *The Cinema of Satyajit Ray* (New Delhi: Vikas, 1980), p. xi.

9

TEEN KANYA (THREE DAUGHTERS): The Shorter Form

Three Daughters (Teen Kanya) was made in 1961, based on three stories by Tagore. For foreign distribution Ray decided to remove one story, *Monihara*, reducing the running time from over three hours, and retitled the movie *Two Daughters*. The remaining two episodes, *Postmaster* and *Samapti*, have sometimes been dismissed as slight or lacking in dramatic interest. This opinion seems curious, for though the two short films are very different, each achieves its objectives with great skill and one, at least *(Postmaster)*, is a small gem. *Two Daughters* also reveals Ray as an accomplished humorist.

Postmaster examines the relationship between Nandalal, a man from the city who has been transplanted to rural India in his job as postmaster, and Ratan, a ten-year-old who serves him. The humor and poignancy that the film generates comes from the simplest of paradoxes: Nandalal is the child and Ratan the adult. *Postmaster* is, unlike its companion piece *Samapti*, a two-character film with a fine simplicity of setting as well as narrative.

The opening scenes of the film serve to demonstrate Nandalal's uneasiness in his new situation. He locks his small box of personal possessions on every occasion; he refuses to accept a genial offer from the village men to join a musical evening; when he goes to bathe in a nearby pond, he encounters a snake skin and retreats in alarm. A harmless local crazy man appears, heavily bearded and in rags, and crouches in front of him, making strange noises. Nandalal is terrified, but Ratan commands the crazy fellow to desist and he marches off in the style of a British soldier, carrying his fly-fishing rod like a weapon. This scene, the first fully comic one in the film, demonstrates Ratan's strength and Nandalal's uncertainty. Subsequently, we learn that Ratan is an orphan who has had to survive on her own, and that Nandalal is experiencing, at the age of about 30, his first extended period away from his mother. When he goes to bed on his first night, he hears strange night sounds, as well as sounds from the crazy man, and cries out in a trembling voice for Ratan. Later on, she gazes longingly at a photograph of his family and says she wants to be like his sister, who, he answers her, can sing and write. He is moved when Ratan sings to him and he begins to teach her to write. But Nandalal's bout with malaria puts an end to their relationship. He has refused to take his malaria pills, and after Ratan nurses him through his illness he applies for a transfer. The little poem he gives her acknowledges their affection: "Ratan is a little dear/She's like a sister to me here" (we would add that she's more like a mother). He is, however, unaware of how keenly Ratan is experiencing his leaving. When the new postmaster arrives, he asks him to give her a rupee and then thinks better of this idea and goes looking for her, but she passes him by on the road.

The end of the film makes clear that Nandalal has been so eager to return home from this strange environment that he has been unaware of his own feelings for Ratan as well as hers for him. Though he's treated sympathetically by Ray, he stands as the best example in Ray's films of the undeveloped man. He won't take his malaria pills, not because they are bitter, as he tells Ratan, but because he unconsciously desires to return to his mother and family. In the meantime, he needs Ratan as a mother figure, and she is more than capable of playing that role. (How many solitary men has she taken care of in her job as postmaster's servant? They have been her "family," for she has no immediate or extended family.) Two details from the film demonstrate her motherly strength. In the dark, stormy night of Nandalal's illness, Ray places a soft, steady light on her face as she nurses him. After the illness has subsided, she gets Nandalal to take a malaria pill by first taking one herself—the perfect gesture of a mother to a child.

Cinematically, this film is interesting. There is very little dialogue. Aside from the brief opening exchanges between Nandalal and the former postmaster, the first 15 minutes work largely in pantomime. There's an early eight-shot sequence in which we watch Nandalal enter the house and unpack. He wanders shiftlessly, examining the contents of the house, fingering the scales for weighing letters, peeling an old month off the calendar, and finally pulling out a family picture from his suitcase. These slow-paced shots reveal his uneasiness and early twinges of homesickness very well. There's also a fine treatment of his reaction to Ratan's singing. As he lies half asleep listening to her tender, childish voice, the camera closes in on him and he opens his eyes slowly; he's very touched by what he hears (and by all the things Ratan does for him). It is all the more surprising, therefore, that he almost tries to leave without saying good-bye to Ratan. The final two shots of the film present his awakening to how much she means to him; they're the high point of the film. In the first shot, Ratan walks by him on the road, head averted. She's carrying water to her new master, her face still streaked with tears. Nandalal softly speaks her name as she passes, and is holding the rupee to give to her. He watches her walk away. In the second shot, Ratan has stopped in the distance to look back at him. As she turns to go on, Nandalal's face is turned from the camera. He slowly turns toward us and we see that he's upset. The impact of his loss of her is beginning to dawn on him. Still holding the rupee in the fingertips of his upraised hand, he begins to move slowly down the road, the camera moving with him. When he hears Ratan say to his replacement, "Master, here's your water," he stops and looks back once more. His lower lip is trembling slightly and he swallows hard as he walks away, slowly putting the rupee in his pocket. He won't forget about her as easily as he had thought.

Two things remain in the mind's eye after seeing *Postmaster:* the evocation of rural Bengal and a sense of Ratan's loss and her strength. Nandalal's simple, one-room house and covered porch, the muddy road flanked by dense trees and vegetation, the village elders enjoying a musical evening— all of these, simply presented, give us a memorable sense of place. But the final memory is of Ratan: of her strength, intelligence, caring, and endurance.

Samapti, the second part of *Three Daughters*, is a comic treatment of the marriage process. As with *Postmaster*, the film involves painful elements, most of which attach to its central subject, the change in a young woman from rebellious tomboy to wife.

Amulya, freshly out of college, returns home for a visit to his mother who wants him to get married. His visit to a potential bride from a proper family proves disastrous and involves some slapstick effects. The whole family is extremely tense (the father laughs nervously all the time); the girl is unattractive and cowed by parental and cultural pressure; Amulya winds up coughing up his food onto the head of the dozing grandfather. Amulya is attracted to a local girl whom his mother considers a horror. Mrinmoyee, nicknamed Puglee, is pretty and vital but she doesn't conform at all to the role of a proper bride. She spends her time swinging, playing with her pet chipmunk, and mocking Amulya from a distance. On their wedding night, she admits to Amulya that she's been forced into the marriage, mainly by pressure from her mother. She then leaves their marriage room and spends the night near her swing by the river. Brought back to the house, she wrecks the marriage room and Amulya dejectedly tells her that he is going to leave for Calcutta. During their separation, Mrinmoyee undergoes a profound change and, when Amulya is lured back by his mother, he finds her fully willing to be his wife.

As this summary suggests, *Samapti* involves the conflict between parents (in this case, mothers; as in *Postmaster*, there are no fathers) and children regarding marriage. The scenes between Amulya and his mother are uniformly comic: She brings sweets which she puts into his reluctant mouth, she musses his hair while he grimaces. Her adoration is both welcomed and barely tolerated by him. The conflict between them when Amulya chooses Mrinmoyee is played out in the broadest terms. Their anger quickly escalates into comic melodrama. The conflict between Mrinmoyee and her mother is more serious. The mother beats her in one very short sequence. She's determined that their poor family not lose its chance to make connection with Amulya's wealthy family. Mrinmoyee's change does not occur as a result of external pressure; Amulya's kindly response to her rebellious rage when she wrecks their room makes some part of her want to change (she expects to be beaten by him; the darkest part of her perhaps wants to be beaten). The change itself is presented by two dissolves: Mrinmoyee lies on her side, her face deeply shadowed and grieving; her mother chastises her for having an evil karma and says "no one will want you now." After a slow dissolve, we again have a close-up of her painful face and hear her mother comfort her ("such is our fate"). A fast dissolve shows her still lying on her side, but now her face is softened and smiling, suffused with well-being and new strength. A hand moves into the frame holding the dead chipmunk for her to see but she barely notices. She has made the full transition from girlhood to womanhood. The two dissolves are nearly a direct quote from *The World of Apu*, in which Ray shows us Apu's grieving after Aparna's death. Their placement in *Samapti* is both apt and powerful. A less successful throwback to *The World of Apu* (which was made only two years earlier) involves the wedding scene. In both scenes we have the lovers, in traditional marriage costume, placed in various positions around a large wooden bed in the decorated marriage room. Ray's handling of the scene in *The World of Apu* is much more fluid and subtle than in *Samapti*, perhaps because, in the former film, the married couple are actually able to communicate their feelings for each other. In any case, the infrequency of similarities of visual procedure between films illustrates how little Ray is interested in repeating himself, how much he wants to stretch himself.

Amulya's and Mrinmoyee's return to their marriage involves the rejection of maternal influence. In the last sequence, Amulya's mother mounts the stairs with some food for the young couple, only to have the door slammed in her face. From now on, her attempts at interference will be blunted as the couple go on to make their own life. Amulya is different from Nandalal, the mother-attached hero of *Postmaster*. Rather than go along with the safe or proper bridal selection his mother has made (as Nandalal will probably eventually do), Amulya follows his instinctive choice of someone very different from himself. Mrinmoyee's "wildness" points up his conventionality. Her ability to grow into womanhood without losing her spark, coupled with his intelligence and strength, suggest that their marriage will maintain its vitality. In this sense they are really like Apu and Aparna before their tragedy. If Nandalal's relationship with Ratan is a radical example of male dependence on womanly strength, then Amulya's patient and kindly treatment of Mrinmoyee presents a counterbalancing example of male strength.

Visually, Amulya is associated with interiors while Mrinmoyee is associated with the outside, particularly with her swing by the river. His room is full of books and pictures of his favorite writer/heroes. It contains his gramophone on which he plays his favorite music. He wears wire-rimmed glasses and takes a broad intellectual and philosophic view when he talks to Mrinmoyee in their marriage bedroom scene. Her "place" is in the open spaces by the river, where she keeps her chipmunk and where she can swing to her heart's delight. After she steals out of the bedroom by climbing down a tree in the moonlight, she goes to her swing and Ray gives us a short but intensely lyrical presentation. As the orchestra and flute give out a spiritual melody, we have three shots of Mrinmoyee vigorously swinging. These shots are intercut by point-of-view shots of the moonlit, cloudy sky from a swinging camera. The fourth and final shot is a long shot of Mrinmoyee sitting on the ground in the early morning with her head and arm on the swing. She's sleeping as the river flows by in the background. This sequence, and others like it, suggest in their use of space, a certain wild freedom about her. Amulya is right to be attracted to this freedom, for, if anything, he has a tendency to be too constrained and philosophical.

Because *Monihara*, the third part of *Three Daughters*, has a running time of nearly an hour, Ray evidently decided to delete it from the other two films and to show them as *Two Daughters*. *Monihara* isn't as strong as either *Postmaster* or *Samapti*, but it's a well-rendered treatment of the Tagore story on which it is based. A ghost story, *Monihara* is perhaps chiefly interesting not only for the way it evokes the supernatural, but as a prefiguration of *Charulata*.

The ghost story itself is narrated by a schoolmaster/writer whom we first see visiting an imposing old house on a windy, gloomy day. He encounters a shrouded figure by the river and speaks to it of ghosts, joking that he doesn't know if he believes in them or not, and going on to say that he has written a ghost story anyway and wants to read it because it's about the former residents of the old house. This small prelude to the story prepares the viewer very nicely in its use of the looming house, the mysterious figure and sound of the wind. The story itself involves Phanibhusan Saha and his wife Monimalika, or Moni. Thirty years ago, the two took possession of the house and its jute mills. Moni's insatiable desire for gold jewelry becomes a problem when the jute is destroyed in a fire and Phanibhusan needs money. Instead of giving him back some of her jewelry, she leaves with her cousin, a handsome young man, only to return as a ghost at midnight to retrieve a gold necklace her husband had bought for her. Phanibhusan is left in a state of terror, having seen a skeletal hand take the necklace from his bedside table.

Ray presents this ghost story in the style of an atmospheric melodrama. The setting consists almost entirely of the darkened interiors of the old house. These confined and brooding spaces are a good visual approximation of Moni's obsessiveness. She's often placed in proximity to stuffed birds and to a portrait of her husband's dead aunt whom she resembles (there's a suggestion that the aunt lives on in her). She believes she's cursed because she can't have children, and probably also because of her hunger for gold. Though she performs some wifely duties such as flower arranging and (in a fine sequence, typical of Ray) singing to her husband, she is often distracted. In an interesting early shot, she is standing in a window nearly dissolved in light as her husband slowly enters the room. Like those light-filled shots of Daya at the end of *Devi*, there's a suggestion that she's already in another world. Phanibhusan doesn't understand how far gone she is. Perhaps others might find her a bit odd, he says, but he is comfortable with her. He's a practical man, interested in the manufacture of jute, and an innocent. He often wears white and moves toward the lamplight while Moni stays in the semi-darkness. Moni no doubt leaves him because she's bored with him and because she fears she'll lose her gold. She tells her "cousin" that she'll die if she loses the gold and then, in a sexual gesture, slowly opens up her dress to reveal that she is wearing all of it over her sari. The scene is full of intense emotion and heavy breathing on her part. When she returns at midnight to reclaim the necklace, Ray really turns on the melodramatic effects: a shot of fresh flowers dying, the sound of her footsteps moving toward the bedroom, the creaking hinge of the bedroom door, and finally the skeletal hand. With the ghost story proper now over, the writer laughingly addresses the shrouded figure, who tells him that many of the details are false and that he should know because he is Phanibhusan (that is, a ghost). At this, the writer scrambles away in terror, leaving his umbrella and his book.

At the level of pure story, *Monihara* is a good ghost tale. At another level, it is a cautionary tale about what can happen to a man if he lets his wife get out of control. In this aspect, the film has a sexist bias (women are gold-hungry and greedy—prone to excess), unusual for Ray but typical of many old stories and folk tales. The schoolmaster/writer breaks in several times to point out how foolish the husband is in not dominating his wife and that he deserves his fate. In looking at all of Ray's work, *Monihara* is also interesting as a forerunner of *Charulata*. As a study in sexual and spiritual disaffection shot within darkened interiors, the film points ahead to Ray's later masterpiece. Many important elements differ in the two films (in *Monihara*, the husband is rejected by the wife) but the basic sexual triangle is present with the appearance of the cousin. There is also a particularly effective musical score by Ray based on a simple theme, which he uses throughout the film and most particularly in Moni's song.

10

KANCHANJUNGHA:
Ray's First Examination
of Contemporary India

Kanchanjungha (1962) is especially important as Ray's first treatment of contemporary India. Up to *Kanchanjungha*, Ray had examined his country through the meditative distance of time, a point of view he is most comfortable in. The film thus posed certain problems for Ray, and it is interesting to note that he increased his risk taking by using color for the first time and relying entirely on his own story and script, also for the first time. *Kanchanjungha* was a significant experiment for Ray. Part of the reason for the success of the film lies in Ray's intelligent decision to balance the risks by establishing a certain comfortableness in the filmmaking process: He chose to set the film in the familiar context of his own class, to shoot the film in the familiar setting of Darjeeling, and to employ actors he had worked with before, such as Chhabi Biswas *(The Music Room)* and Karuna Banerjee *(Pather Panchali* and *Aparajito)*.

The subject of *Kanchanjungha* is social change in contemporary India. The story is extremely simple but full of human subtlety. Indranath Choudhury's youngest daughter, Monisha, is being courted by an eligible suitor approved by her father. Her decision to reject him overturns Indranath's authority, and all it stands for, for the first time. The central scene that most clearly reveals Indranath's position occurs late in the film. In a long monologue, Indranath tells the young commoner Ashok about his pride in his success as a chairman of five companies. First he sends Ashok, like a servant, to fetch his muffler. He imagines that Ashok wants to use his influence to obtain a job, and at this point Ashok does. Indranath speaks about the importance of sports and the sporting spirit (a British contribution). After he speaks about the importance of influence for anyone working to get ahead, he then tells a story about his behavior during the movement to obtain independence from England. He had three friends who engaged in violent resistance against the British; one was killed and the other two rotted in jail. He tells Ashok that he did not rebel, and that as a result he now enjoys "the fruits of independence," including great wealth and a British title. Standing silently beside Indranath, Ashok looks more and more troubled. When Indranath finally offers his influence, Ashok turns him down. A moment later, Ashok slaps his forehead as if to awaken himself to what he has done. He has impulsively responded to Indranath's empty, self-satisfied declarations. To Ashok, a poor tutor, and to us, Indranath has revealed himself to be morally bankrupt.

The full extent of the devastation resulting from Indranath's tyranny can be seen in his family. His wife, Labanya, is depressed. An accomplished singer, she no longer practices her craft; instead she forces her sad face into a smile when Indranath tells her to brighten up. His oldest daughter, Anima, an actress, is unhappily married as a result of another of Indranath's arrangements. In the only interior scene in the film, Anima's husband, Shankar, tells Monisha to marry for love. Amil, Indranath's son, is a foolish playboy—clearly unable to establish himself in any independent relationship to his father. Only Monisha, the youngest child, has a chance to make something of her life. Her potential health is intimately connected with the process of separation from Indranath's power.

The first one-third of the film is made up of relatively brief scenes introducing the major characters. These scenes have a quickness and economy that sets the stage very well for the drama of Indranath's fall from power. The final two-thirds of the film is made up of a dozen scenes of dialogue, usually between two people. These scenes are shot on the paths and in the parks near the hotel in Darjeeling where the family is staying, and they tend to have a similar pattern in which the camera moves back and forth between the speakers or follows them slowly as they stroll along, talking.

Ray has avoided interior shooting in order to give his film more visual flair and variety—almost as if he felt the need to use the outdoor ambience to lighten the heavy emphasis on dialogue. Compare, for example, the interior scene between Shankar and Anima and almost any of the later outdoor scenes. In the interior scene, characters move in and out of the room (Monisha comes in at one point, and then leaves); there are brief snatches of dialogue and an elliptical process of exchange which has a greater weight of implication than the later, talkier scenes. If *Kanchanjungha* has a major weakness, it is its talkiness; its script has the feeling of a stage play, and a rather unusual stage play at that, for the unities of time, place, and action are observed precisely. There is no foreshortening of time; the film covers an hour and a half of the last afternoon of the Choudhury family's stay in Darjeeling. Does Ray's unusual reliance upon dialogue betray an uneasiness in his first examination of the contemporary scene? Nevertheless, all the dialogue scenes are well handled; none seems to go on too long.

The most cinematically interesting of these scenes involves the long exchange between Indranath and Ashok, which I referred to earlier. This scene is introduced by the first long pause in the film in which landscape carries the burden of implication instead of dialogue. There are four long takes of the landscape as the mist rolls in. The film then shifts to a pattern of cross-cutting between Labanya, sitting mournfully by herself in the mist, Anima and Shankar in an embittered discussion in the park, their daughter as she takes a pony ride around the paths (the daughter's progress on the paths is used as a linking device to these different family groups), Praneb and Monisha as he presses his courtship, and Indranath and Ashok. Each of these groups is experiencing simultaneously its own form of crisis: Labanya is contemplating whether she'll submit once again to Indranath's in-sistence—this time about Monisha's future; Shankar and Anima are talking about separation and divorce; Monisha is feeling more and more suffocated by Praneb's friendly but persistent pressure about marriage. Characteristi-cally, Indranath is the least aware that he, too, is facing a crisis. He goes on and on about his own past prowess in cricket, the importance of sports in general, the decline of modern standards of work, and the disruptions of the marketplace by strikes and riots. The central shot of this sequence lasts one minute and seventeen seconds. Indranath and Ashok appear at the far end of the path. There's a twisted iron railing in the foreground. The mist comes down the mountain obscuring the two men as they walk slowly toward the camera. Gradually the mist dissipates and the two are sharply revealed as they come to a halt near the railing. This shot is a miniature of the whole final two-thirds of the film, in which the visuals underline the ongoing pro-cess of clarification that is occurring among the different family groups. As Ashok stands listening to Indranath's fulsome declarations, he finally sees Indranath for what he is. There's an implication here that Indranath is not as secure in his self-concept as he'd like to be. When he says, "I have lived. I exist. I have a title from my former masters of which I'm very proud," there's a sense of deep uneasiness behind the confident mask. Like most tyrants, he needs total compliance in order to feel good about himself. As a slavish imitator of British values he has never found his identity in his native Bengali soil. Unconsciously he's aware of his imposture. He never once looks at Ashok until the little "nobody" turns him down. He's off in his own world of arrogant superiority, and yet he deeply needs Ashok's respectful attention. *Kanchanjungha* is, in this respect, a political statement about post-independence India, in which pervasive manifestations of the imperial past persist. The film suggests that many of the "movers and shak-ers" of modern India (the Indranaths and, to a lesser extent, the Pranebs) continue to worship at the shrine of the Raj, even though their time is passing. Indranath is like Sir Boren, the titled member of the board of directors in the later *Seemabaddha (Company Limited)*, though Sir Boren's im-itation of the British imperial style is given a comic turn.

After Monisha walks away from the frustrated Praneb, she hides behind a tree in the mist-shrouded central square, her body shaking with emotion. An Indian bagpipe band, in kilts and all, is playing in the square. It is a further manifestation of the British influence (in this case, Scottish; for, as Indranath informs Ashok, Darjeeling was transformed by a Dr. Campbell from a village into a civilized hill station). The wild, agitated music is well-suited to Monisha's inner state. Later, when Ashok recounts to Monisha what happened between him and her father, he says he can't fully under-stand why he rejected Indranath's offer of influence. "Perhaps it's this place that made me do it," he says, referring to the magic of the misty landscape. Ashok's story inadvertently gives Monisha the courage to reject Praneb and resist her father. More importantly, Ashok's comment about the landscape emphasizes the significance of Ray's use of landscape and color in *Kanchanjungha*.

The mountain setting of Darjeeling does more than provide visual variety; it is an essential device of meaning. The movement of the film from early sunlight to increasing mist, to a final clearing, is complementary with the growing complication of relationships between the characters. The sunny afternoon gives way to evening mists and shadows, dissolving the clear outlines of people and things. These relationships are, as usual with Ray, finely shaded. Anima's and Shankar's decision to repair their unhappy relationship for the sake of their child seems the least satisfactory. Their unhappiness seems so pervasive that no amount of hopeful change can redeem it. Monisha's situation at the end is improved. Praneb withdraws his suitorship with tact and sensitivity. Monisha invites Ashok to consider her a friend and to visit her in Calcutta. Labanya resolves to resist Indranath's plans for Monisha. The last close-ups of Indranath show his anger and disbelief at what has happened. Behind him, in the final shots of the film, the great mountain of Kanchanjungha finally stands revealed. Indranath has been waiting for days to see it, but he is preoccupied with other matters. The final clearing away of the mist in late afternoon is, as I've suggested, the visual complement to the resolutions of the various complications within the family. Indranath's inability to see the great chain of mountains is typical of him. Like Praneb, he is essentially out of touch with his physical environment; the landscape holds no special meaning for him, whereas for Monisha and Ashok and Jagadish, the bird watcher, the physical setting is wonderful. Their love of nature causes them to be drawn together in the process of natural selection which the film dramatizes, much like the process of pairing-off which occurs in *Days and Nights in the Forest*, to which *Kanchanjungha* can be seen as a forerunner. In this sense, Indranath and Praneb, the pragmatists, though they may have money and power, are the losers. The spiritual and romantic sensibilities of the others enable them to fare better. Monisha's friendship with Ashok is a sign of her vitality. She won't cancel herself out as her mother has. And even Labanya, sitting in the mist, breaks into song before she decides to go against her husband. The landscape affects her, too. It should be added that in his depiction of the landscape, Ray's use of color is as subtle as his depiction of human relationships. The setting of Darjeeling and the mountains nearby is rendered with lovely shading and half-tones. Color is an effective device of meaning in the film. When the great mountain emerges clearly at the end, so do the colors which have been muted by the misty sunlight.

Kanchanjungha is thus a strong statement of women's rights, in the cases of Labanya and Monisha. In Anima's case, this statement is qualified. As a woman who has betrayed her husband with a former lover, her guiltiness is probably the main cause of her timidity with her husband. In any case, when Shankar asks her to tear up the letters her lover has written her (and which she discovers Shankar has read without her knowledge), she does so quickly and then meekly asks, "What will you do now?" She doesn't get angry that he has violated her privacy, nor does she get angry when Shankar implies that he has had affairs, too. Ray's portrait of the unfaithful wife, in Anima, has none of the prideful sensuality we might see in a more Western depiction.

The message of *Kanchanjungha*, though developed with subtlety, is fairly clear: The old ways must give way to the new; the old authoritarian system must allow the young to find their own way in a problematic world.

11

ABHIJAN (THE EXPEDITION):
A Good Man Gone Wrong

Abhijan (The Expedition) was made in 1962, the same year as *Kanchan-jungha*. The film is very rarely shown, even in many Ray retrospectives, and though it's not one of his better films it's an important film in the pattern of his development. Along with the impossible-to-see *Chiriakhana (The Zoo), Abhijan*, according to Ray's response to a question by Henri Micciollo, was created in a difficult financial period.[1] *Devi* and *Kanchanjungha* had not done well at the box office in India. Producers were wary of Ray's work, for the moment, and since friends had acquired the rights to the melodramatic novel on which *Abhijan* is based, financing was available. Ray had written the screenplay for his friends but did not intend to direct. However, since he likes to keep working and had no other shooting projects he agreed to direct. Melodrama is not Ray's strong point and the film shows it. Even though the choice of material was not Ray's, the film nevertheless represents, like *Kanchanjungha*, a period of transition in which Ray is moving away from the great early films (the Apu trilogy, *Jalsaghar, Devi*) and toward a more extensive examination of contemporary reality—a transition which culminates in the urban films *Pratidwandi (The Adversary), Seemabaddha (Company Limited)*, and *Jana Aranya (The Middleman)*.

Abhijan is the story of Narsingh, a taxi driver, who is caught in the bind between his caste and his class. As a Rajput, Narsingh is supposedly strong and carefree; he has two lions tattooed on one arm, and he's proud and fierce as befits his warrior ancestors. He's also a troubled, vulnerable man, however; his wife has left him and he drinks too much. His caste is only one level below the Brahmin (he's a Kshatriya) but his job is that of a lower class. This causes him great problems. He wants to quit driving a taxi and become a gentleman but when he recklessly passes the car of a powerful, local policeman he has his permit taken away and is temporarily left without a way to earn money. He allows himself to be persuaded to transport illegal drugs for a local businessman-racketeer in return for a one-third interest. He has fallen for Neeli, the pretty, innocent sister of a fellow driver, and he wants to be able to show her that he's successful. The racketeer's girl friend, Gulabi, a beautiful former prostitute, is more interested in Narsingh than is Neeli. When Narsingh learns at the last minute that the racketeer is about to be raided by the police, he backs out of the drug deal and goes off with Gulabi. He has abandoned, momentarily at least, his dreams of being a gentleman and recognizes the strong basic values which Gulabi represents.

The opening sequence, before the credits, establishes Narsingh's troubled condition. It's a long single shot in which one of Narsingh's drunken fellow drivers talks to him about his troubles ("So you lost one woman. Get another. Start a new taxi company with me. Things will get better."). Narsingh doesn't say a word; we see part of his anguished face reflected in a broken mirror. He's a fragment of his former self, of his proud lineage and his caste. Still partly drunk, he takes a group of old men on a fast reckless ride to catch a speeding train. The film catches his self-destructive energy very well at this point. In the scene with the policeman, who is shaking with rage, Narsingh refuses to beg to keep his permit; he tells his assistant Rahman that his caste background prevents him from begging. Rahman looks up to him, not merely because he works for him as maintenance man for the car and as a hustler who drums up passenger trade, but because for him Narsingh is a superior person, tall, handsome, full of authority (Soumitra Chatterjee plays Narsingh and Robi Ghosh plays Rahman).

The scene in which Narsingh agrees to work as a courier in the drug deal is played as a straight temptation scene. Laughing and smiling, the fat-faced racketeer gets him to agree that he likes risk and that as a driver he knows that the best route between points is often not a straight one. Despite his reluctance and suspicions he gives in. The lighting in this scene is very dim and diffuse (the film seems to get darker and darker as Narsingh's world nearly collapses). The other strong pull on Narsingh comes from his friend Joseph and his sister Neeli. They are low-caste Christians and very gentle and sweet. They promise a kind of salvation for Narsingh, Neeli as a future wife and Joseph as a steadfast friend (Narsingh has no friends). In one of the more interesting scenes, Joseph takes Narsingh into a rocky landscape and shows him a large, looming boulder which legend says has the power to collect all the evils in the world, leaving the supplicant calm and free. Narsingh has the fantasy of riding horseback in this place, like a Rajput warrior. For all his harshness and seeming cynicism, he's a dreamer and a romantic who hasn't gone totally sour. Neeli, a very good girl and naive, isn't aware that he's interested in her; she's in love with a crippled man and actually asks Narsingh to help them leave in his taxi so they can marry without her mother's objection. The sensual Gulabi is much more suited to him though he doesn't know it at first. One of the better scenes occurs when she tells him about her life and how she was sold by her father into prostitution. Narsingh refuses to consider marriage to her because it would be a further comedown in status. He eventually takes her away only after Joseph has shamed him into rejecting the drug deal.

Abhijan is full of twists and turns of plot too complicated to enumerate here. The film moves at a fairly brisk pace suitable to its action-oriented story, with long takes (more typical of Ray) used appropriately in such scenes as the temptation scene and Gulabi's life story. The deep-focus black-and-white images are very well composed and lighted—in many ways the purely visual element is the best part the film. Ray seems to have felt the need to use music very frequently to accompany his drama. Uncharacteristically, he's underlining his messages in a heavy-handed way. Two scenes are wildly bad. The fight between Narsingh and one of the surly, jealous drivers is not convincing. Ray's characteristic abhorrence of the direct presentation of violence is probably the cause here. The other scene is a howler. As Narsingh is about to rescue Gulabi from the clutches of the racketeer, he has a vision of himself as a Rajput warrior on horseback. There's a sound splice of horse's hooves (in the midst of this realistic scene, the viewer is naturally surprised: where does the horse come from?) as he pursues them in his taxi and then he appears in soft focus in a turban, bobbing up and down on his mount. The horse is not shown; it's like a studio horse in North American Westerns from the 1930s and 1940s, rocking up and down mechanically while an artificial landscape slides by in the distance. Narsingh is evidently having a nice fantasy of being a Rajput warrior at this point. It's an ending worthy of the most conventional Hindi film. It's also conventional (and unconvincing) in its suggestion that Gulabi will make Narsingh's life good, without Narsingh having to take a close look at himself. At no point in the film does Narsingh ever examine himself and ask in what way he might have caused his own difficulties. He's the same at the end as at the beginning. The interior dimension—so strong in most of Ray's work—is missing.

Abhijan doesn't bear much of Ray's personal stamp. It's a fairly conventional film and a good example of the collaborative nature of filmmaking, in which, as often happens, a fine filmmaker is asked to step in and rescue a faltering project. Nevertheless, Ray was involved in the film from the start. His decision to direct material uncongenial to his natural style is a strong indication of his need to keep working. Marie Seton, who was present while Ray was making the film, reports his high enthusiasm for the project.[2] He may have felt the need for a popular film—a natural feeling after the relative lack of success of *Devi* and *Kanchanjungha*. *Abhijan* illustrates a cardinal dimension of filmmaking, one often overlooked by film critics: the extent to which aesthetic choices are dictated by economic conditions.

NOTES

1. Henri Micciollo, *Satyajit Ray* (Lausanne: Editions l'Age d'Homme, 1981), p. 288.

2. Marie Seton, *Satyajit Ray: Portrait of a Director* (Bloomington: Indiana University Press, 1971), p. 68.

12

MAHANAGAR (THE BIG CITY): The Woman Leads the Way

Mahanagar (1963) shows Ray's indebtedness to Italian neorealism better than any other of his films. As its English title, *The Big City*, indicates, it is an extensive look at urban life. Ray's determination to capture the daily rhythms of one family's threadbare existence in the city has a quick pace, saturated with realistic detail, without any of the lyrical or meditative rhythms we had noticed in his earlier films. Such rhythms would, of course, be inappropriate to a city setting. *Mahanagar* is one of Ray's longest films, and it feels like a long film. It is also worth pointing out that *Mahanagar* has relatively few open-air shots of the city streets. It's a film of interiors, shot mainly in the studio; and though it deals with city matters, the city itself is largely absent. The film suggests a reluctance to engage fully the environment of the city (and, by implication, its poverty, pollution, and savage inequality). Ray has argued that this reluctance—at least in the early films— was caused by the near impossibility of shooting in the streets without immediately drawing a crowd and damaging the shot.[1] Clearly there is more to it than this. The urban environment and its attendant social and political tensions were not entirely congenial to his sensibility.

Unlike Ray's earlier films, the plot of *Mahanagar* is fairly extensive. The Majumdar family lives in a tiny, three-room apartment. Subrata, an accountant in a new bank, doesn't earn enough for his mother, father, sister, wife, and son to live on. Arati, his wife, obtains a job as a salesgirl after Subrata enthusiastically helps her with the letter of application. When Arati proves successful, Subrata feels insecure and resentful. His father, Priyagopal, takes an even more negative attitude toward Arati's success and puts pressure on his son to force Arati to quit her job. Subrata applies for an additional part-time job and types up a letter of resignation for Arati. When his bank fails and he loses his job, he hastily tells Arati not to hand in the letter. Arati is given a promotion and asks for a raise, which she receives. Her boss, however, has a violent prejudice against Anglo-Indians, and when he fires her friend Edith, Arati hands him the letter. Subrata understands and supports her. The two of them face an uncertain future in the big city without fear.

The early scenes of family life in cramped quarters stress both economic poverty and family love and affection. In a natural style we've come to expect of him, Ray gives us the momentary glances of affection and humor between family members. Subrata pulls his sister's hair and kids her about her interest in "domestic science." It's clear that he and Arati love each

other, despite the tension caused by their poverty. Subrata's mother is devoted to Priyagopal. As a member of the older generation, she would never
think of going to work. Priyagopal has his old cronies in to talk about cross-
word puzzles and to complain about old age. Subrata is devoted to his
young son, Pintu. When we are given a long take in which Arati and Subrata wordlessly commiserate after a storm of criticism from the aged parents, we realize how much the film is made up of short sequences detailing
the business of family life. These quick rhythms evoke life in the city. As
there are few long takes in the film, so there are almost no long shots. We
are confined to settings within the home, the office, the washroom (where
the women workers can communicate in privacy). It is a film of interiors
and has the feeling that it was shot largely in the studio. There are even
relatively few street scenes, in which we have a sense of natural light as
well as extensive space. The soundtrack is busy with a mixture of sounds
(a radio playing next door, a car or motorcycle going by).

Two supporting roles particularly deserve attention. The Anglo-Indian,
Edith Simmons, wears high heels and a skirt, while the other saleswomen
wear saris. She speaks English and asserts the demands of the salesgirls that
they receive a commission for their work. She represents a westernized
femininity, both friendly, direct, and assertive. Arati sees her as a role model
and likes her. It's no accident that she resigns when Edith is fired; she sees
herself in Edith. Their boss, Mr. Mukherjee, is energetic and friendly. He
has a good salesman's liking for people, but as an administrator he is now
restricted to his desk. He admires Arati and even offers to help Subrata
find work. His prejudice against Anglo-Indian women seems unaccountable
at first. He implies that they're whores. When he fires Edith, he is acting
out the sexist prejudice earlier displayed by both Priyagopal and Subrata.
He can't stand Edith's westernized ways and her assertiveness. He'll toler-
ate Arati's demands as long as they come from a woman who displays the
traditional Bengali dress and manner (she pleads with him for a raise; she
doesn't ask directly). For all his warmth and humor, Mukherjee stands as a
warning about the limits of women's aspirations in Bengali society.

Mahanagar moves toward depth of statement in its incomplete examination of the relationship between Subrata and Arati. Their marriage is able
to survive because Subrata, partially by force of circumstance, is finally
willing to accept Arati's status as a working woman, capable of self-deter-
mination as well as bringing in money. The modern marriage in *Mahanagar*
stands in sharp contrast to the marriage between Bhupati and Charulata in
Charulata. By using the same actress, Madhabi Mukherjee, as female lead
in both films, Ray seems to be making a statement about progress in wom-
en's roles from the nineteenth to twentieth centuries. Arati, in fact, seems
stronger and surer than Subrata. She is quickly offered promotion while he
remains in his accountant's job, unaware of the shaky condition of the bank
he works in. He's kindly but somewhat dreamy. Ray's decision to use Anil

Chatterjee as Subrata contributes to our sense of his weakness. Chatterjee's soft, chubby face has a kind of boyish petulance and sensitivity; he hasn't fully grown up. Ray had used him earlier in the role of the dependent Nandalal, who is mothered by little Ratan in "Postmaster," the first part of *Two Daughters*. After the bank fails, Subrata is chided by a family friend who tells him that in his position he should have known about the financial shakiness of the bank. When Arati brings home presents for everyone in the family, he remarks in self-pitying and melodramatic tones, "exit husband, enter wife." This self pity is a direct inheritance from his father, who is always complaining about being a "back number." He's naturally concerned that his wife will replace him in the position of economic power. Her gain in strength seems to him to diminish his own. He makes Arati throw out the lipstick Edith has given her. Purely by chance he overhears Arati support him in a conversation with a handsome man in a tea room. This incident helps him see that Arati is not trying to overthrow him. Ray's camera brings out her beauty very forcefully when she tells him that she means to be his loyal wife. Arati is able to be wife, mother, and wage earner without enormous stress or conflict within herself. Her growth in strength is admirably dramatized by Ray. Subrata's own growth is not nearly so well presented. When he supports Arati's impulsive decision to resign her job, he shows an unusual strength and calm, considering the harried and depressed man we've seen a few scenes earlier. Perhaps Arati's sureness is carrying him along. In any case, it's he who says in the final scene, as they both face the city without jobs, "We have lost our fears." His break with his father over the issue of Arati's working is not dramatized. Perhaps Ray felt that this important matter would deflect attention from the emphasis upon Arati's growth. Nevertheless, the omission of attention to Subrata's own growth constitutes a serious flaw in our understanding of his and Arati's developing relationship.

Ray seems to have intended Subrata to stand as a contrast figure to Arati—his weakness highlighting her strength—rather than have them both grow in strength and thus mutually enable each other. We do have an early sense of Subrata's growth. His attitudes at first are conventionally sexist. He jokingly tells his sister not to bother studying because "you'll end up in the kitchen like the rest." He has seen his mother comfortably accept the traditional role of the housewife, and that is what he expects of Arati. He tells Arati he doesn't want her to take a job because she is too attractive and "a woman's place is in the home." When he cheerfully searches the "want ads" with her, he is not fully aware of how he'll feel when she gets a job. His growing uneasiness is subtly presented when he interrupts Arati's first interview with Mukherjee by phoning to see if everything is going all right. He is comforting himself with the phone call as well as showing concern for Arati. He is willing, nevertheless, to use the money he's earning to buy Arati some clothes so that she can feel more fashionable at work. He is caught between the family's need for money and his own desire to maintain traditional ways. His turnaround at the end, as I have suggested, doesn't seem fully prepared for. Oddly enough, instead of a scene or two dramatizing the change, we are given a touching scene in which his father repents his harsh judgment of Subrata and Arati. The old man has collapsed while climbing the stairs to see his eye doctor and is recuperating at home. His near brush with death seems to have caused his change of heart. What is odd about this scene is that it occupies the place where a scene demonstrating Subrata's change might be. From this angle, the father seems to be acting not only for himself but for his son; it is as if he's momentarily a substitute for Subrata, or Subrata is an extension of him. Subrata's change evidently occurs without the necessity of a break with his father—a dubious development from the Western point of view, but one which is entirely in accord with behavior within the closely woven extended family in India. A Westerner who is used to different patterns of family behavior (sons and daughters choosing away from parental values and leaving home) may have some difficulty here. The drama of social change in *Mahanagar* is all the more interesting for a Western viewer because it takes place in the context of the Indian extended family. The changes take place and yet the family is preserved in an intimate relationship with one another. Perhaps Priyagopal's repentance releases Subrata and enables his change. Nevertheless, one still wishes for one or two scenes dramatizing Subrata's change toward the end of the film. The film would have had more dimension for such scenes.

The visual feeling of the film is one of acutely observed detail. Ray's social realism doesn't reach the resonance of DeSica's poetic realism in *Umberto D* or *The Bicycle Thief*. There is no sense of subtext or of the mythic dimension of the Apu trilogy or *Jalsaghar*. Cinematically, there are some brilliant details: Arati lying in bed at night as the camera pans up to reveal Subrata in profile, smoking behind a dense curtain of mosquito netting (Subrata's torment and confusion is perfectly evoked in this image); or Priyagopal's collapse on the stairs, in which we see the porter turn toward the camera in alarm at what he sees and then, in the next shot, we're given Priyagopal's cane as it bounces and clatters down the stairs. As usual with Ray, some of the best scenes involve long takes with little dialogue. The longest shot in the film, for instance, lasts nearly two minutes and presents Arati and Subrata as Arati attempts to leave the house for work for the first time. First we see Arati entering a doorway and finding her son, Pintu, lying discouraged on the bed. His mom is abandoning him. She tries to comfort him and even tries to bribe him with the promise of a toy, but he struggles out of her grasp. As the two of them move left, out of the frame, Subrata enters the doorway and slowly and pensively puts betel nut in his mouth (some oral comfort). As he stands nearly paralyzed in the room, Arati comes behind him into the doorway and leans against it, weeping.

There is the far-off sound of a bell tolling the hour; Subrata slowly looks at his watch and says dejectedly that they must catch their train. This shot has both a fluidity of movement within the frame and a stillness (or minimalism) of human response which makes it very absorbing. The viewer's eye catches the subtlest detail. The sequence closes with a series of shots which show Arati and Subrata slowly leaving the house until Pintu releases them by asking what kind of toy Arati's going to buy.

Mahanagar is a good first attempt by Ray to portray life in the city. Its story of radical change within the context of the extended family is affectingly told. Not until *Pratidwandi* ("The Adversary," 1970) and *Janya Aranya* ("The Middleman," 1975) did Ray bring his full powers to the subject of the city.

NOTE

1. Interview with Satyajit Ray, Calcutta, January 4, 1988.

13

CHARULATA:
The Seeds of Reform

After three films examining contemporary India, Ray once again moved his subject back in time and made one of his most successful films in *Charulata* (1964). The film is set in 1879 and, in part, it examines the early days of the movement for independence from England. Based on a novella by Tagore, "The Broken Nest," it dramatizes the power of imaginative writing as an agent of self-growth. Most importantly, the film examines the secondary status of educated women in India, and shows the growth into strength of its central character, Charulata. The film was very popular in India, and Ray has several times referred to it as his finest.

The opening section dramatizes Charulata's loneliness and boredom. Childless, she is living with her wealthy husband Bhupati, who seems totally preoccupied with his political newspaper. As she wanders shiftlessly around the house, we see her bored irritation, but we also see her pleasure in reading and note that she has a lovely musical voice as she hums softly after picking up a book. She is clearly a woman of sensitivity and intelligence who finds herself reduced to peeping out in the street through opera glasses. She even peers at her husband through the glasses after he walks by without noticing her. The opera glasses suggest that she is both distanced from life and that she has a noticing eye. The interior setting of the house, with its heavy Victorian furniture and its ornate velvet wallpaper, accurately presents the historical period but it also suggests an interior environment that is oppressive and confining, much like Charulata's own interior life. She lives in a genteel prison of her own and her husband's devising. Yet she is not fully conscious of her situation. This is the way educated Indian women have always lived. Her love for Amal, the poetic cousin of Bhupati, changes all this.

Nor is Bhupati conscious of his own situation. He is obsessed with his newspaper, *The Sentinel*, which he produces in the ground-floor rooms of the house. He is extremely idealistic, high-minded, and unworldly, though warmhearted. He feels keenly the injustices which India is suffering under British rule (the land tax, the poll tax, the lack of political representation). In an early scene, he reads an editorial which speaks nobly of patriotism, duty, and truth and then informs Charulata that he'll explain his political ideas to her "some day." He regards his wife as a pretty household ornament. When she gives him a handkerchief she has embroidered for him (she spends a good deal of her time embroidering), he asks her where she found the time to do it. He seems totally unaware of her condition until she confronts him with it by asking mournfully whether he really thinks she doesn't have time on her hands. He tells her he has no need for poems or plays because "I've got my Charulata." He is completely antiliterary and abstracted. His unconsciousness and high-mindedness combine to make his awakening the most abrupt of the three major characters. This awakening occurs in two stages. First, Charulata's brother steals money from him after Bhupati has naively given the malcontent the keys to his safe on the principle that he will be happier working for the newspaper if he has more responsibility. Bhupati's discovery of the theft shakes him deeply and his confession to Amal of his disillusionment in his brother-in-law's trust creates the second stage, for Amal and Charulata have been on the edge of acting out their love. Amal's abrupt departure so upsets Charulata that she bursts out in grief and is observed by her husband. The interior regions of his wife's life finally stand revealed to him.

Bhupati's lack of interest in imaginative literature is closely tied by Ray to his lack of interest in the inner life of himself and others. In one scene he asks Amal to read one of his poems and then fails to comprehend even the title, "Light of the Moonless Night." Is it something scientific? What kind of light, exactly, is Amal getting at? He seems to have no sense of the figurative dimensions of language (the one example we have of his newspaper writing, the editorial Charulata overhears, is extremely abstract and dry). After puzzling over the title to the poem, he abruptly advises Amal to accept an arranged marriage with a girl from a well-placed family (Charulata is standing, anguished, in deep shadow as this is going on). Bhupati sees Amal as a hopelessly impractical dreamer. He doesn't see that Amal has a sensitivity to others that he himself lacks. Indeed, Ray has drawn the two leading male roles in such sharp contrast as to suggest that the film is an allegory, Bhupati representing the rational and public man, Amal the poetic and private man, with Charulata in the central mediating position between the two.

Like Apu of *The World of Apu* (also played by Soumitra Chatterjee), Amal has some of the properties of a Shiva figure, a flute-playing, singing, and dancing god—a god of creation and destruction. He can't understand at all why Bhupati wishes to criticize the government in his newspaper, not because he is timid but because he is completely nonpolitical (though both he and Bhupati are passionate admirers of Raja Rammohun Roy, the founder of Brahmoism and an early leader in the independence movement). He loves to sing, as does Charulata, and at least one of the scenes is constructed around his singing of the ballad "I know you, I know you, O Mademoiselle" in such a way that it is almost like a scene from a musical. He's witty and playful—a young university graduate interested in having a good time after earning his degree. He accepts Bhupati's request that he encourage Charulata in her literary leanings with a kind of feigned reluctance (he calls it a "tax" upon his newfound independence). The scenes between Amal and

Charulata in the middle of the film have a light and airy quality (the garden/ swinging scenes in particular) as compared with the darker interior images toward the end. We see Charulata beginning to love Amal before he realizes it. They are kindred spirits. Amal stimulates Charulata's literary interest by his own writing but not in the way Bhupati had imagined. Amal publishes an essay he wrote and which he promised her he wouldn't publish, and this violation of trust provokes Charulata to begin her own writing. Her love for Amal becomes absolutely clear to him when, after her writing is published, she says she'll give it all up for him. His abrupt departure, after Bhupati's betrayal by his brother-in-law, is a brutal termination of their relationship from her point of view. He doesn't leave her a note or tell her why he must go. He merely instructs Bhupati, in a letter, to tell her to keep on writing. Amal's behavior, in the end, is a mixture of honesty and carelessness, even caddishness. He's still entirely a vain, callow young university graduate enjoying his freedom and experimenting with life. His behavior forces Charulata to continue her process of growth on her own. His creative energy helps her begin writing, and his destructive energy forces her to separate from him and find her own way.

Charulata's growth, as I've suggested, is the central action of the film. Her potential for growth is indicated by Ray's use of her sister-in-law Manda as a contrasting figure. Manda is pretty but uneducated (she can't read) and somewhat coarse. She sticks with her husband Umapada even though he's weak and corrupt. Manda is attracted to Amal but he is not to her. With a touch of mockery, he calls her "conservative woman" and Charulata "liberal woman." Umapada is, however, a more significant figure than his wife. He's the only purely evil character in all of Ray's films. He resents Bhupati's circumstances—and his idealism—and coolly plots to help himself to Bhupati's money as well as ruin the newspaper. He's not disturbed, or driven; his malice is calm and rational. There's a relaxed sensuousness to him in the scene in which he's lying down, stroking Manda's arm, chewing slowly and taking deep, comfortable breaths as he hints to her of his plot.

Charulata's growth is linked throughout the film to the act of writing. The scene in which she begins to write is connected entirely with events in her childhood. As she sits pensively on the swing, crumpled pages of her writing lying around her on the ground, Ray uses a series of dissolves from images of smooth water, a sailing boat, an old woman spinning cotton on a wheel, a moving playground wheel full of children lighted by sparklers, running children, masked figures from a religious ceremony or a carnival shot from a low child-view angle. These images are vivid and somewhat disturbing, like a child's first experiences. Charulata is instinctively acting out Amal's earlier observation that she might use her earliest memories as a subject for her writing. We don't know exactly what she writes, though the next scene tells us that she has published something, for she playfully taps Amal on the head with the same magazine he has published his first piece in, and shows him her name in print. After presenting him with slippers she has embroidered for him, she tearfully tells him she published her writing to please him and that she'll stop writing if he wants. She is offering herself as a second-class woman, content to sacrifice herself for her man. She hasn't essentially changed from the lonely and bored woman of the opening sequence who conceals herself in order to support her husband— except that she knows she has a proven skill which she can use to define herself and give herself strength. Her proposal, later on, to Bhupati that she write and edit the literary and cultural section of a new newspaper he wants to start is a clear sign of her growth. As the custodian of Bengali culture in Bhupati's new effort, she will balance his interest in politics with her own rich aesthetic sensibility. Her cultural nationalism—her embodiment of the Bengali sensibility in her songs and in her graceful movement— seems even stronger than Bhupati's nationalism, which is characterized by his worship of things British, as seen in his style of dress, his fascination with British politics, his use of the English language in his newspaper. Her section of the new newspaper will be in Bengali and will show the power of Bengali traditions. Bhupati's enthusiastic response to her proposal is a sign that they may be able to reconcile their difficulties.

Of the three central characters, Charulata emerges the strongest from her growth into awareness and strength. As a mediating figure between Bhupati and Amal, she combines a poetic sensibility with a sense of the public dimension of India's problems. Compared with her, each man seems incomplete. Ray's unpublished essay, "On Charulata," makes it clear that he sees Charulata as a far better writer than Amal.[1] She brings more growth and maturity to her writing. She stands as another example of woman's strength in Ray's world. Speaking of her, Ray has said, "A woman's beauty, I think also lies in her patience and endurance in a world where men are generally more vulnerable and in need of guidance."[2] Charulata's character is further defined in the much later character of Bimala in *The Home and the World*. Bimala also stands between her idealistic husband Nikhil and a more opportunistic version of Amal in Sandip. The many similarities between the two films (in historical period, in visual confinement to ornate Victorian interiors) even suggest that the later film is another (and less successful) version of *Charulata*.

Charulata is the film which best illustrates Ray's careful scenic preparation before shooting and the superb coordination he obtained with his longtime art director, Bansi Chandragupta. In an interview in *Montage*, Chandragupta talks about the detailed drawings Ray gave him concerning the interior space of Charulata's house.[3] The quadrangular courtyard is flanked by verandas which look into the bedrooms. However, only three verandas were constructed because—given the carefully plotted camera positions Ray knew he would shoot from—only three were necessary to suggest a quadrangular space. Charu's bedroom and its adjoining veranda were built on a six-foot-high platform in life-size scale, while the two other verandas were deliberately built smaller to convey a sense of distance and perspective and to accommodate the small (80- x 40-foot) floor space available in the studio. The wallpaper and other Victorian interior furnishings were found by Ray and Chandragupta after scouring the bazaars in Calcutta. Thus in *Charulata*, as in all of Ray's films, limitations were turned to advantages by careful planning before shooting began.

Cinematically, *Charulata* is something close to perfection. Every scene is exquisitely evoked in terms of lighting, camera movement, and (above all) acting. The first of several sequences I want to examine in some detail is the opening one in which Ray presents Charulata's boredom. The sequence is made of 29 shots and lasts seven and a half minutes; it contains no dialogue and very little music. After ordering tea for her husband and shushing her noisy parrot, Charu throws down the handkerchief she's been embroidering and selects a book to read. The camera follows along behind her as she walks slowly toward the window, reading. The rhythm of the shots here is very slow and desultory, befitting her aimlessness. It picks up, however, after she glances out the slatted blind at the goings-on she's been hearing from the street (sounds of street noise are audible in many of the scenes in the house; we are subtly reminded that there's constant life going on out there). In a series of quick shots we see her get her opera glasses and resume peeking out at the street. There's a fine shot (number 13) of her hand swinging the glasses as she moves briskly along the balcony railing. The glasses are shown through the moving railing supports as the camera moves with her (this shot is duplicated later on when Charu carries her first published piece of writing to show Amal; in a sense, her curiosity about the outside world finally issues in creative expression). A series of shots shows her moving from window to window and shows us what she sees: a beggar with a monkey, servants carrying an enclosed sedan chair, a portly man in a dhoti carrying an umbrella. The shots of what she sees have the conventional figure-eight framing of binoculars but, oddly enough, they don't move. It's as if Charu has put the opera glasses between the slats, rather than keeping them back a bit and moving them from aperture to aperture as any enthusiastic viewer would do, in order to keep the object in view. After this excitement, there's a long middle-distance shot of Charu as she turns away from the window and moves very slowly across the room to the piano where she picks out a few notes. The largo rhythm of her boredom has returned. Hearing Bhupati walking along the interior balcony, she moves to the door where she witnesses his passing within two or three feet. He's deeply absorbed in his reading and doesn't notice her. There's a shot of him walking away from her and then a shot of her watching him go. Slowly, hesitantly, she raises the opera glasses to observe him, her upper lip slightly curled. There's a shot of Bhupati through the glasses and then a shot of Charu lowering the glasses as the camera executes a reverse zoom, abruptly distancing us from her. This reverse zoom puts a decisive period to the end of a masterful sequence, but it also presents certain problems. First, why should we be so abruptly distanced from Charu when the sequence has placed us so subtly and tactfully within her boredom and her loneliness? A second issue involves Ray's use of zoom shots throughout the film. There are several zoom shots, some of them quite effective. Others, it seems to me, are questionable and present the only cinematic flaw in an otherwise perfect surface.

The opening shot of the film is, in fact, a reverse zoom. Rather than have the camera back away from Charu's hands embroidering a "B" on a hand-kerchief (the image against which Ray shows the credits), he employs a zoom to show her sitting on a bed. He's clearly experimenting with the shot. There are several effective zooms: when Amal blows into the house with the storm the camera closes on him fast (it's Charu's first sight of him); when Amal rejects Bhupati's suggestion that he marry, the camera zooms in on Charu standing in deep shadow—its movement expressing her exul-tation. And finally, there's a zoom to the grieving Charu collapsed on the bed as Bhupati, who is standing in the doorway, sees for the first time that his wife is in love with Amal. This last shot evokes the perfect function of the zoom shot in the drama of growing awareness—and *Charulata* is nothing if not a drama of awareness, even in the sense of that master of dramas of awareness, Henry James. The trouble is that the zoom is not a subtle shot; it calls attention to itself. When Charu hears Bhupati read Amal's letter, in which no word is addressed to her, she runs to his room and we're given a reverse zoom as she enters the door and then another forward zoom as she sees the new slippers she made for him. The zooms, it might be added, refer most to Charu's mode of seeing; they are part of her way of bringing distant things up close suddenly, as with the opera glasses. They also ex-press what is happening in her world, in which sensations and feelings— and the outside world—are collapsing in upon her, piercing through her sedate, boring (and emotionally frustrating) way of life. They express very well what is going on within her, but they are overused.

The zooms are minor matters, however. Two other superb sequences follow Charu's. Directly after we've observed her boredom, we're presented with Bhupati as he chats with Charu while eating. In one shot lasting two and a half minutes, the camera stays on Bhupati, moving slowly to the right, behind Charu. She's the dutiful, silent wife, listening to her hus-band's ideas about giving her brother employment. All of Bhupati's high-mindedness and generosity and blindness to what is really going on inside Charu is apparent here. More interestingly, even though we never see her face in this shot, we know from the previous sequence what Bhupati cannot see. The third sequence, Amal's arrival, is equally well done and involves some very fast cutting between shots of people hurrying to get things inside before the storm breaks, papers flying in the air, parrots swinging in their cages while we hear the sound of glass breaking, and then Amal's abrupt, tempestuous appearance in a cloud of dust and wind. Significantly, he's a bit of a dandy, with a carefully trimmed mustache and a dark mole on his right cheek like a beauty spot. The first three sequences in the film give us each character precisely rendered.

Two other sequences, which lie very close together, deserve detailed notice. In the first, Charu and Amal are tensely awaiting Bhupati's return from town where he discovers the theft. They know something is wrong. They're also uneasy about their own growing involvement. The first part of the sequence is all done with body language and with the choreographic movement of bodies within the dark, confined space of the house. In the first shot we see Amal reflected in the dark glass of a clock as the camera moves right to show him standing pensively, with Charu well behind him. Ray's manipulation of focal length accentuates our sense of the space between the two characters. As Charu moves toward Amal we see him standing half averted from her in sharp, deep focus. At the sound of Bhupati's arrival, the focus shifts to a medium close-up of Charu standing in profile, with Amal blurred in the background. As she turns slowly toward him, he comes back into focus. The first eight shots of the sequence are entirely without dialogue but heavy with implication. In shot nine Amal finally breaks the silence by asking if Bhupati isn't coming upstairs to the living quarters. As he moves to go to Bhupati, Charu bridges the distance between them by touching him and pleading for him to stay, "no matter what happens." Amal's response of "what could happen?" shows that he's not yet aware of the full implications of their involvement. He has to ask Charu to let him go.

The second sequence follows directly after Amal's conversation with Bhupati about the demise of the newspaper and repeats some of the visual procedure of the earlier sequence. In the first shot we see Charu's face reflected in the dark glass of the door as the camera pans right to Bhupati, who is explaining to Amal his profound sense of betrayal. Ray has Bhupati sit down near a light on a table and lean close to it. He's coming closer to awareness, but still has a long way to go. Shot two cuts to a medium shot of Amal, looking terrible. He feels *he's* the betrayer. He glances down the hall and we see (in shot three) a long shot of Charu about to descend the stairs. As Bhupati continues ("My whole world seems to be crumbling") he rises and comes toward Amal who asks what he can do to help. With eyes glistening, Bhupati tells Amal to stay as he is and invites him to go to the seaside with him and Charu for a few days. On the tenth and final shot Amal lowers his head with a half smile in response to the invitation, as Bhupati moves out of the frame. When he raises his trembling face to the advancing camera his eyes are full of tears. He has barely managed to control himself with Bhupati. His hasty departure that night follows.

Charulata is a fine example of Ray's abilities as an adaptor of a work of literature. Working in terms of key scenes, he reshapes the rather dispersed structure of "The Broken Nest." As he points out in "On Charulata," he also provides more convincing motivation for Umapada's betrayal than Tagore, and he refuses to have Bhupati abandon Charu in the end and go to Mysore (as in Tagore), believing that this is "not consistent with his character as described by Rabindranath."[4] "On Charulata" reveals that Ray can be sharply critical, as well as admiring, of his master. The essay also points up the classical structure of the film, in which there is a distinct beginning, middle, and end. The "exposition" section, as Ray refers to it, ends with the scene at night in Bhupati's office when he asks Amal to help Charu with her literary efforts. The "denouement" begins with Bhupati's discovery of Umapada's betrayal. Ray's script "follows the classical method of screenplay-writing, namely through consecutive rounded scenes."[5] In this, and other films, Ray avoids the modern, expressionist devices of jumbled chronology and shifting points of view.

Finally, I want to comment briefly about the superb ending to *Charulata*. We don't know whether Charu and Bhupati will reconcile; so many painful things have happened to each one. Ray's use of a freeze-frame and stills perfectly evokes the equivocal nature of Bhupati's return home after his grief-stricken carriage ride during the night. Six brief shots suffice. After Charu twice asks him to come in and holds out her hand, we see (in shot one) Bhupati slowly put out his hand and we're given a freeze-frame of his hand about an inch away from hers. The second shot is a still photo of Charu, her head slightly tilted as if in question. The third is a chest-high still of Bhupati's grieving face. The fourth is a still of the servant holding a light. The fifth is a medium shot of the two, their hands nearly touching, in which the camera backs away on the still image to reveal them standing in the doorway. The sixth and last still is the familiar long shot down the hall to the top of the stairs, showing Bhupati and Charulata frozen in the same position as in number five. More than hesitancy is evoked here; the abrupt, fragmentary rhythms of the still shots accurately suggest a relationship in pieces, without wholeness and flow.

NOTES

1. "On Charulata," unpublished essay written by Ray in Bengali and translated into English by Kiron Raha, p. 18.

2. Chidananda Das Gupta, *Satyajit Ray* (New Delhi: Directorate of Film Festivals, 1981), p. 67.

3. *Montage*, special issue devoted to Satyajit Ray, published by Anandam Film Society, Bombay, July 1966.

4. "On Charulata," p. 38.

5. Ibid., p. 14.

14

KAPURUSH-O-MAHAPURUSH (THE COWARD AND THE HOLY MAN):
A Love Story and a Satire

The two films which make up *Kapurush-O-Mahapurush (The Coward and the Holy Man)* were made in 1965, directly after *Charulata*. Though the title suggests that the films are related, they are not at all, other than being based on stories by Premendra Mitra. They were probably coupled by Ray because, as he did in *Two Daughters*, he wished to put together two shorter efforts. Each film, though, runs about an hour and a quarter; together they make for a long evening of film viewing.

KAPURUSH

The more interesting of the two films is *Kapurush* which reveals that, for the first time, Ray is repeating himself both in subject matter and style. It's not too much of an exaggeration to say that *Kapurush* is a retelling of *Charulata* in a modern setting. There's the same love triangle, and Soumitra Chatterjee again plays the young lover, here named Amitabha, and Madhabi Mukherjee again plays the young wife, Karuna. They've been lovers some time ago; and when Amitabha's taxi breaks down and he's invited by Karuna's husband to spend the night, he comes upon her in what is total surprise for both of them. The husband, Bimal Gupta, is a blustering, hard-drinking materialist. He's worked hard to own his tea plantation, and he relishes his possessions. Unlike Bhupati, Charulata's husband, he has little sensitivity and perception. Behind his aggressive cheerfulness and loud laughter, we're allowed glimpses of a troubled spirit. He has everything he ever wanted: money, status, a young beautiful wife, yet he's still, unaccountably, unsatisfied. In his materialism he's as self-absorbed as Bhupati in his idealism. He never becomes aware of the tension between Amitabha and Karuna, as did Bhupati. In part, this lack of awareness is caused by Karuna's guarded and self-controlled responses to Amitabha's renewed advances (it was he who left the earlier relationship). She doesn't break down like Charulata; she's determined to preserve herself this time. The result of such crucial changes to the triangle situation in *Charulata* is a film of much less shading and depth: we don't see each of the characters gradually come to a greater awareness. The film tends to remains static. Bimal remains ignorant, Amitabha remains the suffering lover, and Karuna, the most interesting of the three, manages to keep her integrity, though she pays a price for it.

The first long sequence gives a good idea of Ray's procedure in *Kapurush*.

The trio is having drinks before dinner. The camera tends to place Bimal between the former lovers. He's talking a lot, boasting about his success, but what is really going on is Amitabha's attempt to connect with Karuna. As Bimal gets drunker and drunker, and his platitudes about hard work more boring, the camera slides slowly to one side or the other to show Amitabha's troubled and sympathetic glances to Karuna. He knows that marriage to this good-natured but heavy-bodied, sweaty-faced, thick-tongued man must be hard for her, but Karuna refuses to give him any signal of recognition. Immediately after this lengthy scene, as Amitabha stands troubled in his bedroom, Karuna enters with a water bottle but again fails to respond to his now more overt entreaties. Later that night, after a disturbing flashback in which he relives their breakup, she gives him a bottle of sleeping pills and tells him gently that he won't take more than two pills—an idea he has just advanced to her in his suffering. The next morning, after a breakfast scene which is an abbreviated repetition of the drinks-before-dinner scene, Bimal and Karuna take Amitabha on a picnic before dropping him off at the train. Once again, he makes a series of appeals to Karuna but is rebuffed. After he has been waiting dejectedly for a long time for the train, Karuna suddenly materializes before him (earlier he had asked her to meet him at the station and run away with him), but she has come apparently only to retrieve the bottle of sleeping pills.

As I've suggested, there's a somewhat repetitive, static pattern to *Kapurush*. The breakfast scene repeats the earlier drinking scene; the scene between Karuna and Amitabha when she gives him the sleeping pills repeats the lengthy scene of their breakup. Ray doesn't use interior settings to get inside his characters, as he did so wonderfully in *Charulata*. *Kapurush* isn't nearly as good a movie as *Charulata* is. However, *Kapurush* is good in its moments of wordless communication, or attempted communication, between former lovers. And it's particularly good in a couple of moments of extreme tension. The first occurs when Amitabha gets out of bed and moves obsessively toward Karuna's and Bimal's bedroom door where shadows are moving in the light that comes from under the door, only to knock over an object on a side table. There's a self-torturing element to Amitabha that is well evoked here. Another brief episode involves Bimal more directly. He's sprawled out asleep on a rock after having taken some swigs from his flask at the picnic. A cigarette burns like a fuse between his fingers. He'll wake up when it burns down. A low shot places his hand in the foreground while in the background Amitabha makes yet another feverish attempt to reach Karuna (he ends up writing her a note asking her to meet him at the train station, and Bimal never sees what is going on).

Of the three major characters, the portrayal of Karuna is easily the most interesting and most ambiguous. In part, like her predecessor Charulata, she represents the middle-class Bengali woman trying to find a position of strength in the modern world. Her husband may look upon her as a possession, but Amitabha's attitude, involving as it does all his uncertainties and self-absorbing torments, promises no surer ground. She must make her own way. This she accomplishes by a monumental act of self-control, which looks at times like coldness and malignity. Unlike Charulata, she clearly doesn't want the excitement and turbulence that Amitabha promises. She appears to have come to terms with the limitation of her life with Bimal. And yet, there are contradictory signs. In the before-dinner scene she understands at once the signals Amitabha is sending her and refuses to comply. Moments later it's she, not a servant, who enters Amitabha's room with the water bottle and again refuses to engage him. Is she testing herself? Is she working him over? Surely she must be angry at Amitabha for bursting into her calm and resigned life. Her visit to the railway station seems the most gratuitous act of all. Retrieval of the sleeping pills is not the motive. She must know how brutally this will arouse, then destroy, his expectations. Is she paying him back for his earlier rejection, so painful to her? When Amitabha is riding in the backseat of the jeep and she places her hand on Bimal's shoulder, Karuna is clearly signaling Amitabha where she stands, or would like to stand. Because she reveals so little of herself in words, we have mainly the visual aspects to rely on. Toward the end of the film, in the picnic and jeep scenes, she wears very dark glasses which totally hide her eyes and a silk scarf which hoods her hair and neck. She is, by design, nearly completely hidden. But when she goes to the train station, in the most powerful scene in the film, Karuna is not hidden. Without dark glasses or scarf, she shows Amitabha her suffering face. Bimal's and Amitabha's suffering is totally revealed (but not superficial); her suffering is hidden and may be the greatest of all. This is the price she pays for her control, her self-preservation.

MAHAPURUSH

Mahapurush (The Holy Man) is the comic foil to the darker tonalities of *Kapurush*. It's a satire on the theme of the false guru, an idea Ray was to make reference to in two of his later films. The guru, Birinchi Baba, is presented as a fraud from the opening scene; there's no interest in suggesting that he might be real, at first, and then giving us a gradual unmasking. The film stays in one key, broad satire and farce, but within that key it's often very funny.

The story involves the quick conversion of a rich man. He has lost his wife and his moorings. Meeting Birinchi Baba on the train, he immediately becomes a disciple, to the consternation of his daughter, Buchki. The guru moves into the rich man's house and begins to give audiences to respected community leaders, some of whom are recruited by a cynical uncle who acts as a shill for a cut of 10 percent. Buchki's lover, Satya, is dismayed that Buchki herself seems to have been converted, that is, until he receives a note from her indicating that she can't leave the house unless the guru is unmasked and her father forced to come to his senses. Satya and his chess-playing friends resolve literally to smoke Birinchi Baba out. They start a fire during one of his audiences. In a panic he drops his act and is kicked out by the rich man and his friends.

The film is at its best in its zany, slapstick passages. The opening sequence, which actually begins behind the credits, establishes the comic note immediately. The train has stopped at a station for a few moments and Birinchi Baba stands on the train's steps smiling and throwing sweets (a kind of divine offering) to an adoring, gaping multitude. Even the conductor, who hops about nervously, won't blow his whistle until he receives a sweet. There's a nice low shot from within the train of Birinchi Baba extending his bare foot, big toe raised, to be touched by his worshipers as the train pulls out. In a few shots Ray has established the issue of gullibility. The believers are as ridiculous as the one who dupes them. This idea carries over into the next scene, in which Birinchi seduces the rich man. He tells him he has lived for centuries, that he's on familiar terms with the ancient gods, and he commands the sun to rise just before it actually comes up. He also exploits his ability to move each hand in opposite circles while he speaks his mumbo jumbo. The rich man immediately goes down on his knees to him.

Even some of Satya's friends are not immune to the lure of the guru. As two of them play chess, a third remarks that he needs to find a good "baba" (god-man). He's the one who later throws himself at Birinchi Baba and asks to be transported back to 1914 so he can make lucrative investments. The chess players joke about the various babas floating around: an electricity baba, a chili baba, and others. Presumably the chess game demands the kind of intellectual rigor that would resist the pull of a Birinchi Baba. At any rate, one of the friends agrees to help Satya by going to see a professor who is married to Birinchi's sister. The visit to the professor has the same comic verve as the opening scene. The professor at first appears to be nuttier than anyone we've seen so far. He's conducting a scientific experiment in his home, boiling grass in a large bucket (he calls it protein synthesis). He speaks in a stutter and smiles all the time. The scenes with the professor don't go all the way into the zany absurdity of a Marx Brothers farce, though they move in that direction. The professor sees Birinchi Baba as a fraud, however, and says that Birinchi Baba claims to have educated Einstein and chatted with Chekhov. Like the chess players, he's essentially a rationalist.

The scenes in which the guru gives audience are also done with skill. They're basically a repetition of the opening train scenes, though they use language more fully and adroitly. In one, Birinchi Baba uses his reverse hand circles to expostulate on the paradox of time ("all is flux") and to assert that he's had an argument with Plato. His assistant (played by Robi Ghosh) sits at his feet, comically echoing his movements in the manner of a fanatic disciple. In his final audience, just before he's exposed, the guru says he talked with Jesus and that he pities him ("poor fellow; he died for nothing"). His assistant weeps in sympathy. It's one of numerous witty references to different religions in the film. When we see the two resting after one of their performances, the assistant walks around with false arms strapped to his torso and the guru has a smoke and talks about business. They have to jump quickly back into costume when the rich man knocks unexpectedly on the door of their room. After they are kicked out, they walk down the road at night, the assistant's false arms draped with the guests' handbags which he's managed to make off with.

Mahapurush, like parts of *Parash Pather* (the party scene, for example), shows Ray working successfully at the far end of the comic spectrum—in the area of broad, slapstick effects. It doesn't have the fine, mixed comic tonality of *Postmaster*, *Jana Aranya*, or *Days and Nights in the Forest*, but it does show the wide range of his skills in comedy. In its treatment of the false guru it looks ahead to the two detective films, *Sonar Kella* and *Joi Baba Felunath*, in which false gurus and con men are used.[1]

NOTE

1. In *Sonar Kella*, the two con men Bose and Barman have earlier been a team of fraudulent faith healers.

15

NAYAK (THE HERO):
A Star Falls

*N*ayak *(The Hero*, 1966) was made in the difficult period immediately after *Charulata*. It is one of Ray's least successful films. The film is a study of the popular Bengali film industry, using one of its real-life actors, the romantic hero, Uttam Kumar, to portray a leading man whose personal problems illustrate the problems of the industry as a whole. *Nayak* implies that the industry's wholesale reliance on escapist entertainment produces unreality and artificiality as well as corruption and brutality. In its avoidance of any reality or truth, the industry creates lead actors who believe that their romantic roles really represent them, and who are thus out of touch with themselves. We have seen such criticism in the numerous films which have examined the Hollywood of the major studios, including *All About Eve, Mommie Dearest*, and *S.O.B.* The trouble with *Nayak* is that such commonplaces are presented often in a not very interesting way. The film has the feel, in part, of a trite and even strident exposé. In cinematic terms the film is deficient: in almost every scene, dialogue is asked to do the work Ray usually has his camera do, so that we rarely have passages of nonverbal communication which Ray is so expert at in his other films. Moreover, the visuals we do have are not very interesting. Our eyes are confined to bland interiors of train compartments, the dining car, an office, a hotel room. There is no interplay between interior and exterior. It is a film largely shot in the studio; its calculated artificiality doesn't give it any depth. It is dull to the eye. *Nayak* is a thesis film rather than a film of atmosphere and implication. Most of the film is set on a train, presumably in order for Ray to bring his hero into contact with as many other characters as possible without having to demonstrate how they got together; yet, rather than move briskly, many scenes are slow as well as talky. The two crucial dream sequences are probably the weakest element in the film. Finally, and amazingly for a film by Ray, there are actually some short sequences that really don't contribute much and could have been omitted. Yet, for all its defects, *Nayak* is hardly the disaster that a poor film by a lesser director would be. It achieves strength as a study in partial self-recognition on the part of its hero.

The story goes as follows: Arindam Mukherjee is traveling to Delhi to receive an award. The evening before, he has been involved in a nightclub brawl. On the train he encounters a number of his fans, but the person to whom he is most drawn, in spite of himself, is Aditi, a journalist who wishes to interview him for her magazine. After a disturbing dream, Arindam finds

himself telling Aditi revealing details about his career. A second dream un-
settles Arindam even more, and his subsequent conversation with Aditi is
a drunken confession. Aditi rips up the notes she has been taking and says
she'll publish nothing of what he had said. As he leaves the train, he is
mobbed by worshipers who take him to be the hero he portrays in his films.

Criticism of the commercial Bengali film industry is represented both in
the secondary characters as well as in the leads, Arindam and Aditi. Arindam's presence on the train excites everyone to comment on Bengali films.
An old, wizened man, who evidently is an important writer for *The Statesman*, inveighs against all films as immoral. He represents the reactionary
extreme. The wealthy businessman, Mr. Bose, also has a low opinion of
Bengali films. Bose is being assiduously courted by the advertising man,
Mr. Karkar, who wants to land a contract. But Bose is only interested in
Karkar's pretty wife, Molly, who herself is interested in getting into film
and who approaches Arindam about a job. The hustling and manipulation
which surrounds Arindam on the train is meant to represent the cynical
atmosphere of the film industry as a whole. Only Bose's sick daughter re-
tains a credulous attitude; she believes that Arindam's presence has helped
to cure her. Like the mob that engulfs Arindam when he arrives in Delhi,
she represents the naive and gullible attitude that the industry needs from
its audience.

Arindam may exploit such gullibility but he is portrayed, most of all, as
self-exploited. In their first encounter, he puts Aditi off; he doesn't want to
reveal himself in print for fear he'll lose his audience. The scene subtly
suggests that he can't reveal himself because he hasn't looked into himself;
he's been too caught up in acting out his film roles in real life. Out of his
hearing, Aditi calls him a hot-house flower that can't bear too much natural
light. The main process of the film involves exposing him to this light.

Nayak is a history of Arindam's career as presented in five flashbacks as
well as an examination of his psyche in the two dreams. The first scene
suggests that Arindam is in difficulty. In a conversation with his long-time
assistant Jyoti he both curses the film-going public as fools and says that
his newest film is largely trash but that it should succeed "if only because
I'm in it." His nervousness (he's smoking constantly) suggests that he's worried about the success of the film and fearful that his career may fail. This
mixture of cynicism, egotism, and anxiety characterizes his state before he
boards the train. As he opens up to Aditi, the flashbacks depict his earlier
career. The first three flashbacks involve well-known actors who have been
his superiors. His career began in the theater, where his mentor, the actor
Shankarda, angrily criticizes him for a growing interest in film. In the earliest flashback he warns Arindam about "the nasty side of films, the business side," and tells him that in the world of film you're either up or you're
down. Shankarda is presented here as a man of traditional values—a wise,
older, father figure. When he dies suddenly at a religious festival (he's a

religious figure to Arindam as well as a fellow actor) his influence diminishes and Arindam decides to go into film. The next two flashbacks involve the actor Mukanda Jahiri and are designed to illustrate Shankarda's warnings. Mukanda is an egotistical and tyrannical father figure to Arindam. After they have rehearsed a father-son scene in front of the camera, he abuses Arindam about his acting. Mukanda is at the top of his career and uses his powerful voice to intimidate everyone on the set. Arindam knows, however, that Mukanda's day is passing because he can't adapt his stage actor's techniques to film. In the next flashback, a transformed Mukanda comes to visit the now successful Arindam to appeal for his help in obtaining a role. He's been out of work for four years; he looks gaunt and his voice is nearly a whisper.

The fourth flashback illustrates Arindam's anxiety when a political activist, Biresh, involves him in a demonstration which is attacked by government troops. Five years later, when Arindam is now a big star, Biresh gets him to attend another demonstration but when Arindam finds that he's expected to address the strikers, he refuses. He's unwilling to risk his reputation or image by doing anything controversial. The scene is filmed in such a way as to suggest Arindam's cowardice. He sits sweaty-faced in his car, hiding behind his dark glasses (which he wears in many scenes in the film) while Biresh exhorts him to get out and give the poor workers some moral support. When he drives off, the audience is asked to share in Biresh's angry glance. The trouble with this flashback is that Arindam has plenty of reason to refuse Biresh who has lured him out to the strike without telling him where they're going or what he expects of him. The film wants us to see Biresh as an example of Arindam's failed social conscience but instead we're likely to see Biresh's hostility and manipulativeness and to see Arindam's cowardice mainly in his inability to get angry at Biresh. The best way to make sense of the flashback is to remember that it is a part of Arindam's narration of his career to Aditi and that, in this context, he feels disturbed and guilty over just about everything. I don't think it's accurate to read the scene as an indirect manifestation of Ray's own guilt about not treating burning social and political problems (a common criticism of him in Bengal in the 1960s). He had already made *Abhijan* (1962) and *Mahanagar* (1963), tentative forays into the realm of social issues, though his major social statements were still ahead of him in *Pratidwandi* (1970), *Seemabaddha* (1971), and *Jana Aranya* (1975).

The fifth and last flashback shows us Arindam's sexual guilt. The cynical and ambitious Promilla visits him at home, like Mukanda Jahiri, and attempts to seduce him into giving her a film part. At one point she weeps in an anguished fashion, then abruptly stops and laughs mockingly. She's been giving Arindam a demonstration of her acting ability. Though he puts her off, he later has an affair with her which provokes her husband to insult him in the nightclub brawl. Arindam's life is messy.

The two dream sequences are intended to amplify on a less conscious level the uneasiness we see in Arindam in the flashbacks. In the first, he sees a blizzard of banknotes falling to the ground. He walks smiling on the thick carpet they make and then runs, scooping them up in the air. The bright diffuse lighting of the first four shots of this sequence then dims, and the landscape of banknotes becomes dark and forbidding. Arindam, looking troubled, is seen in silhouette as the camera closes in on him. We then hear a telephone ringing as he searches for the source of the noise. A large skeleton hand holding the telephone now appears, then many more hands as Arindam tries to flee to the accompaniment of African drums and chanting. In the tenth shot, he sinks into the banknotes like quicksand. Seeing Shankarda sitting nearby on a hill of notes, he begs for help. Shankarda approaches and holds out his hand but he's made up like a papier-mâché dummy and can't reach Arindam. As we see him go under, he abruptly awakes in his train compartment.

The main problem with this dream is that it functions entirely on the literal level; there's no feeling of the irrational. The message is that Arindam has sold out for money and that the spirit of his old mentor is so dead within him that it can't provide any aid. It's all heavy-handed and, unusual for a Ray film, simplistic. The second dream is really no better. Arindam walks in a studio rendering of an artificial garden at night; he hears mocking laughter and follows Promilla through a white door and eventually into a nightclub where all the patrons are wearing dark glasses. He's accused of being a scoundrel, probably by Promilla's husband, and knocks him down. After waking from this dream Arindam goes to the toilet where he looks at himself in the cracked mirror and begins drinking heavily. The artificial, studio-like setting of both dreams gives them a distant feeling when they should be most consuming. They are didactic and reductive. They don't have the compelling ambiguity of true dreams. A comparison (admittedly unfair) with the first dream sequence from Bergman's *Wild Strawberries*—the masterpiece which deals with the subject of self-recognition—indicates Ray's difficulties here. In Bergman's film, Professor Borg finds himself in an empty section of town, sees a clock with no hands, and witnesses a bizarre accident in which a horse-drawn hearse dumps out a coffin which contains his dead other self. The whole sequence is both real and strange, alive with the irrational. In contrast, Ray's wooden dream sequences seem totally rational, totally thought out on the conscious level. One might even say that they suggest an inability, or at least an uneasiness, in rendering subconscious states. In this regard, Jyoti's remark to Arindam early in the film that "this is the age of Marx and Freud" puts the problem squarely before us. The structure of the film may be based on the therapeutic model (Arindam as patient, Aditi as compassionate but distant therapist), but "Freud" is poorly incorporated in the film. The subconscious remains inert, unevoked in the cinematic text. We do know from the film, however, that

Arindam remains undeveloped and immature in basic ways. He hasn't really grown beyond the need for a disapproving father. Shankarda remains for him an unbending super-ego whom he can never satisfy. That is why he presents himself in a drunken state to the old critic for *The Statesman*, whom he knows (from an earlier scene) hates anyone who drinks and who will undoubtedly vilify him in print. In a perverse way he needs to punish himself, increase his anxiety about his potential failure. In this respect, his screen persona of the romantic hero can be seen as an enactment of his active juvenile fantasies. He simply hasn't grown up. Aditi confronts him with this and, aided by her and his dreams, he begins to take a look at himself. But he doesn't go very far. The film does a good job here, but we must be aware that it also shows Ray's inability, at this point, to speak fully in the language of his time—"the age of Marx and Freud." An inferior product by a major artist, *Nayak* reveals Ray's limitations up to the mid 1960s. He isn't very good at making direct comment on a contemporary subject. In fact, Ray's most potent criticism of commercial Bengali cinema (and Indian popular cinema as a whole) occurs in his best films, not in *Nayak*. These films, by implication, show what true cinematic art really is. Their truth and power show up the falsity of the escapist popular cinema.

The unnecessary sequences are minor but the fact that there are any at all reveals that Ray was not working at top form. The second encounter between Arindam and the old writer for *The Statesman* doesn't contribute anything that the first and third don't present. The chess game between Bose and Karkar also doesn't add anything that we don't already know about their relationship. And the fairly noticeable presence in Arindam's compartment of the fat man who is constantly eating and grooming himself in the foreground is curious. His conversation with Karkar in which he solicits advertising help in promoting his organization for world peace seems dispensable until we realize that he represents the total self-absorption of almost all the characters in the film. His presence is both obscure and heavy-handed. He's another hustler, a replica of the phony guru in *Mahapurush*, the film which preceded *Nayak*.

For all its faults, *Nayak* has real strengths in the depiction of the relationship between Aditi and Arindam. Aditi's honesty and intelligence provoke Arindam to reveal more of himself not only to her but to himself. As she sees his anxiety, pain, and loneliness she relents from her opinion of him as a mere hot-house flower. When he's drunk she stops his confessional flow. She doesn't want him to injure himself; she's aware instinctively that he might even do himself physical injury (a moment earlier, before she arrives, he's been standing at a half-open door looking down from the speeding train at the tracks) and she waits for him to return to his compartment before she leaves. The strength of the scenes between them comes from the way Ray dramatizes the subtle changes going on in each one. These scenes don't function entirely on the verbal level as many of the others do. In a good example, the two are sitting in the dining car while a herd of film fans press up against the window. She's embarrassed and wants to leave, but Arindam advises her to pretend that he and she are actors. He's been acting all his life but the integrity which he lacks, and she possesses, comes from her sense of privacy. She is unable to relax in front of the faces pressed against the window while Arindam conducts himself with aplomb. We're meant to understand that Arindam's smoothness—his "cool"—is really a form of bad (dishonest) acting. Nevertheless, it's necessary to mention that Uttam Kumar's performance as Arindam is very good. As a representative of the blatantly commercial Indian film culture he should, according to Ray's thesis, be a poor actor. But Ray, of course, didn't want a poor actor in the film.

The relationship between Aditi and Arindam looks forward to the brilliant presentation of Ashim and Aparna in *Days and Nights in the Forest*, the film that demonstrates Ray's return to full power after *Charulata*. Significantly, he cast Sharmila Tagore in both female roles, for she represents the enabling female presence. In *Nayak*, however, Ray had yet to prove that he could deal successfully with the problem of modern self-consciousness.

16

GOOPY GYNE BAGHA BYNE (THE ADVENTURES OF GOOPY AND BAGHA): A Children's Story

For pure enjoyment, *Goopy Gyne Bagha Byne* (*The Adventures of Goopy and Bagha*, 1969) is one of Ray's best films. He has referred to it as "my first children's film" and said that he made it for his eight-year-old son.[1] The film was an enormous success in Bengal but not widely (or lengthily) shown in the West. The film is equally pleasing to adults and children, functioning as it does as both serious commentary and pure fantasy. The musical score by Ray is one of its strongest elements; it also has dancing—both staples of traditional Indian cinema. It is based on a fairy story by Ray's grandfather, Upendra Kishore Roy Chowdhury, a well-known children's writer in India. The film also owes a debt to Ray's father, the well-known writer of nonsense verses for children. It's a product of Ray's family heritage as well as a loving gift to his son. It is also a film which is full of creative play—perhaps the most inventive of all of Ray's films. In any case, it has become a classic in Bengal, for when it is revived every ten years or so, it enjoys long runs, and according to Ray, appears to many to be a new film.[2]

The story involves two young men, Goopy and Bagha, who aren't very good musicians (one is a singer, the other a drummer) and who are banished by their respective kings. Meeting in a forest, they encounter the King of the Ghosts, who grants them extraordinary powers so they can travel wherever they wish, always have plenty of food, and perform their music superbly. They go to the kingdom of Shundi where a good king presides over a friendly and peace-loving populace. Not too far away, the king of Shundi's brother presides over the kingdom of Halla. He is a weak leader, easily manipulated by an evil magician and his equally nefarious colleague, the prime minister. He desires to attack Shundi, but Goopy and Bagha fly in via their magic slippers, and their singing counters the evil influence of the necromancer and the prime minister and restores peace between the two brothers. They are rewarded by marriages to the kings' daughters.

Though the film is largely characterized by fantasy, it does have a realistic dimension which can be seen chiefly in the early sections. When Goopy, hoarse-voiced, sings to the elders of his village, we are very nearly back in the rural environment of the Apu trilogy or *Postmaster*, where older men sit under a tree chatting or making music. The villagers, as a joke, send Goopy to sing to the king, who is awakened by his squawking in the early morning and banishes him. Two early scenes now reveal the high level of skill with which Ray rendered his fantasy. The first involves Goopy's meeting with Bagha in the forest. As Goopy timidly enters the forest, we hear a slow but steady drumbeat; the camera moves downward to show water dripping out of a tree onto a drum. Bagha is asleep under the tree. He's startled to see the smiling Goopy, who mimics the stretching movements Bagha makes as he awakes. As they make friends, they're suddenly terrified to hear the growl of a tiger who appears at a distance behind them. They are frozen in fear (Ray uses a long but perfectly timed freeze-frame), but the tiger leaves and they immediately burst into joyful song and dance. The whole scene has a fine, natural movement from tension to relaxed play. Their music leads into the second scene and what is undoubtedly the most brilliant cinematic sequence in this film, the dance of the ghosts. Their music and dancing calls out the ghosts who want to play, too. The ghosts are first shown as black figures emerging from a forest projected in negative. Soon they form into four groupings which Goopy later in the film refers to as "black and white, pale and bright." Each group dances in its turn as the music goes faster and faster. Finally, the dancers begin to attack one another and fall down dead as the sequence moves to its close.

A number of interesting things are happening in this dance sequence, but they happen so fast that they may be hard to catch. It is helpful, then, to have an interview Ray did with *Kolkata* magazine in which he comments on the ghost dance.[3] First, he conceives of the ghosts as representatives from Bengal's past: the kings (shot in blurred images—the "pale," probably because they come from the distant past); the peasants, the "bright"; the British, shot in slow motion and then speeded up somewhat to give them a mechanical, artificial movement—they are the "white," dressed in imperial costumes, moving against a black background; and, finally, the "black," the traditional fat country businessman, "the well-fed Brahmin," as Ray puts it, dancing against a white background. Each group has its own appropriate musical accompaniment (the drum for the kings, the small cymbal for the peasants, the hard, earthen pot for the British, and an instrument much like the Jew's harp for the fat people).

The dance is a kind of thumbnail history of the birth of modern India: the kings and peasants (shot in blurred image by the ingenious device, developed by Ray's cameraman, Soumendu Roy, of having a thin sheet of water move over the camera lens) represent the old India; the British and their local representatives (the fat, black Brahmins, some of whom are carrying the Christian cross) represent the occupying powers. The violence which occurs as the tympanic rhythm speeds up suggests the downfall of all these powers, yet we don't ever see one group attacking another, as of course happened when the British were forced out. Each group remains self-contained. The final layered images of the dancers (from about shot 45 to the close of the 50-shot sequence) show each group dancing in a line above the other. Ray conceives this as a kind of coda in which the groups are "all in harmony with other. Since ghosts would not have an internal conflict, the amity would come easily and it would come through a song."

As complex and highly structured as it is, the dance of the ghosts functions also as a pure visual and musical delight. One doesn't have to notice the underlying historical, moral, and musical dimensions in order to enjoy it. In a sense, it contains the essence of the film, expressing as it does the tendency of people of like backgrounds (the brother kings) to fall asunder and wound one another. The antidote that Goopy and Bagha bring is not only that of music and dance (the artist as healer) but of cooperation; their magic works only as long as they stick together, able to clap right hands as the King of Ghosts has instructed them.

As an allegory or moral fable, *The Adventures of Goopy and Bagha* takes a hopeful look at human conduct. The wolf does not eat Little Red Riding Hood in this fairy tale. The bad king and the good king are really the same man, or different sides of the same man; both are played by the same actor. The bad king isn't really even bad, just manipulated by his evil advisers who are put to rout by Goopy and Bagha. The tiger, which Goopy describes as "burning bright," is not a renderer of human flesh or principle of amoral destruction; the gods' role in his existence is not questioned as Blake questioned it. The general of the king of Halla's army does not really want to fight, and the soldiers themselves and their camels seem singularly lethargic. The people of Halla are sweet and polite, though they cannot speak until Goopy and Bagha remove the curse put upon them. The landscape these people live in is very beautiful, even paradisiacal. The animating spirit of the film is playful and kindly; there is no attempt to frighten or horrify the audience, as in many modern fantasies. It is a comforting fairy tale—nothing grim about it.

The film is at its best when it is most fantastic, such as in the later scene when the evil prime minister visits the magician in his lodgings. The set here is particularly fine in its dark, cavelike dimensions. (Bansi Chandragupta, Ray's long-time art director and close friend, made wonderful contributions here and elsewhere, as did Ray himself, as seen in his many detailed illustrations of costume and set design.) The magician's eccentric behavior as well as his make-up, crazy-looking glasses, and comic skullcap with its looping, insectlike "feelers," help to give a feeling of the dreamlike and bizarre. This particular scene is very reminiscent of certain scenes from two films by Michael Powell, *The Red Shoes* and *Tales of Hoffman*, in which a surrealistic, dreamlike atmosphere prevails. It is possible, as well, that the distorted sets of such expressionist films as *The Cabinet of Dr. Caligari* may have made a contribution.

The Adventures of Goopy and Bagha is an enjoyable entertainment made in that period after *Charulata* in which Ray seemed to be searching for new subject matter and new ways to express himself in film. The joyful ending of the film, which turns from black and white to color as Goopy and Bagha meet their future wives, suggests that this period was not altogether a difficult one for Ray. One could only wish that the whole film had been shot in color, given the visual richness of its sets, costumes, and dances. Ray wanted to shoot the whole film in color but the political and economic crisis in India in 1966–67 (including a strike in the Bengali film industry by workers protesting the invasion of cheap Hindi films) prevented it.[4] More than a fairy tale, *Goopy and Bagha* is also a film which says to children (and all of us) that warfare and aggression are wrong and that we should beware of being manipulated into it by misguided and unscrupulous leaders. When, in *Hirok Rajar Deshe (The Kingdom of Diamonds)*, Ray came to make his most direct political statement against abuses of power, during the state of emergency decreed by Indira Gandhi in 1975–77, he chose to use the mode of *Goopy and Bagha* in order to reach the widest possible audience.

NOTES

1. Chidananda Das Gupta, *Satyajit Ray: An Anthology of Statements on Ray and by Ray* (New Delhi: Directorate of Film Festivals, 1981), p. 78.

2. Author's interview with Ray, Calcutta, July 20, 1985.

3. Quoted in Das Gupta, *Satyajit Ray*, p. 79.

4. Marie Seton, *Portrait of a Director: Satyajit Ray* (Bloomington: Indiana University Press, 1971), p. 283.

17

ARANYER DIN RATRI (DAYS AND NIGHTS IN THE FOREST): Finding the Way

*D*ays and Nights in the Forest (*Aranyer Din Ratri*, 1970) is the most seemingly formless of Ray's films but it is also one of his best. A comparison with *Kanchanjungha*, which it resembles, shows how much Ray had grown as a filmmaker in the eight years separating the two films. Each film deals with middle- and upper-class Indians in a holiday setting and each manages to reveal the essence of its characters in an oblique manner. The regular, almost inflexible rhythm of the two-character scenes which distinguishes *Kanchanjungha* is replaced in *Days and Nights in the Forest* by a subtle, fluid, and apparently random structure which allows a much greater weight of implication.

The story is extremely simple. Four young men drive out from Calcutta for an extended weekend in the country. Having lost their way, they come upon an unoccupied guest lodge and bribe the caretaker into letting them have rooms. The day after a night of drinking in a local native wine shop, they meet Sadasiv Tripathi and his daughter Aparna and daughter-in-law Jaya, upper-class residents of Calcutta, who have a country house nearby. Two of the men are attracted to the daughters, while another seduces a local native girl. In each instance, the sexual encounter strips bare the essential self of the participants. From a series of leisurely, random encounters the film moves carefully, gathering weight and speed, to its final moments of revelation. Small intonations and gracenotes delivered at the opening are amplified in a natural rhythm so that the revelations don't seem forced or contrived. The film has truly been called a Mozartian masterpiece. It also reminds one of Chekhov, in the sense that nothing really happens in terms of plot, and yet everything happens. Sankar Basu's *Chekhov and Tagore* (New Delhi, 1985) discusses the affinity between the two writers and suggests that the influence on Ray may come as much from Tagore as from Chekhov.

A basic structural principle in this film involves symbolic pairing. The four men are divided into pairs, and they in turn pair off with the Tripathi women and the native girl. The first pairing we notice is between Hari, a professional cricket player, and Shekar, a gambler and playboy. As the men drive into the country, Shekar constantly needles and irritates Hari with his comments. He's angry that Hari is sleeping instead of participating in the group. Hari wants to rest; he's still recovering from the breakup of an affair, but Shekar won't let him alone. He's punishing him and wooing him into the group at the same time. Shekar's nervous joke-cracking manner entertains the others. He's been looking forward to the weekend and wants everyone to enjoy it. Of the four, he needs the group the most. Later in the film, when Ashim says he'll have a house one day with a well for bathing, Shekar says, "Yes, we'll all be there to bathe together." He's secure in his role as the group comedian, and he's content to stay in that role. He won't be dislodged from his *persona*, or social mask, into deeper and more troubling areas of experience. In the drinking scenes, he remains sober while the others proceed to get drunk and lose their inhibitions. As a result, he probably has the most pleasurable experience but it's also the least meaningful. While the others become involved in intense exchanges with women, he follows his gambling compulsions at a native fair. He's a comic figure, in part, but he's also a victim of his own superficiality. Delightful and entertaining, he is, nevertheless, barely noticed in the important final passages of the film.

Hari, to whom the undersized Shekar is drawn because of his athletic prowess and "masculinity," experiences the most brutal acting out of his darker self. Like Shekar, he's compulsive but his compulsions play themselves out on the deeper level of pure libido. His lovemaking with Duli, the sensual native girl, is more like a rape than seduction. He drags her away from the country fair into the forest, enjoys her sexually, and then promises her money if she'll come to Calcutta, be his mistress and wear a false hair piece like the woman who has just rejected him. An early flashback shows Hari's rejection. He has responded to a six-page letter from his girl with a curt note. As with Duli, he really isn't interested in communicating with her except on a sexual level. Compared to Shekar's purely social mask, Hari seems all unmediated sexual drive. He's aggressive and more or less inarticulate. After he's made love to Duli, he's attacked in the forest by a man whom he had earlier violently (and wrongly) accused of stealing his wallet. Shekar carries him back to the guest house streaming with blood. He hasn't been awakened into a consciousness of his self-destructiveness by either the blow of his girlfriend's rejection (in this case a slap in the face) or by the blows he receives in the forest. He and Shekar remain, at the end of the film, as they were in the beginning.

The other pair among the foursome has more dimension. While Hari and Skekar are grouped together in one room of the guest house, Ray places Sanjoy and Ashim together in another. Sanjoy, a labor officer in a jute mill, and Ashim, an up-and-coming executive, are old friends. They have edited a magazine together in their student days and each has a quality of fineness and sensitivity which Hari and Shekar lack. The two scenes between them on the porch at the guest house show a calm and comfortable friendship. They're both tall and handsome; indeed, they look somewhat alike. The differences between them are first revealed in the two drinking scenes at the local wine shop. These scenes are designed to show each member of the foursome in his most uncensored state. While Hari sits isolated and brooding in the second drinking scene, Ashim becomes voluble. He's both arrogant and embittered. As he looks drunkenly around the wine shop he speaks about the high-class cocktail parties he has attended; he's proud of his success and yet wryly aware of the artificiality of it. He has played the game and won but he knows that, as he puts it, "the higher you rise, the longer you fall." Ashim is an early version of Shyam, the ambitious executive of Ray's later film *Seemabaddha*. He's something of a narcissist and a cynic, yet he continues to look for meaning in life. Sanjoy is far more restrained; he holds himself carefully and isn't able to let go at all, though it's clear from his sweat-covered face that he's very drunk. Later on, when the men are discovered bathing by the Tripathi women, he's the one who throws himself on the ground, behind the well, and hides from view. He's the polar opposite of the uncensored Hari, who accuses him in the early car scene of being unable to reveal his deeper feelings. When he and Jaya Tripathi, the widowed daughter-in-law, pair off, they seem a possible match. She is warm and outgoing and he responds favorably to her flirtatious gestures. When she invites him in for coffee and then makes an overt sexual gesture to him the film suddenly deepens into poignancy. The desperate loneliness as a widow which lies behind her cheerfulness is revealed. Sanjoy doesn't know how to respond when she puts his hand on her chest; he's paralyzed in much the same way we saw him when he was drunk. The close-ups of his face in both scenes are nearly identical. His essentially reserved and inhibited nature is painfully revealed to us (and to him) as he struggles to recover himself. We know that his experience with Jaya will trouble his consciousness in the future. He has witnessed his limitations in a disturbing way.

Days and Nights in the Forest reaches its greatest force in the pairing of Ashim and Aparna. They are acquaintances from Calcutta, and when Ashim is alone with her, inspecting her "meditation house," he comes on to her and she deflects him. He's attracted to her reserved nature, beauty, and also to her self-contained intelligence. Aparna has qualities the other characters lack. She's thoughtful and knowing and considerate. Ray intends us to compare her depths with Jaya. She's aware, at once, of the vulnerability which lies behind Ashim's vanity and arrogance. In the central scene between them, toward the end of the film, she tells him that she wanted to undermine his confidence and Ashim confesses that he's experienced humiliation by being observed by her in the act of soaping his body. His confidence has also been shaken when the district officer arrives to stay in the guest house, finds the men occupying it without reservations and decides to fire the caretaker. Only when Aparna mentions that the men are friends of the Tripathi family does the officer relent from kicking them out. Aparna further tells Ashim that she saw him doing the "tribal twist," a drunken dance, when she and Jaya were driving along the road at night (the men can't see who is in the car). Ashim goes into an agony of humiliation at this information yet he's also laughing at his comedown. Aparna points out to him that the way he moved into the guest house was a bit childish. Ashim, who is aware of an element of fraudulence in his success in the world, is secretly happy to be perceived in a vulnerable state. Unlike Sanjoy, who nervously retreats from Jaya, he wants to be seen for what he is by such a fine person as Aparna. He's willing to submit to her. And she is evidently willing to submit to him, for she gives up her chance to win the memory game they all play at the picnic in order to allow him to win. When Ashim asks her later why she gave up she tells him she still remembers all the names. Her act is complex: It preserves Ashim's ego in a maternal fashion and yet affirms her strength. She tells Ashim of her brother's suicide and of her mother's death in a fire, and then remarks to him "you haven't really suffered have you?" The process of bonding we witness between them involves Ashim's incompleteness and Aparna's wholeness. It's Aparna who reminds Ashim that his thoughtlessness has nearly cost the caretaker of the guest house his job. She takes him to the caretaker's house where they see the caretaker's wife lying very ill. And she arranges through her father for the caretaker to keep his job. True to the world of Ray's films, the woman helps to guide the man into strength.

I don't mean to suggest that there's an inflexible hierarchy to the pairings which occur in the film—one pair being seen by Ray as morally superior to another. The film demonstrates the surprising interactions which occur between vastly different characters. It celebrates the variety of human interaction, and this variety is most fully represented in the subtle handling of the group scenes. There are a number of such scenes: the four men driving into the country, the two drinking scenes, the two visits by the men to the Tripathi house, the memory game. In each scene Ray's fluid and nimble camera work shows the process of pairing occurring in its most oblique form. The first two-thirds of the film contains the group scenes, and these scenes prepare for the more direct one-on-one confrontations in the last third. This structure gives the film its surprising power.

In the first group scene, the early car scene which occurs on either side of the credits, there's a lot of fast cutting in medium close-up between the four men. Shekar's the catalyst here; he's the one, as I've mentioned, who tends to generate group interaction. As Sanjoy reads a guidebook in a characteristically scholarly fashion, Shekar needles Hari about his sleeping. Ashim characteristically plays a mediating role in this friendly dispute. Later on, at the rest house, Shekar gets them all to agree that they won't shave on the trip. "We'll be hippies," he jokes, indicating once again his tendency to think in terms of the group. In these early sequences, the cutting between shots is extremely rapid for a Ray film but it's not especially noticeable because it follows the interaction between the men which is spontaneous and natural.

Each drinking scene begins with the camera panning along the table noticing each of the four men. In the first scene, Ashim drunkenly accuses Sanjoy of being a conformist. "Go ahead, stay in your rut and be a 100 percent, Bengali, middle-class, conventional, good boy,"—which provokes a laugh of rueful self-recognition on Sanjoy's part. But Ashim is really talking about himself here. He's bitter about the compromises he's been willing to make to be successful. In the second drinking scene he's even more embittered and angry because the Tripathi women have seen him bathing and he feels his carefully made image has been blown (we don't know exactly what his work is, but it wouldn't be surprising to find out that it has something to do with public relations). He forces Shekar to drink and then gets angry at Hari for losing his wallet. Shekar becomes very agitated at this point for he knows what a wretched mood Hari is in and doesn't want him to explode. As Hari stands swaying uncertainly he suddenly breaks into laughter and recounts how he watched his friends caught half-naked and soapy by the women. All the men then burst into laughter and leave the drinking place in high spirits, later dancing the twist on the road home. Hari's outburst, which transforms a depressing evening, illustrates as well as any moment in the film the surprising twists and turns of human interaction.

A good example of the quickness and naturalness of Ray's camera work occurs in the first visit to the Tripathi home. This little sequence involves a white lie Shekar has told about Hari, namely that he was visiting the local church when the men first introduced themselves. Jaya asks Hari if he liked the church and Skekar has to signal him to make the appropriate response. In nine shots covering only fifteen seconds Ray nimbly shows each character being himself. Jaya is outreaching, yet fails to notice that Hari hasn't been to the church. Shekar is, as usual, concerned to present the most favorable social mask, while Hari is a bit slow on the uptake. Only Aparna, who says nothing, notices what Shekar has done. Two quick shots of her face (one raising her eyes at Hari's uncertain response, the other lowering her eyes as she spots Shekar's signal) present her as a perceptive observer.

The memory game is the most interesting and complex of the group scenes and one of the high points of the film. The game is a miniature of the film as a whole in the sense that the players who drop out first tend to have the least profound interaction, leaving Ashim and Aparna at the end. Each player, sitting in a circle, must remember the sequence of historical names mentioned by the others and then add a new name. It's not surprising that Jaya begins the game with Rabindranath Tagore, the most important historical name for Ray. She goes out first, however, in the second turn. Sanjoy, the labor officer, mentions Karl Marx and Mao Tse Tung; Hari, Helen of Troy; Ashim, Shakespeare; Aparna, Cleopatra and a mystery writer, Don Bradman. The names evoke the chooser. When Shekar goes out in the second round, Hari wants to go out, too. Aparna remembers her names with great rapidity and confidence. Memory here is akin to insight, to a life lived thoughtfully. Aparna doesn't smile when Hari and Shekar joke around; she plays the game in earnest, demonstrating her skill. When she decides to go out she says, "I'm stuck like Hari was," preserving both his ego and Ashim's. Ray uses a flexible mix of shots in this scene: from middle distance shots of the whole group when Shekar and Hari go out together, to circular panning shots of the whole group, to quick shots of individuals. When Sanjoy, for instance, goes meticulously around the group assigning names to each player, the camera moves carefully, pausing briefly at each person. This point-of-view shot expresses his meticulousness. After he goes out, the camera turns to his flirtation with Jaya and follows him when he goes to get pillows for the ladies, while Ashim and Aparna continue their competition. The memory game presents each player perceptively and entertainingly. The multiple interactions which occur within it are evoked by the quickness and lightness of the camera's way of noticing. It's as if the camera were acting like an intelligent and perceptive observer who is part of the group but does not speak; the camera moves as this observer's eyes would move. The character closest to this imagined observer is Aparna and yet we see very few point-of-view shots from her. The camera remains a discreet, sympathetic, ironic observer. Renoir's handling of groups scenes must surely have been influential here. The group scenes don't succeed only because of Ray's adroit camera work. The ease and lightness of the camera movement are a product of the same spirit of creative play which animates the script of the film and, according to Soumitra Chatterjee, was the prevailing mood on the set.[1] This atmosphere enabled the actors to perform in a relaxed and natural ensemble. Like his master Renoir, Ray has the ability to bring out the best in his performers by allowing them a freedom of response to one another. In its quality of play *Days and Nights in the Forest* comes closest to the spirit of Mozart and Chekhov.

NOTE

1. Interview with Soumitra Chatterjee, Calcutta, July 19, 1985.

18

PRATIDWANDI (THE ADVERSARY): The Job Seeker

Pratidwandi (also known as *The Adversary* or *Siddhartha and the City*) was made in 1970, the same year as *Days and Nights in the Forest*. It isn't as well-known as *Days and Nights*, one of Ray's masterpieces, but it is a very strong film and it shows us Ray confronting head-on the political and social dilemmas of contemporary Calcutta. His earlier film, *Mahanagar (The Big City)* 1963, was, by the standards of *Pratidwandi*, an indirect examination of the same subject.

Ray lives in a comfortable, but not rich, section of Calcutta, and yet his first films, for which he is justly famous, examined rural India (the Apu trilogy) and an India distanced in time and place *(The Music Room, Devi*, or *The Goddess)*. For a number of years he was criticized for not turning his considerable talents to an examination of the problems of contemporary India, particularly urban India. He seemed to like the meditative and lyrical rhythms of a rural landscape set in the past. Though he lives in the city, he seemed to prefer to look elsewhere. The abrupt, crowded rhythms and dissonances of city life seemed uncongenial to him. As a result, he approached the subject carefully. It took him seven years and eight films before he attempted a realistic examination of a contemporary setting. Of Ray's four city films *(Mahanagar, Pratidwandi, Seemabaddha,* and *Jana Aranya)*, *Pratidwandi* is the finest up to *Jana Aranya*, the city film commonly felt in India to be his best and now sadly out of distribution in the U.S.

In *Pratidwandi* Ray examines a common situation in India: a highly educated young man looking hopelessly for work in the city. Siddhartha has had two years of medical school but was forced to drop out after the death of his father (the film opens, before the credits, with the immediate aftermath of the father's death shot in negative; we see his body carried out of the house, his wife's grieving, Siddhartha standing in front of his funeral pyre). The third scene of the film shows Siddhartha in a job interview and serves to give us basic information about him as well as to point forward to the powerful scene of the final job interview near the end of the film. He's 25 years old, has a B.S. and his medical school training. He's an idealist: He asserts that the Vietnam war is more historically important than the moon landing, when the interview committee clearly wants him to talk about the moon landing. When one of the committee asks him if he's a Communist, he dodges the question by replying that one doesn't have to be a Communist to admire the capacity for the resistance that the Vietnamese people have shown. He stands up for himself but he blows the interview.

Siddhartha is a man in the middle. He's bright and complicated; his responses are thoughtful and more than one-dimensional. He stands between the extremes of his sister Sutapha and his brother Tunu. Sutapha is willing to use her attractiveness to advance herself in her work. She may or may not be sleeping with her boss. Her boss's neurotic wife pays a visit to Siddhartha's mother and all but accuses Sutapha of lewd behavior. Siddhartha stands up for his sister in this scene but he's tormented by her conduct. When she's home, she lies around listening to the radio or reading magazines imagining herself as a fashion model. She totally buys into the materialist culture. As the man of the house, Siddhartha feels he should be supporting his family and influencing its conduct. He's frustrated on both counts with Sutapha; *she's* helping to support the family and being cooperative with the boss. At one point she drags Siddhartha up to the roof terrace to show him a new dance step she's learned. As she dances around in her new dress, he fantasizes that she's dancing with a well-dressed man and that other couples are dancing as well and all the women are smoking. To Siddhartha she's liberated and corrupt and he can't do anything about it. In a controlled rage, he visits the boss's richly appointed house, waits nervously for the boss to appear (the waiting scene is very well presented and looks ahead to the waiting scene for the final job interview) and then has an abrupt fantasy of killing him when he does appear. When the boss leaves to take a phone call, after offering to help him find work, Siddhartha leaves the house in disgust at his own impotence. In the street he encounters a mob attacking the driver of a Mercedes which has just injured a pedestrian. Siddhartha does not join the mob; instead he notices the terror of the young girl sitting in the back seat of the car. He sees both sides of everything.

Tunu, Siddhartha's brother, is the extreme opposite of Sutapha. He's a committed revolutionary and bomb maker. When we first see him he's bandaging a leg wound which may have come from an explosion. (It could have been the bomb which interrupts the newsreel propagandizing the government's efforts to aid the poor which Siddhartha sees when he goes to the movies.) Tunu is an ideologue and a fanatic. Siddhartha tells him he's got a one-track mind and Tunu replies, "You're still rotting away in the same spot, not doing anything." (He evidently believes that it's better to burn than to rot.) Tunu hands him a biography of Che Guevara which Siddhartha gave him a few years earlier. Guevara's picture is on the jacket. In a nice touch, Ray shows Siddhartha's dark and pensive face as it grows a beard and takes on a look very like Guevara. This image suggests that Siddhartha wishes he still had his old revolutionary fervor. Instead, he's distanced from the easy extremes of his sister and brother. He occupies a more difficult middle ground which is crowded with hundreds of job seekers like himself. He pursues his search for employment with integrity but without illusions.

The character of Adinath further defines Siddhartha. A former college classmate, Adinath has turned street smart and corrupt. We first see him rifling the money from a Red Cross donation can. Later he takes Siddhartha to an expensive meal and then to a part-time prostitute. Siddhartha is very uneasy in her presence while Adinath lounges around cracking jokes. Adinath can't understand why his friend would turn down a sexual treat from a beautiful woman. He sees himself as a doer and Siddhartha as a thinker (and by implication, incompetent). After Siddhartha walks out on Adinath, he runs into Keya, another college classmate. She's blown a fuse ironing and doesn't know how to replace it. Keya is a good girl who is played in rather stark contrast to the prostitute and to Sutapha. There's a kind of posed cuteness to her, but also intelligence, fineness, and caring. She's another reason, besides his family, for Siddhartha to hope that his coming job interview will enable him to stay in Calcutta, rather than to take a potential job selling pharmaceuticals in a rural area.

The other details of Siddhartha's situation are rendered very concretely by Ray. We often follow him in the crowded sidewalks via a hand-held camera. We observe him closely with his family and his friends. We know his material condition right down to the tear in his pants which he has repaired at a tailor just before the first interview. His inner world is dramatized no less thoroughly but not quite as successfully. Ray often interjects abrupt fantasy or dream passages to take us into Siddhartha's psyche. The first of these occurs in the second scene (as he waits at the tailor's) when suddenly we see him standing very well dressed in coat and tie in a hothouse full of plants and flowers. This is the way he'd like to be living, wealthy, at ease in his vocation as a student of plant life. When he sees a well-built woman in the street he flashes back to a lecture in medical school on the anatomy of the female breast (the sexual references throughout the film are somewhat stiff). One of the best "inner" sequences occurs when he rests in a temple: he sees a poor woman lying in rags, people in the distance washing clothes in the pond, the way the light rests on the water. Slowly but inevitably he drifts into a memory of his early childhood with his brother and sister. They are playing by a river and looking for a bird which is making a strange call. This reverie is interrupted by a group of American hippies who enter the temple, exclaiming the mystery of India in phony language. The bird-call motif is taken up again as his sister leads him by the hand to watch her dance (she took his hand in the childhood scene). Earlier, he has flashed into this childhood scene when his sister calls out his name sharply (as she'd done years ago) in response to his calling her boss a scoundrel. In the last two instances, the upwelling of Siddhartha's preoccupation about the bird seems artificial and forced. He's too tense and preoccupied with present disturbances concerning his sister to move away into the childhood moment. The flashbacks aren't convincing. Only in the temple scene, when he is resting quietly, does the upwelling seem to occur naturally. Ray is best, as many have said, in the meditative mode. Another

instance of Ray's uneasiness in presenting Siddhartha's innermost being occurs when he and Tunu recall how calmly Tunu observed a chicken having
its head cut off when they were children. Tunu then talks of the guillotine
and public executions in France at the time of the revolution. After Tunu
leaves, Siddhartha has a nightmare in which he sees himself in the guillotine. We see images of the bloody blade being drawn up by thick, hairy
arms which pull the rope, Siddhartha's head on the block, the falling blade.
The brief sequence is very heavy-handed and melodramatic, perhaps suitable to a nightmare, with lots of high contrast lighting. Ray means us to
see that Siddhartha is sensitive in comparison to his cold-blooded brother,
but his means of doing so aren't very subtle. On another occasion Siddhartha asks Tunu whether he remembers "that bird" and Tunu's perfectly
reasonable response is, "What?" "Of course you don't," replies Siddhartha.
He sees, as Ray wants us to see, that Tunu has a one-track mind, that he
only lives in the political present.

Ray's major entry into Siddhartha's psyche occurs in the dream sequence
just after the guillotine nightmare. Siddhartha discovers he has a fever; he
takes his pulse, hears the neighborhood cats' sexual howling and throws
something to silence them, then falls asleep again. The dream sequence
consists at first of a long panning shot of the shoreline in which we see the
interview committee sitting behind a desk (filmed in negative), fetuses in
bottles, Sutapha in a model's pose (in positive), a firing squad, a mob attacking a car, the execution of Tunu by a firing squad, Keya's appearance
as a nurse to help the dying Tunu, and Siddhartha's appearance as he recognizes Keya. All this occurs on the beach at the ocean's edge, with alter-
nating use of negative and positive images. The visual feeling here is more
fluid and dreamlike than the nightmare, but the dream remains a highly
schematic compilation of the day's events within Siddhartha. The feeling
of the irrational, of the strange yet familiar, is largely missing. As in his
earlier film *Nayak*, Ray is least comfortable when entering the subconscious.

Pratidwandi moves toward its conclusion with one of the finest extended
scenes in Ray's later films, and certainly the finest scene in his political/
social films prior to *Jana Aranya*. The whole film carefully builds toward
the second interview scene. There's a subtle merging of Siddhartha's outer
and inner worlds here. The room where the job candidates wait has been
carefully designed. It's a long corridorlike space with few chairs or benches
for the 71 young men who line its walls. Of the three ceiling fans, only one
works and it grinds away with a boring and irritating sound. The heat in
the room is stifling. The atmosphere is one of anxiety and irritation mixed
with boredom. The room's confined, pressure-packed space is an accurate
visual replication of the internal condition of Siddhartha and the other applicants. Ray's camera shoots down the narrow space or tracks along its
length showing us the benumbed men. The sound track is effective, too.
Along with the fan, the sound of the pacing of one candidate as he moves

up and down the corridor adds to the tension and the feeling of time's slow passage. This candidate wears a dark business suit and is very tall and handsome. He's got it made and other candidates (dressed in slacks and light colored shirts) all sense it. In a very nice passage, a small group of them speculate hopefully that he might have some defect, a stammer perhaps. This little sequence has a comic dimension that one misses in Ray's social/political films. But even this paragon is worn down by the waiting; he removes his coat and begins to slump. A candidate passes out, and Siddhartha forms a group to ask for more chairs. When they walk into the interview room the committee immediately spots Siddhartha as a troublemaker ("We can't provide seventy-five chairs; if someone passes out he's not tough enough for the job"). They ask his name whereupon the other applicants move quickly out of the room. Siddhartha's reply that he's not here for himself indicates that he sees himself as part of a collective. He continues to wait in the stifling corridor, standing between two signs in English, "Strikers" and "Non-strikers" (his middle position is still not resolved). The film then cuts to a series of images: a shot of a rag-covered figure lying on the sidewalk, shots of the American hippies smiling and playing with finger cymbals, shots of a slum shantytown and of the breezy, sunny living room of a rich house. We instinctively understand that these shots are from within Siddhartha and they indicate the great polarities between wealth and poverty which he is sensitive to. His meditation has a strong element of overt political commentary on Ray's part, but it's closely enough attached to Siddhartha's recent experience (the boss's house, the temple scene) to function successfully as a record of his inner movement. At this point, Siddhartha looks down the hall and sees the waiting applicants as skeletons (all save the tall, handsome one who remains in his dark suit). It's the most arresting image in the film but it's damaged by the use of the voice of the medical school lecturer offering some platitudes about the function of the skeletal system (by this point in the film we know that Siddhartha has a clinical imagination and where it comes from). Still, the scene has enormous power. Siddhartha's hallucination is easily and naturally rendered by Ray. It grows out of the claustrophobic environment of the waiting room and Siddhartha's internal anguish. The inner and outer are perfectly fused here. Ray seems at his best when he examines the borderline area between full consciousness and sleep—in daydream or states of mediation—rather than those more purely subconscious states of dream and nightmare.

When the committee calls for a lunch break, Siddhartha snaps. He storms into the interview room and wrecks it and then walks out. When next we see him he's on the train going to his pharmaceutical job in the country. He's writing a letter in his head to Keya ("I don't expect to be comfortable here or even happy. . . ."). As he sits in his simple hotel room he hears the bird call and goes out on the porch. The regular rhythm of a funeral chant is heard as he looks out into the calming space of the rural landscape.

Something is dying in him and something is being reborn. The funeral chant at the end is in Hindi, not Bengali.[1] We have moved to the state of Bihar where new possibility awaits Siddhartha.

At the end, Siddhartha has rejected collective political action and returned to the basic rhythms of life. It's as if the emphasis has shifted from the social/political concerns of *Pratidwandi* to the universal matters contemplated in *Pather Panchali* and the Apu trilogy. All the impetus toward political action is there for him but he cannot follow it. Perhaps this is due to the distancing factor involved in his clinical imagination—his tendency to see human behavior in anatomical or even mechanistic terms. More likely it is due to Ray's own predilection for meditative distance in which the function of political action takes on an ephemeral and illusionary quality. For Ray, Siddhartha's contemplation of the bird call is finally more important than his joblessness. The most basic and persistent questions inhere in the bird call and not in the social and political problems which the film describes. The bird call evokes the feelings of wonder, of the potentiality of life, of first sight and first hearing. It suggests that Siddhartha's childhood is still alive (as Sutapha's and Tunu's are not) and that he has a chance to recapture or revive the essential vitality within him. The ending of *Pratidwandi* is ambiguous, but somehow we know that Siddhartha will survive and grow in strength.

This ending was not satisfactory to the more politically radical members of Ray's audience in India. For them, the logical arena for Siddhartha's further growth would be political activism. But for Ray that growth could only occur in what is for him a more private region. The film presents in compelling detail all the reasons for radical politics and then rejects those politics.

This is a good place to comment on Ray's uneasiness with political activism. Ray's touchiness on the subject is best seen in a 1982 interview with Udanyan Gupta.[2] Gupta points out that Ray's "most outstanding achievement has been his depiction of women in a cinema overpopulated with vacuous sex objects and silent sufferers." He then elicits from Ray that film can't effect social change, and that you can't say certain things directly because of the censors. Ray then comments on the characater of Tunu—the most politically radical figure in all his films. He says Tunu becomes uninteresting because he's so totally subsumed in his cause, that his radicalism "makes him part of a total attitude and makes him unimportant." His dismissal of Tunu is accompanied by the contention that he has made clearer political statements "than anyone else, including Mrinal Sen," one of India's leading filmmakers and a passionate activist and critic of Ray. Ray then goes on nearly to deny his Brahmo heritage ("I don't even know what being Brahmo means") and to put down the Bengali film audience by saying that they're only used to dross.

The uncharacteristic anger and testiness of Ray's replies in this interview suggest a defensiveness which is, in part, an acknowledgment of his limitations when it comes to politics. It's here that we see the chief difference between Ray and his mentor Rabindranath Tagore, for Tagore was extremely active in political resistance to British control of India—even to leading demonstrations in the streets. Tagore believed he could help change the world, an idea totally foreign to Ray.

NOTES

1. Ray points this out to Henry Micciollo in the latter's *Satyajit Ray* (Lausanne: Editions l'Age d'Homme, 1981), p. 306.

2. Udanyan Gupta, "The Politics of Humanism," *Cineaste* 12 (1982):24–29.

19

SEEMABADDHA (COMPANY LIMITED): The Price of Success

Seemabaddha (1971) is a thesis film, unusual for Ray. Perhaps this is why it isn't quite as successful as its companions *Days and Nights in the Forest* and *Pratidwandi*. Still, it moves, at the end, to a moral complexity not found in *Pratidwandi*. The film examines the life of an upwardly mobile corporate executive, Shyam Chatterjee, in Calcutta. The opening images suggest that Shyam's life is subject to immense pressures toward conformity and compartmentalization. In the initial sequence prior to the titles we see the huge, high-rise office building Shyam works in. It's like a gigantic beehive rising out of the street. Shots of the assembly-line production system give a sense of repetition and replication. Shyam's son is shown dressed exactly like his boarding-school mates in shorts and a sweater. We see workers at rows of desks, a list produced by an automatic typewriter, a sterile office corridor off of which each executive has his space. Ray even uses the split screen to give us the titles and at one point shows multiple, compartmentalized images of Shyam's activities as he narrates his early history. "My future is completely tied to that of my firm," he says. The world of *Seemabaddha* is technological, but it's a place where things break down, telephones don't work, elevators fail to operate and the upwardly mobile come to taste the sourness of ambition. The film recounts the price of success.

Shyam, as played by Barun Chanda, is extraordinarily handsome, tall, graceful, and charming. He has a disarming smile. He knows he's attractive and knows how to use it. Ray wants us to be taken with him and then gradually to see him. He also wants Shyam gradually to see himself. In an early scene he enters his office to discover that the fan has been left on. He abruptly tells the office boy that he'll dock his pay if it happens again. He's tough and even ruthless. Later in the film he jokes with the personnel manager about how big a funeral wreath the manager would have sent had a night watchman died as a result of his severe wounds from a bomb explosion during a strike Shyam and the manager had arranged to happen. It should be added that Shyam is very upset when he first learns of the watchman's injuries and that he goes to visit him in the hospital. He's a good man damaged by ambition. Shyam is also a loving father. When he reads his son's letter from school his face lights up. He's kind to his wife but doesn't tell her about anything going on at work, or anything going on inside himself. He's nice to his fellow workers, flirts with his secretaries, and knows how to play up to members of the board of directors. He'll listen smilingly to Sir Boren's (boring?) humorous account of how he held up delivery of a paycheck to a famous British general during the occupation. (Sir Boren is, of course, an Anglophile from his Rolls Royce to his studied role as an eccentric.) Shyam speaks Bengali and English with equal ease, often switching back and forth between the two. His bosses are British. In fact, the company is British owned—a reminder that well after independence England still pulls many of the strings in India's economy. If he becomes a director, he'll be the first Bengali employee in the company to do so. He must conform to British customs. He is liked by his friends and correctly perceived as a young man on the rise. At a party he and his wife Dolan give, we see them share their views: "The city is doomed" (but we are comfortable); "The whole system is rotting." "They don't want jobs, they want revolution." He's good at image building, his own as well as his company's. We see him presiding at an ad conference reviewing a TV spot for the ceiling fans they produce (that the ad is a witty parody of TV advertising is no surprise given Ray's early experience in the advertising industry). The film suggests that one of the sources of Shyam's ambition may be his instinctive discomfort at his compartmentalized existence. He'll play the game according to the agreed categories because he's good at it, but he'll also play outside the rules when the prize warrants it. He likes the stimulus of the corporate fast lane. As he says to Tutul, his sister-in-law, he likes risk and danger and is aware that, like a jockey pressing for the finish line, he may commit a foul accidentally. He finds himself more and more deeply attracted to Tutul and his remark about the jockey is a subtle reference, which she understands, to their growing involvement. The danger of this involvement is linked with his determination to get a company directorship at any price. When a large order of ceiling fans bound for Iraq is found to be defective, subjecting the company to heavy penalties and loss of prestige, it's Tutul who lightheartedly suggests that Shyam arrange for trouble at the factory in order to avoid the penalty. Since his directorship is on the line, he acts at once through the personnel manager to foment a strike, thus closing down the plant temporarily and avoiding the penalty. The plan works and Shyam gets his directorship, but his climb to the top is strenuous and costly. In one of the most effective scenes in the film, Ray has him return the day of his appointment as director to his high-rise apartment only to discover that the elevator is out of order. Most directors would give a highly abbreviated treatment to Shyam's progress on foot up the stairwell, but Ray presents an extended passage without music of Shyam laboring up flight after flight. It's almost a symbolic sequence (Shyam's hard climb upward) and the effect is surprisingly powerful. Soon after he has climbed exhausted to his apartment he experiences his moment of mutual recognition with Tutul.

Tutul is the other major character in the film. She's from Patna, visiting her sister in the big city. She's educated, intelligent, and thoughtful. Since she's played by Sharmila Tagore, the knowing Aparna of *Days and Nights*

in the Forest (and the perceptive Aditi of *Nayak*), the viewer may assume
that she's morally aware. She says she's a student of psychology. When she
hears from Dolan about how much Shyam will be paid if he gets the directorship, she's somewhat stunned and remarks in an aside "the poet Tagore
got that much when he won the Nobel prize," and adds thoughtfully, "it's
always nice to get what you want." Though she appears to be morally
aware, the viewer should be careful of any quick assumptions. She admires
all the conveniences in her sister's apartment, the fans, the hot water system. Dolan points out to her that their eighth-floor apartment is high above
the dust and noise of the streets, and that there aren't even any insects up
that high (and, of course, we're given to understand, no revolutionary up-
heaval). She's thrilled by Calcutta and all it offers. She goes to the beauty
parlor with Dolan and goes to the races with Shyam, where their conduct
is flirtatious and she quickly develops a liking for the betting action. Compared to her, the pretty Dolan seems plain and conventional. (Dolan actually seems to become plainer in appearance as the film goes on, just as
Tutul becomes more beautiful—a calculated strategy by Ray's make-up
person.) She's witty and more than a bit coy, particularly about her boyfriend in Patna who's a revolutionary. She tells Shyam that she's come to
observe "someone who's not a revolutionary," meaning himself, but she's
really come to see her sister and to see if she cares as much for Shyam now,
after all his success, as she did six or seven years earlier in Patna. She's on
uneasy ground from the start and complicates matters by suggesting to Shyam
that he arrange for trouble at the factory. When she comes to visit him at
work he asks her why she didn't tell him about her friend and she replies
that she would have if there were something to tell. They're in the elevator
and, as people do in elevators, they're not facing each other when they
speak. There's an obliquity to the scene which suggests both that they are
knowingly avoiding the full complication of their relationship and that, in
part, they're not entirely conscious of the complication. In this scene, Tutul
asks Shyam to get her a job in his company and then she'll move to Calcutta. Though she's speaking playfully, she's making a major move for him
here. At the end of the film she's finally fully aware of her complicity with
Shyam and is deeply upset. It's important to see that Tutul is nearly as
compromised at the end as Shyam. She doesn't have the moral wisdom of
Aparna and Aditi (Sharmila Tagore's other roles); she's been sucked into
the excitement and glamour of Shyam's "life-style" (the verbal corruption
is appropriate here). Ray has remarked that "she will probably go back to
the revolutionary because she's so completely disillusioned with the other
kind of life she has witnessed."[1] Still, it's impossible to imagine Tutul participating in revolutionary action. Such action is distant to her, as it is to
Siddhartha in *Pratidwandi*, and to Ray himself. At the end she hangs between the world of bourgeois success and the world of revolutionary rebel-

lion. Her situation is more tragic than Shyam's; he still thinks he knows what he wants. In this sense she's a more interesting character than he is. But Ray is more interested in Shyam's difficulties than he is in her existential dilemma.

Seemabaddha is at its best in three key scenes which depict Shyam's and Tutul's growing complicity. In each scene Ray is working in comfortable territory—a region, one might add, where many directors would and do have difficulty. In each scene the objective is to portray the growing complicity in nonverbal ways, through lighting, carefully staged movement, facial gestures, and so on. Each scene must accurately, and seemingly accidentally, suggest the great weight of the unspoken. We've seen Ray handle this masterfully in *Charulata* and *Days and Nights in the Forest*, so it's no surprise to see him bring it off here. In the first scene, Tutul and Shyam have risen early and they have tea together in the sunny living room. Tutul has her hair down; she's beautiful and pensive. They don't say much but their glances and their movement around the room suggest affection and mutual attraction. The whole scene has the desultory rhythm of small talk and the underlying feeling of things left unsaid. In a briefer passage later on, Tutul stands in her doorway in deep focus and says good night to Shyam in the foreground of the darkened living room. He looks across the room to her but says nothing. As he turns slowly toward the camera the focus shifts slowly to him and we see his anguished, smiling face. He moves out of the frame and we're given a long look at the empty living room, a light breeze blowing the curtains inward. The painful complexity of their relationship is perfectly evoked here. The shot of the empty room, so typical of Ray, contains the reverberations of the exchange which has just occurred. In the final scene of the film Tutul comes slowly out of her room into the darkened living room, pauses to look out of the window (a characteristic gesture on her part), and then sits down near Shyam. She's looking sorrowful and pensive and he looks that way, too. She gives him back the watch he had earlier given her in the early morning scene (she no longer wants to live by his system of orientation) and Shyam slowly covers his face with his hands. The slowness of his gesture here is like the slowness of his turning away from Tutul's good night—both movements splendidly dramatize the growing weight of complication between them. They are both finally aware of their mutual culpability and they're both devastated. No dialogue is necessary in these last two scenes (which were very likely shot close together); they accomplish what they have to in purely visual terms. They're very reminiscent of that other film of dark interiors, *Charulata*. In this respect, it's useful to note how much of *Seemabaddha* is shot in interiors: either the antiseptic environment of the office building or the enclosed space of the apartment. This isn't Ray's favorite setting; he likes a more open space. But he does a good job, particularly with the living room, which we see in many different manifestations: dark, brooding, sunny, peopled with friends and family—and, most memorably, empty with the wind blowing the curtains.

In other scenes, however, Ray is less secure when he attempts to depict Shyam's and Tutul's inner anxiety. After Shyam has returned home the day he learns about the defective fans, Ray has him look up at the ceiling fan in his living room. He sees the broken neon sign of a fan turning (which he had earlier taken Tutul to see, expecting it to be working properly—a piece of rather stiff foreshadowing) and he then sees the stamped word "rejected" jumping nearer and nearer. It's almost as if Ray is parodying an American B film from the 1940s. Again, Tutul comes toward an awareness of her compromised state in a nightclub with Shyam and Dolan. As the camera moves slowly in upon her troubled face, the film cuts back and forth to a half-naked dancer doing the hula (she's the prostitute from *Pratidwandi*). The juxtaposition of images of the dancer and Tutul is heavy-handed in the extreme; a Victorian would understand it.

Ray's handling of the strike at the factory owes a certain debt to the Eisenstein of *Potemkin*. There's even a quote from the Russian film when we see the food for the workers being dispensed through a small rectangular slot. Significantly, the strike begins, as in *Potemkin*, over complaints about the food. Ray uses a fast-cut rhythm of shots to suggest the progress of the strike. This isn't, to say the least, Ray's most comfortable cinematic rhythm but he makes it work.

Finally, *Seemabaddha* advances an idea subversive and new to Ray: that the body or the face, is not the image of the soul. In all prior films the characters have proved to contain their essential beings in their faces and in their bodies; they are what they seem. *Seemabaddha*, that examination of corporate image-making, suggests that beauty and attractiveness may be only skin deep.

NOTE

1. Quoted in Chidananda Das Gupta, *Satyajit Ray* (New Delhi: Directorate of Film Festivals, 1981), p. 93.

20

ASHANI SANKET (DISTANT THUNDER): Starvation Comes on Slowly

*A*shani Sanket, or *Distant Thunder*, was made in 1973. The film examines the mass starvation which occurred in Bengal in 1943 as the result of the war with Japan. It measures the incremental coming on of starvation from the vantage point of a small Bengali village. The caste system plays an important part as the context for the drama, for the two central characters, Ganga and Ananga, are the only Brahmins living among the lower caste peasants in the village.

Ganga's gradual conversion from an attitude of aloof superiority to a compassionate sense of community is the most important narrative element in the film. There are two elements that influence him to change: his wife Ananga's compassion for the suffering of others and his association with the starving Brahmin Bhattarcharji.

Ganga's situation early in the film reflects his comfortable sense of himself as a superior person. He's the priest, doctor, and teacher to the village, the only educated person there. "These people are ignorant," he remarks to Ananga while she serves him dinner. When a sick peasant visits him the next day he gives him a haughty lecture, muttering all the while about the peasants' stupidity. The villagers *are* ignorant, but Ganga's own education is spotty at best. He doesn't seem to know where Singapore is (he places it somewhere in India); he misquotes a few lines of Sanskrit poetry in a pompous tone and claims he knows Sanskrit very well. He's able to get away with this because the villagers look up to him, placing him always in a superior position on a clean mat on an elevated porch when he comes to visit them, while they sit in the dirt. Soumitra Chatterjee's performance as Ganga is very evocative here. His stiffness and pomposity make him a comic figure. He clears his throat loudly when he wishes to speak to the villagers. When he's negotiating with a man from another village who wants him to perform religious rituals so that the village will be spared an attack of cholera which has broken out nearby, he walks up and down his front porch sucking on his pipe, his posture slack, scratching himself, glancing portentously over the top of his glasses, mournfully counting up the cost to him of such a service. His play-acting helps him get his price. He's canny and calculating. He knows he has found a good deal in this small village and he means to make the most of it. His slack posture and constant pipe-sucking suggest an almost narcissistic self-indulgence. He's really not aware of the feelings of other people. He's always ordering his young students to get their parents to supply him with something, a piece of food, a haircut; in this way he's paid for his teaching. He's a bit of an operator, and his sense of his own superiority assists him.

The fragility of Ganga's sense of superiority is seen in his relationship with his wife Ananga. Though he's the active man, performing his various roles and bringing in the food and money, while Ananga largely tends to their small house, she's really the stronger of the two. She's not only very beautiful; her calmness and placidity suggest an acceptance or acquiescence of whatever fate may bring. This attitude, which may in part be the product of her woman's experience as a second-class citizen, is a very valuable one to have when faced with a hopeless situation such as the coming starvation. It allows her to feel connected to the others she sees suffering around her, while Ganga scrambles around trying to find rice for her and himself. She doesn't have any children to worry about, either. In an interesting early scene, her friend Moti, an untouchable from the village she and Ganga have recently moved from, tells her "it's your turn to have a baby now." Ananga is standing within the darkened interior of her house and Ray gives a medium close-up of her distressed face. It's clear that she's deeply troubled about not having children. Whether this has anything to do with the quality of self-absorption we sense in Ganga remains to be seen. The fact remains that Ananga has a fuller knowledge of life's tragedies than her husband, even though he has more education and can play the knowing man, explaining to her in authoritative tones about the war and how planes fly. Her toughness is fully revealed when she refuses rice from her close friend Chhutki, who has made herself sexually available in order not to starve. Ananga is more morally courageous than anyone else in the film. That she stands for the vitality of life is made abundantly clear in the opening images of the film. At first we see a shot of light reflected off the surface of water, then gradually, as the camera subtly shifts its position, we see beneath the surface and gradually perceive a human hand limply rising until it breaks through the surface. Our immediate sense is that this is an image of death— the dead hand of a drowned person (there's a pattern of hand images throughout the film, culminating in a silhouette shot of a dead hand and forearm at the end). The hand begins to move slowly and sensuously and, as the camera backs away, we see that it belongs to Ananga who is bathing with friends in a nearby pond. The movement here from death to life is the reverse of the movement of the film as a whole.

If the portrayal of Ananga seems at least partially idealized, the portrayal of the starving Brahmin Bhattarcharji does not. He's an ambiguous figure, fully human. An older man (he says he's 69 and has a large family), he's pitiable in his starvation. But he's also canny and manipulative as he insinuates himself into Ganga's and Ananga's household. (Who wouldn't do the same in his condition?) He sees that they have more than he and he shows no compunction, as a fellow Brahmin, about helping himself. He's not entirely likable. He represents Ganga's most severe test: whether he can reach out to help another suffering human.

The visual center of the film involves Ray's portrayal of Ganga's relationship with Bhattarcharji. Three scenes are important here. In the first, Ganga is traveling home in a bullock cart from the village threatened by cholera where he performed his services. As he nods sleepily to the rhythm of the cart, the camera pans down to show us a new red sari he's acquired for Ananga as part of his price. He's also been paid in rice. There's a medium side shot of the oxen's legs moving as they pull the cart and a shot of the cart wheels moving slowly. A shot from within the canvas roof of the cart shows Bhattarcharji approaching from the rear. The key shot in the sequence then occurs: a long side shot of the cart moving and a man approaching it. The cart and the man are small dark objects rendered in silhouette under a huge evening sky filled with monumental clouds. There's a sense of the precariousness of human existence in this shot; the cloudy sky suggests, as do the earliest shots of storm-clouded sky behind the credits, that a disaster may be approaching. Another implication is rendered visually as well: the eternal, on-going meeting between the man who has and the man who needs. Ray's use of silhouette shots at this point in the film (and at many other points) suggests that Ganga and Bhattarcharji are both individuals and, at the same time, archetypal forms. In a series of medium close-up shots, we see them in silhouette as Bhattarcharji explains his situation to Ganga. The camera is low, the men's outlines cast against the sky. We can't see facial details of either man as we hear Bhattarcharji explain that he's old and starving and that the Japanese have taken Singapore and thus cut off the flow of rice. After Ganga gives him rice, Bhattarcharji characteristically asks for more and then asks Ganga's name. The scene closes with another long side shot in silhouette of the wagon as it moves slowly away from Bhattarcharji under the massive, threatening sky.

In the second scene Bhattarcharji makes an unannounced visit to Ganga's house, while Ganga is teaching, and tells Ananga that he's a Brahmin and he's come for lunch. Ananga promptly serves him the food she was expecting to eat (without saying anything, of course). While Bhattarcharji eats greedily, we're able to have our first close look at him. He's gaunt and sharp-featured, with slightly bulging eyes and a voluble tongue. After asking for a second serving, he takes a nap on the front porch. When Ganga discovers Bhattarcharji asleep, he's very irritated. Ananga is amused at this situation and tries to mollify her husband. Bhattarcharji, once again, explains his dilemma to Ganga and asks for rice which Ganga says he can supply through a friend, but only if he can pay for it. Bhattarcharji says he has no money and slaps his forehead moaning that he and his family are going to starve. His message to Ganga is pretty clear: We Brahmins must stick together. But it's a message Ganga rejects. He moves to the far end of the porch and sits smoking his pipe, his back half-turned to Bhattarcharji, sending surreptitious glances at him. The camera is positioned at a slight angle to the porch so that Bhattarcharji sits in the left foreground of the frame while Ganga occupies the middle ground at the right. This single shot lasts 41 seconds, and it's pure Ray. It's a long, leisurely shot in which nothing important seems to be happening and yet in which everything is happening. There's no dialogue, only the desultory, scratchy sound of something like radio music in the distant background. Bhattarcharji slowly wipes his bare feet with his hands and knocks out dirt from each shoe before he puts it on. He seems to take an eternity to do this; he's putting the pressure on Ganga, but he's also completely dejected since, for him, Ganga is the last hope of survival. Finally he rises to leave, thanking Ananga for lunch. As he walks away from the house, Ananga speaks urgently with Ganga and Ganga finally calls him back.

The third scene occurs immediately after the second, after a time jump of several hours, for it's now evening. Bhattarcharji slurps noisily out of a bowl (the sound track is keyed up here) as Ganga and Ananga watch. Ganga looks extremely unhappy. There's a slow pan shot to the left, beginning with Bhattarcharji's shoes tilted against the wall, as we listen to his explanation of why rice is beginning to be in such short supply. He says that the authorities (presumably British) are diverting rice to the army. In other words, this famine they are all beginning to experience is a planned one. He knows more about the world than Ganga. His insinuations make Ganga increasingly uncomfortable. First, he implies that since Ganga has no children, he can better afford to be generous. Ananga, standing in the doorway to their bedroom, keeps sending warm and encouraging glances to her husband. She wants him to be less irritated with Bhattarcharji. She also knows that he too is sensitive about their not having any children, and that Bhattarcharji's appeal for generosity is also a form of bragging. Bhattarcharji then implies that, as the only Brahmin in his village, Ganga has found a good deal and knows how to use it. Ganga defensively replies that his job is very exhausting. At this moment, he has had it with his guest and walks away into the bedroom to Ananga. The whole nighttime dialogue is filmed by Ray as a kind of reverse silhouette—the faces and bodies of the two men brightly lit from the side, against a very dark background. The harshness and clarity of the images accurately reflect the tension between the two men. The scene ends with Ganga telling Ananga not to take pity on any old fellow who comes along. As he says this, he pushes the door shut so that Bhattarcharji cannot overhear their discussion. The noise of the door seems to awaken Bhattarcharji, who has been lying on the porch. There's a close-up of his face as his eyes pop open. He turns his head slowly toward the door, and we see his suffering face. It's a simple and extremely poignant shot.

Ganga's change of heart toward Bhattarcharji is accompanied by his gradual awareness of the severity of the crisis facing them all. He witnesses a riot over rice at the local market in which he is flung to the ground. He is forced to permit Ananga to lower herself by working at the local rice-husking mill so that she can bring home a palm full of rice as her pay. He sees the growing number of starving people who come by his house begging for food, or gathering snails to eat from the local ponds. He witnesses the aftermath of an attempted rape on Ananga when she is out in the countryside with her friends gathering leaves and roots to eat. He ministers to Biswas, the wealthiest man in the village, after he is attacked by robbers who want to find out where Biswas has stored his rice. Slowly Ganga comes to see the enormity of their fate. His final acceptance of Bhattarcharji occurs just before they are all engulfed by the starving horde and is prepared for by the depiction of the death of Ananga's friend, the untouchable Moti—the last crucial visual episode in the film.

Moti's death is introduced by a series of very grainy still shots of starved bodies, the only time in the film Ray uses documentary images. We next see a shot of still water lying between little muddy ridges of land. Moti's reflection in the water then occurs, but it is broken into fragments by the ridges. The camera moves upward to show her, half-dead, staggering along even though she's using a staff. She lies down near the large banyan tree near Ganga's and Ananga's house. Ananga is summoned by a neighbor, and Moti tells her that no one is left in their former village. She also repeats to Ananga what she said in the beginning of the film: "Don't touch me; you'll have to bathe." This time she speaks in a slow and dreamy fashion; she's semi-conscious from starvation. Ananga leaves food beside her, but Moti is too weak to eat. It is late afternoon, and there's a golden light as sunset and dusk come on. There are a series of shots of Moti as she dies quietly and open-eyed. Ganga comes and takes her pulse (the silhouette shot of her hand and forearm), and then leaves to arrange for her cremation. A young girl, who has been watching from behind a bush, runs up and snatches the food.

This death scene is interesting in several ways. First, Ray chooses to present it in relation to Chhutki's submission, for rice, to the scar-faced man at the local kiln. There's a good deal of cross-cutting between the two incidents. The effect is to show the viewer the increasing pace of the famine. Second, Ray splices into Moti's death a number of shots of butterflies and dragonflies resting on blades of grass. These shots are designed to place the death in a continuum of natural events. Their effect is to distance viewers from the immediacy of Moti's death (and the other deaths which are to come), and to remind us of the more universal context in which the starvation is occurring. We have seen shots of butterflies earlier in the film and pan shots of the lovely countryside accompanied by the distant, steady beat of the rice mill. They seem to say that no matter how horrible and tragic the starvation is, life will manage to go on. A Western director might treat the subject of man-made starvation by showing anger at the authorities who created it, but Ray shows no anger, only total sympathy with the sufferers. Even Biswas, the local rice-hoarder, is treated with understanding and humor rather than anger.

As Ganga walks away from the dead Moti, he sees Bhattarcharji and his family coming along the road. He tells Ananga that they must take them in and that "there will be ten." Her response, "No, eleven," tells him that she is pregnant at last. This turn of events avoids becoming the conventional film cliché (popping the news to a surprised husband) because of the tragic context in which it occurs. Ananga and Ganga are most unified in their love just before they go under. It is also a symbolic event: Ganga learns of the pregnancy at the precise moment he is finally able to reach outside of himself.

Ray's use of silhouette shots dominates the end of *Distant Thunder*. We see the silhouettes of Bhattarcharji and his family coming along the road. The camera then backs away to show us silhouette shots of dozens and then hundreds of starving people. A title card tells us that 5 million died in Bengal of starvation and epidemics in what has come to be known as the man-made famine of 1943.

Ray surely meant to suggest, in these final images, that Ananga and Ganga die in the mass starvation, and yet a large number of viewers of *Distant Thunder* seem to feel that they somehow survived. We don't see their silhouettes join the vast army of shades, but do we need to? The problem here is that, of the foreground characters in the film, only Moti actually looks as if she is dying of starvation. Chhutki is plump and round when she visits the scarred man at the kiln and then leaves her family to go with him to the city "in order to eat." Ananga herself is both full-bodied and very beautiful; she looks more like a movie star than a peasant. Ananga and Ganga don't seem haggard or lacking in energy at any time, even though they've had no rice or other staples for quite a while. It is worth noting, for instance, that Ganga doesn't take Moti's untouched food after he discovers that she's dead. In this sense, it could be argued that Ray has kept the starvation at too great a distance. Ananga's pregnancy may suggest to a hopeful viewer that they will go on and have a family. The documentary photographs which introduce Moti's death, and her death itself, may not have sufficient weight, in the context of the whole film, to convince the audience of what is surely to come. Nevertheless, *Distant Thunder* remains a powerful study of moral change as the caste system is impacted by deprivation. The film looks forward to *Sadgati*, Ray's later effort for television.

Finally, it should be pointed out that *Distant Thunder* is one of Ray's most violent films and that the violence is presented powerfully—contrary to Ray's usually uncertain treatment of violence. The riot over rice which Ganga observes is a convincing representation of mob violence. The nighttime attack on Biswas is more typical of Ray, since we hear more of the injury done to Biswas than we see. The attack by the rapist upon Ananga is, however, one of the best presentations of violence in all of Ray's work. We see his stiffened, slightly trembling fingers with their overly long nails, and the burning cigarette, just before he makes his attack (it is almost a duplicate of the shot of the neighbor's hand before he makes an advance to Sarbojaya in *Aparajito*). The hand-held camera shows the attack itself in all its frenzy. The most graphic part of the rape comes when Ananga's friends return to rescue her and beat the rapist to death with their staves. We see the bloody marks on his back through his shirt and hear the heavy sounds of their blows. Ray uses a number of fast cuts here. As he struggles to get away in the stream, we see the blood flowing away from his weakening body. A shot of his lifeless hand, partially submerged, closes the scene. The shot is related to the other hand shots in the film, particularly the opening shots of Ananga's hand in the water.

21

THE INNER EYE and *TWO:*
Two Short Films

The short documentary *The Inner Eye* (1974) describes the work of one of India's most important painters, Binod Behari Mukherjee. Ray studied with Binod Behari at Santiniketan and was influenced not only by the master's paintings and drawings but also by the example of his courage and vision, for Binod Behari was born with severely defective vision and became completely blind at the age of 53, though he continued to work. The film was written by Ray and is narrated by him as well. The film opens with shots of a tile mural the artist designed for Santiniketan and shows him feeling the tiles to make sure they are being properly placed. There's a brief sequence showing his domestic habits and then the film moves back in time to show Binod Behari's earliest paintings and drawings. Most of the documentary concentrates on the murals he made for Santiniketan. A beautiful ceiling mural done in earth colors of a pond surrounded by scenes of local rural life near the school is intercut with actual scenes of rural life. The artist's decision to use contemporary rather than the usual mythological subject matter is noted, as is the influence of Japanese painting upon him. A few fine paintings and sketches of Benares are shown, and Ray comments on Binod Behari's ability to "catch the essence beneath the surface." A second mural dealing with Indian religious figures is shown and described as the only example of epic Indian art in the twentieth century. The artist's work after he became totally blind is particularly interesting: small clay figures, a fine semi-abstract human figure done with a nearly continuous line, colored paper cutouts in the style of Matisse.

The Inner Eye amply presents the rich visual production of Binod Behari's life. His art is an example of fine work done under great handicap, of a creative response to hardship. As the artist himself has written: "Blindness is a new feeling, a new experience, a new state of being." Most of all, the documentary stresses Binod Behari's ability to paint from an inner vision, whether he could see or not.

Ray's own inner vision, so eloquently rendered in his best films, first found expression at Santiniketan, the school for the arts (some have called it a creative ashram) founded by Rabindranath Tagore. *The Inner Eye* is thus a tribute to the school as well to one of its finest teachers.

Two is a short (13 minutes) dramatic film without dialogue. Made in 1964 for Esso's television program "World Drama," *Two* is the second part of three sections, the first a short on ballet and the third a short on Ravi

Shankar. These sections were made by other directors. *Two* isn't particularly interesting from a visual standpoint but it does have some interest in terms of Ray's social message. The film dramatizes class conflict between a rich boy and a poor boy. The rich boy, whom we see playing with his toys shortly after his birthday party, attempts to intimidate the poor boy by displaying his possessions in a highly competitive fashion. His failure, finally, to silence the poor boy's flute playing amounts to a defeat.

We first see Budu, the rich boy, in an up-angled shot. He's standing on the balcony of his large, spacious house, wearing a Mickey Mouse hat with his name on it. He waves to someone driving out the driveway. He's like Pikoo on his balcony (in *Pikoo's Day*) at this moment, but he doesn't have Pikoo's wit and sensitivity. In fact, he's rather unattractive—pudgy, light-skinned, heavy in his bored movements. He's drinking a bottle of Coke, and throughout the film he's always eating or chewing gum. He's a good example of the over-privileged rich. There's something destructive in his boredom when he saunters into the house and begins to burst the party balloons by lighting matches. His attention is attracted to the dark-skinned poor boy when he hears his flute, and we see that the poor boy lives in a shack in a field next door to Budu's house. He silences the poor boy's flute by aggressively blowing a party horn, and then silences his drumming by producing a mechanical monkey who plays the drums (the large number of automated toys Budu has suggests both wealth and an underlying passivity in his pleasures). The poor boy appears jumping up and down in the costume of an African native (mask, bow, and arrow). The shot of him here is a near duplication of the shot of young Apu as an African when he demonstrates what he's learning in school to his mother. Budu responds by appearing in his window in various costumes, finally shooting a toy machine gun at his opponent. He then produces a real air rifle and shoots down the poor boy's kite, smiling triumphantly and sticking out his tongue afterward. He's wearing a painted mustache at this point and it's exactly like the mustache of the tyrant King Hirok in *Hirok Rashar Deshe*. There's little charming about him, even though he's a child. He turns to play with the toys on the floor, starting his robot, and then hears the flute again. He hasn't been able to silence the poor boy. Pouting, he turns away from the camera and sits on the bed dejectedly as the robot proceeds to knock over his toys and we hear the slightly mournful sound of the wind blowing in the room as the film closes.

Budu's defeat is tinged with sadness. He's imprisoned in his room with his lifeless mechanical monkeys and robots. He may have the power of his material possessions but it's a dead, impotent power. The poor boy's power is essentially nonmaterial; his spirit remains indomitable. But the poor boy remains an idealized figure. We don't see him in his shack, and there are much fewer (and briefer) shots of him than of Budu, whom we see in detail in his natural habitat. The film doesn't gloss over the brutality of class conflict but it does, as a parable, imply the idealized message that the meek can defeat the rich and powerful. Perhaps Ray conceived of children as the audience he was aiming at in *Two*.

22

SONAR KELLA (THE GOLDEN FORTRESS): A Detective Film

Ray's most important early experiences as a film viewer were almost entirely with American films of the 1930s and 1940s, the work of Ford, Capra, the American films of Lubitsch and other European directors. He loved the American development of different film genres. Whereas Kurasawa was mainly attracted to the Western, Ray chose the detective film as the genre he wanted eventually to work in. The other major influence is the Sherlock Holmes stories, several volumes of which occupy a place in Ray's library. His detective films, *Sonar Kella* and *Joi Baba Felunath*, are unusual adaptations of the genre in that they are films for children as well as adults. Children and childhood are important to an appreciation and understanding of both films.

Sonar Kella (*The Golden Fortress*, 1974) is Ray's first attempt at the genre and though it's entertaining it's not entirely successful. It's too slow, but not in the sense that Ray's films are usually said to be slow. Its episodic structure is often a random one. There's no drive to it, no sense of urgency and little, if any, suspense. It is almost successful in its comic passages which largely have to do with a popular mystery writer and with two villainous criminals. A somewhat simplified version of the plot is as follows: A young boy Mukul disturbs his parents by staying up many nights drawing pictures of things he says he knew in his past life—a camel, a peacock, a golden fortress in which there is a large cache of precious gems. A garbled account of Mukul's unusual situation is published in the newspaper and two crooks, Barman and Bose, manage to get rid of one Dr. Hazra, a parapsychologist who is accompanying Mukul in search of the fortress. Felu, a detective, has been hired to protect Mukul. Felu sets out on his search accompanied by his young cousin Tapas and the mystery writer Lalmohan Ganguly. Eventually, after many twists and turns, Felu exposes Barman and Bose as frauds and rescues Mukul from their clutches. According to conventional formula, there are one or two exciting chases in a film, the last one toward the very end. However, Ray turns the whole film into one long, extended chase in which we follow Felu's pursuit of Mukul and the crooks through a number of different settings, some of which are indeed spectacular, such as the cities (and forts) of Jodhpur and Jaisalmer.

In part, the film is calculated to appeal to boys. It's a boy's adventure story, an exciting outing away from daily routine. Tapas is allowed by his parents to leave school for the search. His father says that Felu is a better teacher than any of his schoolteachers. (As Tapas looks up to Felu, so Felu looks up to Uncle Sudhir, a white-haired gentleman who knows a great deal about parapsychology and who remembers that Dr. Hazra exposed a fraudulent faith healer and his assistant several years earlier.) The film is also about learning from wise teachers. It has a kind of moral dimension to it. Ray wants to instruct children as well as entertain them (this is also true of *Joi Baba Felunath* and, especially, *Hirok Rajar Deshe*). Some of the episodes within the extended chase, the camel ride for instance, may be good fun for youngsters but they are too random. *Sonar Kella* is the only film by Ray which could have used judicious pruning at the script stage.

The performances of Ajoy Bannerjee and Kamu Mukherjee as the con men Barman and Bose add a great deal to the film. They're comic in a ridiculous way and sinister at the same time. Both are bald and have dark fringe beards and mustaches. They're an evil Mutt and Jeff, the old comic book characters. Bose isn't too bright. He tells Lalmohan that he shot wolves in Africa, and he wears a shirt which has as its design the pictures of scattered playing cards—a perfect sign of his mental state. He's a clown but also a hit man. He pushes the kindly Dr. Hazra over a ledge and then immediately goes into a kind of comic pantomime to explain to Mukul how the "bad man" disappeared. Barman is the brains of the duo. He's short and speaks in a muted, menacing singsong à la Peter Lorre. He isn't very bright, either, for he turns Mukul against him at the end by unaccountably trying to shoot a peacock they run across in the golden fortress (perhaps Mukul really has lived at the golden fortress). We're not surprised when Felu deduces that they are the faith healing team that Dr. Hazra exposed a few years earlier.

The mystery writer Lalmohan is also a fine comic touch. He's so involved in fantasy that he can't distinguish reality when it presents itself. Felu points out to him that some of the details in his novels are inaccurate and tells him that if they survive their search for Mukul his next novel will have more substance to it because it will be based on real experience. (Ray explores this motif even more fully in *Joi Baba Felunath*.) Lalmohan is unfailingly cheerful and enthusiastic but he's also a bumbler. He makes an unnecessary move which allows Bose to escape when Felu has him trapped. He learns from Felu, too.

If the film can be said to have a subtext, it involves the presentation of Felu as a seer or perceiver of the truth. The mystery he confronts is not merely concerned with the whereabouts of Mukul; more centrally, it involves the business of seeing into a child's mind. Felu is better at this than anyone else, including Dr. Hazra, Barman (who hypnotizes Mukul and gets him to reveal that the golden fortress is in Jaisalmer) and the sympathetic journalist who interviews Mukul and his parents in a very early scene. In a sense, Felu releases Mukul from his obsession with a past life by rescuing him from Barman. Amid the glowing stones of the fortress at Jaisalmer, the usually somber Mukul breaks into joyous laughter. He has not only been rescued, he has found the spiritual "home" he's always been aware of (with its actual peacocks and camels). The film endorses the idea of preexistence. Felu likes action; he packs a gun and is prepared to use it if necessary, but he's also a contemplative, meditative man. In our first sight of him he's standing on his head, doing yoga. In the key scene in the film he's standing above a table lamp, his face lit from below, meditating out loud to Tapas about the necessity of finding out what is in Mukul's mind. He's able to fit odd pieces together to discover what Barman learns by hypnotizing Mukul. Like Sherlock Holmes, there's a mystical, intuitive element to him which enables him to understand children. It's this kind of understanding on Ray's part which enabled him to make an enjoyable detective story for them.

23

JANA ARANYA (THE MIDDLEMAN): Urban Corruption

*J*ana Aranya (*The Middleman*, 1975) is the last of the group of films that examines life in Calcutta in social and political terms (the others are *The Adversary* and *Company Limited*). As an examination of unemployment among young B.A. graduates, it's closest to *The Adversary*, though it lacks *The Adversary*'s anger. Instead, it is a kind of black comedy, in which scenes of sympathetic comedy deepen and darken into an attitude of tough-minded survival. *Jana Aranya* is also a much closer look into one aspect of the Bengali economy: the world of the small trader or middleman. It's as if Ray took Siddhartha's middle position (politically speaking) in *The Adversary* and translated it into more concrete economic terms in *The Middleman*. The film is generally regarded in Calcutta as Ray's truest, most real depiction of Indian urban life. It's too bad that it has been out of distribution in the United States for several years, though it is available in England and in France.

The story centers around Somnath, a bright student who does poorly because his examiner needs a new pair of glasses and is tired and distracted by family interruptions when he reads Somnath's final B.A. exams. As a result of a mere "pass," Somnath finds his chances in the job market to be impossible. Like Siddhartha in *The Adversary*, he finds his job interviews absurd and disillusioning ("What is the weight of the moon?" he is asked in one). He runs into an old friend, Bishu, who persuades him to try work as a small trader or middleman, renting a desk in Bishu's office. At first, he makes a sale or two and is pleased with the money, but soon he learns that he's expected to provide the purchasing officers he talks to with liquor and women. A sensitive young man from a strict background, he balks at what he considers to be pimping, but finally goes through with it in order to land a big contract. His return to his troubled and brooding father, with whom he lives, dramatizes the heavy price he must pay for any economic success.

This brief recounting of the somber story (based on a story by Shankar, who also wrote the story from which *Seemabaddha [Company Limited]* was made) doesn't capture the film's kindly and understanding comedy. We first catch the comic note in a scene in which Somnath and a school chum sit smoking outside a soccer match (they're too poor to buy a ticket). As the crowd leaves the match, the two men joke that you can tell if a man has a job by the way he walks. They notice different categories of men: a clerk, a manager, a B.A. with first-class honors who definitely has a job. When they shout out to the B.A, asking him if he's a first-class graduate, he misunderstands and shouts back the name of the team who won the game, to their amusement. Even the sequence in which a number of recent graduates send letters applying for jobs has a comic dimension, though a grim one. We see Somnath mail a letter, then we see several others do the same, then we see bags of letters which are emptied into huge piles in the sorting office. Soon we learn that there were one million letters applying for ten job openings! A satirical note is struck when Somnath and his school chum go to see a member of Parliament who leans back relaxedly in his chair and gives them a series of platitudes about patience and the examples of great men from Indian history.

The comedy reaches its high point when Somnath meets a series of small traders, each of whom attempts to educate him in the ways of middlemen. These traders have their mailboxes crowded together on the wall near the ground-floor office door. Bishu, the first of them, is genuinely kindly to Somnath. Like any successful salesman, he's a good, enthusiastic talker and he likes helping a young and somewhat naive fellow get a start. He tells a funny story about a middleman he knew who once even bought an elephant, thinking he might make a quick sale. But Bishu goes off on vacation, leaving Somnath on his own. Next comes Ashok, an accountant who tells Somnath how important it is to know how to please the purchasing officers he deals with. As he jokes about human foibles, Somnath listens smilingly, with an open mouth. This cheerfully cynical view of life is an eye-opener to him, coming as he does from the university and a sheltered family life. His final "street tutor" is Mitter (brilliantly played by Robi Ghosh in a role very much like his performance as Shekhar in *Days and Nights in the Forest*). Mitter is introduced as the archetypal middleman: successful, canny, full of brisk nervous energy. He's the one who suggests that Somnath will land a big contract only by providing the purchasing officer, Goenka, with a prostitute. Up until they go searching for a suitable woman, Mitter seems completely in command; but when the search proves more difficult than expected, we begin to see him unravel.

This section of the film has the feeling of a good, semi-documentary look into the world of prostitution. First they visit an attractive married woman who works in part to provide money for her drunken husband, who returns early and refuses to let his wife go out. Next we see a widow who plays madam for her two daughters. Finally, we see a low-class neighborhood where a suitable young woman who works in a traditional whorehouse is available. As Mitter becomes more and more frustrated and sweaty-faced, we realize the cost he pays for his economic success. Earlier he has claimed to Somnath that he is happily married with three children and that he doesn't feel compromised by what he does. Toward the end of the search, however, we see him pleading anxiously to the "madam" to let one of her daughters go to a hotel (she refuses). By the time they reach the third prostitute, he remembers an important meeting and leaves Somnath to carry on. He's momentarily sick of the whole business and walks away. Somnath's position at this moment is complicated because he recognizes the prostitute to be his school chum's sister, though she denies it. She's clearly working to help support the family, whom we've seen in an earlier sequence which establishes that they are much poorer than Somnath's family. After a good deal of hesitation, he leaves her at Goenka's hotel room door with a generous amount of money. He can't regard her, or any woman, as a mere commodity in a business transaction as Mitter had earlier suggested.

The prostitution section functions to create the central tonal shift in the film. It dramatizes Somnath's darkening predicament in a cheerful atmosphere of salesmanship, camaraderie, jokes, fun, and corruption. The hunt for a prostitute deepens our sense of the darker side of this world of amusing hustlers. *Jana Aranya*, finally, has none of the hard-bitten, streetwise amorality of a culture steeped in the payoff, the bribe, the sweetener, the "mordida." It has an ironic awareness of the pressures that force a young man of a certain fineness to begin to compromise himself. In the apt words of one critic, it's a "sour, witty, tough, individual comedy."[1] Ray's moral attitude in the film is both realistic (this is the way middlemen operate in India) and idealistic (let's take a close look at the underside of the smiling commercial culture of the middleman and note how it damages a fine young man). The irony of the film, like an electric charge, crackles in the gap between the realism of what is and the idealism of what might be if there were more Somnaths in the world.

Part of the pleasure of *Jana Aranya* comes from watching Somnath learn about life outside the university and his family. His tutors, the established middlemen who take to him and advise him, are all vividly rendered comic types, from the placid, world-weary accountant Ashok, to the agitated, chain-smoking Mitter. Life is a hustle, they agree, and the more invention you bring to the hustle, the better. There's a cheerful energetic cynicism to this section of the film. Ray's middlemen are as sharply and affectionately observed as the rural characters of the Apu trilogy. *Jana Aranya*, in fact, reveals that Ray can be as comfortably at home in the city (his actual living environment) as in the countryside.

Somnath is a serious young man who is not only unemployed but rejected by his only real love, a beautiful young woman who has finally given in to her family's insistence that she marry a doctor because he is well-established, whereas Somnath is not. We want to see him recover from these blows, and at first he seems to be doing so. At the end, however, he is as troubled as at the beginning. He feels he has betrayed not only himself but his father. The series of father substitutes, beginning with Bishu and ending with Mitter, who advise him have not enabled him to move toward independent life. Directly after he leaves Kauna at Goenka's hotel door, the face of his father appears in a dissolve. His father is uppermost in his mind at this guilty moment (the super-ego), and he returns home to find his father brooding in the semi-darkness (a characteristic posture). It is worth pointing out that the dissolve to the father's face is a far more subtle and convincing entry into Somnath's consciousness than Ray's more overt and clumsy entries in *Nayak* and *Company Limited*.

The first shot in the film, which seems unrelated to what follows, is of his father climbing the stairs to the family flat. The father is the dominant figure in Somnath's life. He's an unhappy man who seems to cling to his unhappiness. He doesn't like change. An educated Brahmin, he has retired from life and lives mainly through his sons, particularly Somnath. He's proud of the fact that his family has never been in business and has always been highly educated, but he recognizes Somnath's need to find a job. He tries to arrange a marriage which would guarantee that Somnath would manage a cement store, but Somnath wants to try his luck in the wider world. The father says he has never recovered from the loss of his wife in an agonizing illness and from the loss of his religious beliefs. When he learns that Somnath may be involved in the standard business practice of bribery, he tries to prevent him from continuing such practices by saying that he might do something rash if he hears of further actions. This threat of self-destruction is a major power play and is intended to knock Somnath into line. It occurs when the family is at dinner and the elder married son keeps bringing up the subject of bribery in order to confront the old man with the real world.

The family is shot with harsh frontal lighting against a black background, and there's a harsh, unsettling quality to the scene. Somnath says almost nothing; he's more closely tied to his father than his brother is. Part of his initial pleasure at working as a middleman undoubtedly involves his sense of freedom from his gloomy house and from his feeling that he has failed to live up to his father's expectations of him. He's a good son. After talking to Bishu, he asks his father for permission to try his hand at commercial life, and his father gives it, though reluctantly. Bishu's office is light and airy, with lots of action (even the office boy has a little pawnbroking action on the side). It's a far better place to be than hanging around the dark house reading the want ads and preparing fruitless letters of application.

The father may be morally right, but his attitude seems to have no place in the world Somnath is entering. He may be a kindly man, but he seems depressed and even reactionary; his unworldliness is even less help to Somnath than the coaching given by Somnath's surrogate fathers. They may be amoral or immoral, but they have vitality. It is better at this crucial moment, after having suffered two staggering blows, that Somnath move in their direction than in the father's. If one asks whether the father is the moral center from which the film speaks, the answer, I think, is no. The film posits several attitudes toward existence and acknowledges the validity of each of them. In this sense it is a more complex statement (more real, less schematic) than *The Adversary*, where Siddhartha's brother and sister are each presented as having extreme and compromised attitudes. Its realism is actual, not ideological.

An important influence on Somnath's family is his sister-in-law, Kamala. Her loving and understanding attitude toward Somnath helps to soften his harsh judgment of himself. When he tells her his job may involve pimping, Kamala tells him that anything he does will be all right with her. She's full of understanding and acceptance as well as strength and sanity, but she doesn't fully understand Somnath's situation.

In terms of visual interest, the film is strongest in the scene in which Somnath confesses to his sister-in-law. The brightly lit realism of the early scenes of the film—a kind of street realism in which we move along, looking at the shops of small traders and then eventually at the traders themselves—gives way here to a more carefully controlled visual procedure. This isn't to say that Soumendu Roy's camera isn't effective in the first part of the film. As Henri Micciollo zestfully points out, it's very eloquent: *"la caméra . . . se fait ici fureteuse, fouineuse, toujours à l'affut de detail insolite, mobile et légère, marveilleusement disponible"* ("the camera is marvelously functional, searching avidly, moving freely and lightly, nosing around, always on the look-out for strange, telling detail").[2] These aren't exactly point-of-view shots but they do suggest the excited hunger of Somnath's eye as this new world opens up for him. To return to Somnath's confession to Kamála: this scene is best understood when considered in the context of the scene which precedes it; his breakfast with Mitter in which the latter—eating, smoking, in constant movement—quizzes him about his attitudes toward sweetening the deal with Goenka. In brisk, self-assured style he tells the thoughtful Somnath that he's naive, that "even a baby" wouldn't make the mistake he'll make if he turns down the chance to arrange the contract. The pull here for Somnath is to go along with Mitter's plan because it will help him "grow up" in the real world, not the world of the grieving, depressed father. He has uneasily persuaded himself to follow Mitter's strategies when he talks with Kamala. The scene uses 23 shots. The opening shots show the father listening by candlelight to a meditative song on the portable radio (perhaps there's been a power outage as happens from time to time in Calcutta). The rest of the room is dark. In the second shot, we see a very subtle freeze shot of the unshaven father, holding his head in one hand. As he slowly moves his hand away from his face, there's a cut to Kamala's hand carrying a candle which she puts down on the table, the light illuminating a very pensive Somnath. He is presented visually as being in nearly the same position as his father. In the fourth shot Somnath moves his finger slowly through the flame and Kamala asks him what's the matter. When he tells her his job involves pimping, she excuses him by saying the job was forced on him and that she'll never think of him as doing anything bad. She's being sisterly and supportive, not really giving him an objective response or seeing the situation as he's experiencing it. Somnath's face, shrouded in darkness, seems even gloomier in contrast to her cheerfulness. In shots 19 and 21, he stands in dim profile in front of a mirror and turns slowly to look at himself. When the light in the room goes on at the end of shot 21, it abruptly terminates a conversation in which only partial communication has occurred.

The nine-shot ending to the film is unresolved and full of irony. When the father learns that Somnath has landed the big contract from Goenka, he shows relief (in shot seven) by sinking back in his chair, wiping his eyes and sighing, "at last, it's such a relief." His face is half in shadow from the late light coming through the window, and he doesn't hear the depressed tone of voice in which his son utters the news. His relief is misguided. Kamala's facial expression suggests that she is at least somewhat aware of the price that Somnath is paying. In the last shot, we are given a medium view of the father down the length of the room as he bows his head and sinks forward toward his radio, from which music comes as the shot moves slowly to total darkness.

We don't know what will become of Somnath, but we do know that what he has gone through with Mitter and his school chum's sister has left him full of nausea. He will find his way, most likely, but it won't be easy in the complex and ambiguous world the film presents. Unlike Siddhartha at the end of *The Adversary*, Somnath's middle position between Mitter and his father is unresolved. The most appealing hero of Ray's Calcutta films, he is left alone, facing his predicament.

NOTES

1. Alan Brien, quoted in *Satyajit Ray: An Anthology of Statements on Ray and by Ray*, ed. by C. Das Gupta (New Delhi: Directorate of Film Festivals, 1981), p. 109.
2. Henri Micciollo, *Satyajit Ray* (Lausanne: Editions L'Age d'Homme, 1981), p. 209.

24

SHATRANJ KE KHILARI (THE CHESS PLAYERS): The British Takeover

Probably no other film reveals Ray the classicist better than *Shatranj Ke Khilari* (*The Chess Players*, 1977). The film has a careful balance and symmetry, moving from the public to the private, from the celebrations of the royal court to the entertainments of the men in the street. It even holds its highly various modes of representation (comedy of manners, animated cartoon, historical drama, documentary, song and dance) in a balanced design. Ray's use of the chess game as a metaphor is both elegant and economical. In its exquisite proportions, which are in harmony with its rich visual surfaces, the film takes an unusually calm and serene view of the subject of radical, and often violent, historical change.

The Chess Players was a particular challenge to Ray on two counts: it was his first historical film and his first in Urdu. Based on a story by Munshi Premchand, the film examines the British takeover of India in 1856. The public dimension of the film involves the capitulations of King Wajid Ali Shah of Oudh to the British East India Company and the policies of Lord Dalhousie as carried out by General Outram. The private but complementary dimension concerns two comic nawabs (Indian Muslim landlords) by the names of Mirza and Meer whose devotion to the game of chess causes them to overlook their best interests, as the king has overlooked his country's interests. The film's message is that the British were able to take over because the kingdom and its citizens were ripe for the taking. And yet Ray maintains a carefully balanced position in regard to the historical drama. General Outram and King Wajid, the central figures in the film's public dimension, are both revealed as fully human; neither is a villain.

Two scenes are important in revealing Outram. In each, Ray presents an extended dialogue between Outram and a member of his staff. The first scene serves to give the audience background information about King Wajid. Outram is talking to his assistant Weston, an old-time India hand who speaks the native language and knows the regional culture. When Outram reads Weston a briefing report on the king, his Scottish accent becomes more and more clipped and judgmental as he discovers the king's fondness for women, dancing, music and song, and even poetry. He asks Weston if he knows any of the king's verse, and Weston obliges by quoting a beautiful poem by heart. As we hear Weston's sensitive reading of the poem, the camera moves into a close-up of his emotion-filled face. But Outram is unimpressed; it's clear to him that the king is a decadent hedonist who doesn't know how to run his kingdom. Outram's contempt for the king's artistic pursuits gives energy to his strategy: "We're going to take over," he tells Weston.

A later scene in which he talks to his doctor reveals a different side of Outram. Here he displays a bad conscience about the takeover and the violation of the treaty with the king. He doesn't want to interview the king for fear that their discussion would result in war and bloodshed. The aggressiveness of the Scottish warrior in Outram is checked by a sensitivity we don't see in the earlier scenes. Another reason he resists the interview is that he doesn't want the formal embrace of greeting the king always gives him. He's worried that the king's perfume will nauseate him and permeate his clothing (he tells Weston that he couldn't get the smell out of his clothes for two months after their last interview). He says the king "should be in purdah like his women folk." He sees the king as weak and effeminate as well as immoral. He sees himself as a real man. There's a strong implication here that his uneasiness around the king is a sign of his own incompleteness. He's the kind who has a violent hatred of homosexuals. He hasn't integrated the feminine side of his own being. The final scenes of the film show that, for all his strength and aggressiveness, he is really the weaker man.

The king is as divided against himself as Outram. The two are opposites, but it is Wajid who comes close to being a genuinely tragic figure. He loves his people and their culture but he is incapable of preserving the kingdom against the British. An accomplished poet, he represents the sweet flowering of a culture just before its disintegration. Ray's portrayal of historical change in *The Chess Players* is most successful, and most poignant, in its depiction of the music and dancing in the palace just before the king's downfall.

The key scene here is an exquisite performance of dancing by a beautiful, ornately dressed girl, which occurs just before the prime minister (Victor Banerjee) informs the king that Outram intends to remove him. The scene lasts about seven minutes and looks, out of context, almost like part of a documentary on classical Indian dance (like the wonderful dance sequence toward the end of *The Music Room*). It is made up of 28 shots, most of which refer to the dancer, her musicians, and the king's response. In shot 8, the king moves his head slowly in rapt appreciation; the lengthy shots of the dancer, averaging about 12 seconds, give us the same response. Intercut with these shots are shots of the sorrowful prime minister, who moves toward the king as the dance moves toward its close. In shot 25, the dance having just ended, we hear the chimes of an ornate clock (they're the British sequence of notes marking the hour and contrast vividly with the Indian music we've been hearing). In shots 26 through 28, the king tells his prime minister "only poetry should make you weep," and the minister's response is finally to tell the king that he will no longer wear the crown. The king has witnessed his last dance, a form of aesthetic perfection enacted for him on the eve of the destruction of his court and the rich culture it has created. Ray's purpose at this point is twofold: he wishes to show the necessity of change (and to give us its bittersweet taste), and he wishes to resist change by preserving the beauty of the traditional dance as a remnant of the past (hence its documentarylike quality).

King Wajid's long speech to his ministers is a mixture of confessional ("I've ruled badly") and blame ("You have thrown dust in my eyes"). He admits his naivete and shows his sensitivity and strength by singing a song of loss and sadness. He's not afraid to reveal his weakness. When, after much agonizing, he finally decides to abdicate, Ray shoots the scene in the rich, late light of a deep, golden red sunset with many long shots of the landscape flowing into space. The king's lengthy speech is a kind of soliloquy which is balanced by Outram's soliloquy to his doctor in the next scene.

King Wajid brings to my mind the feudal landlord Biswambhar Roy of *Jalsaghar (The Music Room)*. Both are aware that they represent the end of a way of life which exalts beauty, and yet both are unable to prevent the forces of change from destroying them. Ray presents their situations in much the same way: with beautiful passages of music and dance and with long, leisurely shots into deep space. *Jalsaghar* is a film in one key, however, and *The Chess Players* has many keys and many modes of representation, though it's not the better film.

One mode, that of animation, is used to present the early history of the British takeover in India. In a witty and elegantly drawn sequence (not drawn by Ray), we see a large head popping ripe cherries into its mouth. A narrator's voice reads to us from Lord Dalhousie's writings to the effect that all the British have to do is wait until the various kingdoms in India ripen, then they will fall into the British mouth.

Another mode is that of comedy. The poignancy of King Wajid's fate is balanced by the portrayal of Mirza and Meer, whose obsession with chess is like the king's obsessions with beauty and pleasure. Unlike the king, who sees what is about to happen, Mirza and Meer don't see a thing. Theirs is a comedy of manners bordering at times on slapstick. Meer won't admit to himself that his wife, a chess widow, has taken a lover. When he finds the lover under his wife's bed, he swallows the story that the man is hiding from the army. Mirza also neglects his beautiful wife in favor of chess. After Mirza's wife hides their chessmen, the two devotees go to a friend's house to play; but only the death of the friend's father, replete with exaggerated groans and weeping, prevents them from resuming their game. Finally, in desperation, they adjourn to a quiet village outside of town. They soon fall to quarreling over a remark Mirza has made about Meer's wife's infidelity. Cursing each other as kitchen slaves and grass cutters, Meer suddenly pulls out a pistol and grazes Mirza with a shot. At this precise moment, the British troops make their appearance and the two idle landlords learn that the kingdom has fallen. Shrugging their shoulders, they admit their superfluousness ("How could we fight the British army if we can't deal with our wives?") and decide to resume their chess game.

The Mirza and Meer sequences integrate with the rest of the film on a thematic as well as a dramatic (or musical) level. The landlords are blind witnesses to historical change; they experience from a distance what Outram and Wajid experience as central players. Their perspective is much nearer to that of most men and women. History happens all around them without their awareness. Their comic scenes provide a contrasting tonality to the poignant scenes involving Wajid and Outram. Such counterbalancing is nearly musical in method and is typical of Ray's strategy throughout the film. The counterbalancing also suggests that *The Chess Players* is, in part, a meditation on the nature of history. As major players, the king and Outram have reason to see themselves as "making" history. But they're also chess pieces, moved by the greater forces of economic expansion of the East India Company and the "God-given" manifests of the British Empire under Victoria. The pawns, Mirza and Meer, don't see themselves as historical agents; yet insofar as they represent the sophisticated decadence of the land-owning class of Lucknow, they, too, in little, contribute to Oudh's inability to resist the British.

Two minor characters deserve mention. The first is Nandlal. In an early scene he explains to Mirza and Meer the history of the game of chess and tells them that, though the game is Eastern in origin, the British had adapted it to new rules. He also informs the two that the East India Company is planning to take over the kingdom. He functions to establish the basis for Ray's use of the chess metaphor and also to indicate an awareness of what is about to happen, despite Mirza's and Meer's obliviousness. The second character is the handsome boy, Kalloo, who helps the chess players find a place to play in the quiet village. Like Nandlal, he points up Mirza's and Meer's foolishness by asking them if they plan to fight the British because they both have brought guns. Kalloo is upset that the British have triumphed. Unlike the two players, he would offer resistance to the British in the name of national pride. His spiritedness is of the common people.

The final scene between the king and Outram is a masterpiece of subtle character delineation. It is a formal scene in which Outram comes to thank the king for telling his subjects not to resist the British takeover and to demand that he sign the new treaty which takes his crown away. The scene is made up of 29 shots, many of them brief glances between the king and Outram. The fineness of the sequence involves our sense that beneath the formal language of state, there's a passionate nonverbal dialogue going on between the two antagonists which is rendered visually. As Outram presses his demands, the king (in shots 8, 10, and 12) looks away from him, almost as if he were not there. These shots of his face are like those in the sunset-drenched light after he has decided to abdicate. When the king turns his pained-filled face to Outram, in shot 17, the camera closes on him and, in 18, we see Outram withdraw his glance and look down uneasily. The king then raises his eyes to Weston, Outram's aide and translator, and Weston, too, looks away. Both of the British are uneasy about what they are doing. The king then rises slowly and hands the hastily risen Outram his crown. He's flabbergasted by this breach of protocol and sputteringly tells Weston to tell the king that "I have no use for that" (the crown). In the final shot, the king stands proudly and speaks fully for the first time: "I can bare my head for you, but I cannot sign the treaty." There is great dignity and strength in his behavior here—something truly kingly. In contrast, Outram looks diminished, outclassed. In defeat, the king shows more strength—he's more of a *mensch*—than his conqueror. But that has always been the king's strength, this poet of the ephemeral, of the passing moment of beauty.

The last shot of the film shows Mirza holding up the chess queen and speaking of Queen Victoria's triumph. The British have indeed taught the Indians to play by new rules. The end of the film has an elegance characteristic of the whole. In its careful proportions, the film suggests a meditative distance from its subject matter. The violence of the British takeover, culminating in the War of Indian Independence of 1857, is hardly suggested as is the suffering of the common people under King Wajid's neglectful rule. In his first (and only) full treatment of historical change, Ray chose a moment in the distant past and used all his strategies to invoke "the pastness of the past."[1] His method and goal are the direct opposite of a filmmaker like Bertolucci in *1900*, in which a frantic, angry, political energy animates almost every frame. *The Chess Players* avoids becoming a political tract, but it lacks any sense of the raw and turbulent energies released in a period of abrupt change.

Although not one of Ray's best films, *The Chess Players* remains a moving and entertaining examination of history. As an elegy upon the theme of change, it suggests, like *The Music Room*, that there is a genuine sadness in the destruction of the old forms of beauty and of culture, and that the future by no means promises a replacement of these old forms by anything better. Ray has none of the modernist's excitement and relish in the creation of new forms, shocking and disturbing as they may be. He is a classicist in his response to turbulence and change.

NOTE

1. Interestingly, in an interview given shortly after making *The Chess Players*, Ray speaks of his desire to make another historical film set in the seventeenth century. Interview with Karen Jaehne, "Positif," June 1979, p. 36.

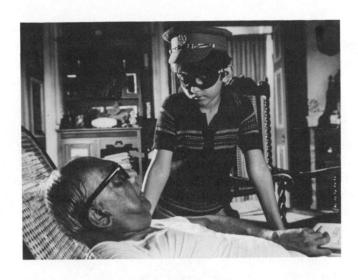

25

JOI BABA FELUNATH (THE ELEPHANT GOD): More Detective Action

Ray may have been thinking of Huston's *The Maltese Falcon* when he made *Joi Baba Felunath (The Elephant God)* in 1978. Both films involve a detective's search for a priceless antique statue, but the resemblance really stops there. Huston's film has a driving rhythm and a witty, cynical hard edge; it's a film for worldly wise adults. Ray's effort is at least partly directed to children; it has a more leisurely structure and a much softer feeling to it, though it's by no means formless. The movement of the plot is less random than *Sonar Kella* and, as a result, there's a greater sense of urgency to the film. It's the better of the two detective films. In his second attempt at the genre, Ray made a more accomplished effort.

The plot, briefly summarized, involves the theft of a small gold statue of Ganesh (the Elephant God—a potent symbol of good fortune and wisdom in Indian mythology) by the evil Maganlal, a smuggler of valuable antiques, from the Ghosal family residence in Benares. Detective Felu, his young cousin Tapesh, and his friend, the popular mystery writer Lalmohan Ganguly, happen to be vacationing in Benares and Felu is engaged by Umanath Ghosal to find the statue, which had been given to Umanath's great-grandfather by a former king of Nepal. In tracking down the statue, Felu unmasks a phony saint by the name of Machhli Baba, who is in league with Maganlal. He also deciphers the riddlelike utterances of Umanath's eight-year-old son Riku. He forces a Ghosal family friend to admit his complicity in the theft and finally, by brilliant feats of Holmesian ratiocination, he proves that only a copy was stolen while the original statue remained safely in a bank vault.

In a nice structural parallelism, the progress of Felu's solution is associated throughout the film with the finishing of an elaborate statue of the goddess Durga by an accomplished old artist. Felu's pursuit of the truth (he's an artist in his own way) is thus likened to the authentic religious rituals performed by the artist—as opposed to the bogus rituals and mumbo jumbo of Machhli Baba, which many of Benares intellectuals and important citizens seem to swallow. Felu is a kind of seer; he's able to gain Riku's confidence (childhood here being a state of basic truthfulness, though guarded by fantasies such as Riku's belief in popular figures like Tarzan, the Phantom, and Captain Spark) and to determine that at one point Riku hid the statue of Ganesh in the statue of Durga.

A further structural device involves scenes investigating that staple subject of detective stories: What is real behind the facade of appearance? Thus we have the first scene in which Machhli Baba holds court, to the accompaniment of marvelous music and singing, and in which he appears to be an authentic religious figure, though Felu has his doubts. Directly after this scene there's a comic interlude involving a heavily muscled bodybuilder who's Felu's and his friend's roommate. Lalmohan Ganguly is mightily impressed with this physical specimen; he takes him to be both strong and brave, but is he? Later on, when a threatening note arrives at the room, the bodybuilder takes off in a hurry. Lalmohan, on the other hand, proves to be much braver when he submits to the knife throwing of one of Maganlal's henchmen. As in *Sonar Kella*, Lalmohan is used as a counterfoil to Felu; as a mystery writer he lives in a world of fantasy and appearance while Felu pursues the the real. He's the center of much of the comedy in the film, such as when he admires the bodybuilder, or when he has the knives thrown at him after fearing that Maganlal has served him a poisoned drink. He's the laughable player to Felu's straight man, the Watson to Felu's Holmes.

One of the best early scenes in the film involves Maganlal's visit to Umanath Ghosal, in which he attempts to buy the statue and then indirectly threatens to steal it. It's a lengthy scene but evocatively sinister and threatening, with lots of side lighting and dark shadows in the corners. It's at this point, as the only flashback in the film later shows, that Riku tells his grandfather that an evil man wants to steal Ganesh. He has overheard part of the conversation, but, more importantly, he's instantly aware of Maganlal's malevolence. Though, like Lalmohan, he lives in a world of fantasy based on the mysteries he's read, his childish instincts are true. Another good, long sequence involves Felu's pursuit of Machhli Baba, this time without his false beard and wig and guru costume, into the labyrinthine corridors of an old Benares house. The editing in this sequence builds suspense very well and the complicated passageways are a good visual rendering of Felu's difficult progress toward a solution of the case. There's a fine point-of-view shot when Felu enters a darkened room from a sun-filled exterior and finds Maganlal there; for an uneasy moment the room remains dark and then, as Felu's eyes become accustomed, the figure of Maganlal slowly emerges. This is an excellent opening to a strong sequence in which Maganlal attempts to bribe and threaten Felu to drop the case. Another fine scene involves Felu's questioning of Riku, in which he puts the boy at ease by asking how Captain Spark allowed the statue to get away. He's immediately able to enter the child's world. He tells Riku that he can see into people and things not through X-ray vision, but because of his powers of mental observation, and that the mind is more powerful than a gun. Jit Bose's performance as Riku in this scene, and throughout, is perfectly natural and convincing. Needless to say, Ray's ability to work with child actors is legendary. All in all, *Joi Baba Felunath* is an accomplished adaptation of a Western genre. Its pacing is sometimes slower than the Western detective film. There's a tendency to hold the shot momentarily after an action has occurred, a Ray signature.

Some of the scenes, such as the lunch in which Felu and Tapesh kid Lalmohan about his fondness for fantasy, are interludes or side trips—minor distractions from the main action. It's an Indianization of a Western form and not at all unpleasing.

There are some minor loose ends in the film, however. How does Felu manage to have an airplane tattooed on his arm like Machhli Baba when he apprehends Maganlal by posing as the false saint? (He's a true seeker and seer, Machhli Baba a fake.) There's also a very unlikely coincidence when Felu recognizes the man who poses as the saint. We aren't shown why he manages to identify this man. More importantly, we're left in a quandary as to why grandfather Ghosal allows the whole detective adventure to continue when he knows all the time that the real statue is safely in the bank. At one point he even tells his son Umanath that he suspects him in the theft (Umanath is having business difficulties). Is the grandfather merely whimsical, as suggested earlier in the film, or is he playing games in an attempt to catch Maganlal and others? His failure to announce right away that the stolen Ganesh is a copy ultimately causes the death by stabbing of the old artist; presumably by Maganlal or one of his henchmen (true to Ray's world, we don't see the actual stabbing). We're plainly not asked by the ending of the film to fret about such questions. The last words are given to Riku. He's learned Felu's lesson very well, for as he raises his toy gun he proclaims that man's greatest power is in his mind. At the sound of the gun, the pigeons burst from a parapet overlooking the Ganges—a reprise of the famous shot from *Aparajito*.

For all its excellence and pleasureableness, *Joi Baba Felunath*, like *Sonar Kella*, has one major omission—not to say defect: There are no women in it. Why Ray omits women from his detective films, when they're so important in all his other films, is a mystery even Felu or Lalmohan might not be able to solve. Is it, perhaps, that Ray considers the sexual and social complications Felu and others might get into to be a distraction from the main problem of solving crime? In *The Maltese Falcon* and other films in the genre, women are alluring and profoundly untrustworthy. In Ray's detective films they are nonexistent. Felu, the truth seeker, the seer, is a celibate. In Ray's detective films women neither help nor hinder men in their search for truth as they do in all of his other films. Is Felu a successful seer *because* he is a celibate? He certainly bears a resemblance to certain ascetic holy men, though in appearance he looks totally different. In any case, a rich dimension to the detective genre is missing.

26

HIROK RAJAR DESHE (THE KINGDOM OF DIAMONDS):
Political Protest

"There are almost no good films in India for children," says Ray.[1] *Hirok Rajar Deshe* (*The Kingdom of Diamonds*, 1980) was designed to remedy that situation. Like its predecessor, *Goopy Gyne Bagha Byne*, to which it is a sequel, the film is full of song and dance and fantasy. It's also a contemporary fable, with heavy emphasis upon its political message. It's an "entertainment," as Graham Greene called some of his lighter fiction, but it's also the only film in which we see Ray as a political activist—a role he usually avoids at all costs. Soumitra Chatterjee, Ray's leading actor, has referred to *Hirok Rajar Deshe* as Ray's "only political film."[2] It's an angry response to the emergency decreed by Indira Gandhi in 1975–77, in which censorship and police control were severe and intolerable to most Indian intellectuals. The anger is barely masked by the entertainment. In this way, presumably, the film could get by the government censors.

The film can be described as falling into two fairly distinct parts. The first is comprised of five sections which are fairly static and rhetorical (as opposed to fluid and cinematic)—very much like a stage play. Most of these early sections take place in ornately designed interiors (Ray, of course, contributing to these designs) such as the good king of Shundi's palace and the council chamber of the bad king of Hirok. The effect here is almost claustrophobic, and perhaps it's intentional. Goopy and Bagha are eager to leave the palace and go on the road again because they're experiencing claustrophobia as well. When we finally reach the school teacher Udayan's open-air classroom, after having been confined to the Shundi palace, and the King of Hirok's chamber, it's like a breath of fresh air. The ornateness of the costumes and the wall decorations in the enclosed scenes tends to bring the visual surfaces up close, crowding our eye. The long speeches, sometimes interspersed with song, crowd our ear. The king of Hirok is a thinly disguised version of the modern political tyrant. His diamond mines are manned with forced labor. His peasants are poverty-stricken and cruelly taxed. He bans the dissenting voice of one of his singer-poets. His advisors are yes-men whom he keeps in line by giving or withholding diamonds. He has a scientist-professor who runs a kind of ministry of propaganda and disinformation called the mumbo jumbo room in which a brainwashing machine attempts to control the thoughts of his subjects through the use of rhymed couplets (for the peasants: "I shall miss a meal a day/So my taxes I can pay"; for the miners: "Miners must be underfed/Miners fat are miners dead"). Utpal Dutta's performance of the king is intentionally overacted;

he's a caricature, a cardboard cutout, though Dutta manages to bring out cleverly both his overbearingness and his insecurity at the same time. Ray has cannily shown that his insecurity feeds his tyranny, and this makes him seem more real as a tyrant—less a comic book caricature. Like Stalin, his deep-flowing suspiciousness and paranoia whets his slaughtering knife— though the absence of blood makes him a mild tyrant compared to Stalin. In contrast to the king, Udayan teaches his young boys a process of free inquiry, to the accompaniment of birdsong and in a natural setting. He's a free, secure man in an idealized, idyllic setting. When one of the king's ministers attempts to indoctrinate the class, Udayan closes his school and retreats to a cave in the nearby hills where he is discovered by Goopy and Bagha. The three then plan a successful rebellion against the king.

The reappearance of Goopy and Bagha seems to loosen the film's rather rigid structure. In the last part of the film there are a larger number of shorter scenes, as opposed to the long set pieces of the first part. There's a greater feeling of cinematic play, such as when Goopy and Bagha sing to the king and his court and Ray cuts both with the rhythm and against the rhythm of their song to the faces of the listeners. Or, most prominently, when we see the mumbo jumbo room with its highly inventive equipment and the massive brainwashing machine out of whose mouth are growled the rhymed couplets the king wants to plant in his subjects' heads. The reference here, of course, is to the government's control of the press and other media.

Hirok Rajar Deshe leaves the viewer with a good feeling; it's not meant to frighten or disturb the children in the audience. Its songs are cheerful and appealing. There's no brutality in the king of Hirok's tyranny—only brainwashing. There's one fairly violent sequence in which the soldiers destroy a shantytown of poor people. Ray has said this scene is based on his own observation of the government's attempt to cover-up scenes of urban poverty along the route taken by Soviet leaders during a state visit to Calcutta.[3] When Udayan and Goopy and Bagha defeat the brainwashing machine with their songs (and a little bribery of the soldiers with diamonds they've stolen from the treasury—another note of realism) the king himself participates in pulling down the massive statue of himself. Even tyrants are reformable; no one is beyond the pale. Ray seems to be calling for the people to rise up (an extraordinary act for him) and help the misguided leader to change his (her) ways. The film isn't as good as *Goopy Gyne Bagha Byne*, however. In his zeal to transmit a message to his audience, Ray robs *Hirok Rajar Deshe* of the full sense of play which animates its predecessor. There's nothing as inventive and inspired in it as the dance of the ghosts in *Goopy Gyne*. It's as if Ray felt an insistent need for political commentary after the detective adventures of *Joi Baba Felunath* and the examination of the historical past in *The Chess Players*. In any case, the value of the film for children as a political antidote to tyranny may be doubted. On the whole, the film operates entirely on the level of rational discourse ("just to keep his crown/The tyrant king must keep them down," says Udayan toward the end). As a fable, as a fantasy, it lacks the irrational and disturbing qualities which Bruno Bettelheim has pointed out are the basic properties of the most compelling fairy tales.[4] There's no wolf in it, no dark forest in which children become lost, lie down, and are covered up with leaves. It's a comforting fable, full of wit and humor, the vigorous play of language, and good intentions.

NOTES

1. Interview with author, Calcutta, July 10, 1985.
2. Interview with author, Calcutta, July 12, 1985.
3. Henri Micciollo, *Satyajit Ray* (Lausanne: Editions l'Age d'Homme, 1981), p. 320.
4. Bruno Bettelheim, *The Uses of Enchantment* (New York: Knopf, 1976).

27

PIKOO'S DAY:
An Awakening

*P*ikoo's *Day* (1981) is a short film (25 minutes) made for French television but it is also, as Ray acknowledges, one of his best efforts. Ray was visited by Henri Fraise, a French television producer who was in Calcutta making a documentary about Mother Theresa, and given carte blanche for a half-hour film. He decided to adapt one of his own short stories. The story involves the diary of a young boy of about seven or eight and the boy's innocent apprehension of events which occur around him. He writes a diary, in his childish fashion, because he sees his grandfather, with whom he's very close, keeping a diary. In translating his story for the film Ray totally avoided the diary; there is even no voice-over narration giving us the words of the diary. Instead, the adaptation is totally cinematic and visual.

The film examines a young boy's experience of momentous events in the context of random everyday happenings. Pikoo's day is almost a day like any other day. He's granted an unexpected holiday from school and so stays home, playing in the house and in the garden, managing to make an interesting day for himself. He plays with his marbles, chats with his grandfather, visits the servants, and draws in his coloring book. On one occasion, after waving good-bye to his father, he simply stands on the balcony observing the desultory traffic in the street (the camera shows us a vintage car passing by, a rickshaw, a man walking his dog, several men carrying what appears to be a grand piano). On another, he makes a series of telephone calls to random numbers. Ray's presentation of randomness is important to an understanding of the film. He's interested in showing us how a young boy—or anyone for that matter—undergoes his first experience of the harshness and unfairness of life. Pikoo's witness to the death of his grandfather and the troubled affair his mother is having with her lover is embedded among the random events of his day. He can't "name" these big events; he can't say " 'dadu' is dead," or "Mom is having an affair." His knowledge is instinctive and embryonic; it's the beginning of his real knowledge of the world. His knowledge, and the events which give rise to it, occur by the way, as if the big events and the little events of his day are all jumbled together as in real life, the big events sliding up obliquely catching him unaware. Ray's presentation of Pikoo's experience (it's perhaps too inflated to speak of his "awakening") is thus profoundly unmelodramatic and real. There are no fanfares of trumpets, no sobbing strings, to announce the big events. In *Pikoo's Day* Ray catches unerringly the mixed character of existence.

The first scene of the film establishes the context of alienation between mother and father within which Pikoo will experience his day. The father discovers a button missing from his fresh shirt and curtly throws it on the bed where the mother is sitting. He asks why Pikoo is still at home and the mother replies that he's been given an unexpected holiday. "Won't this cause problems for you and your boyfriend?" the father casually asks (he's found a strange hair on his pillow). It shortly becomes clear that this is the first signal he has given that he knows about her affair, and this fact profoundly affects her relationship that day with her lover. Thus, though Pikoo is absent from this scene, it crucially affects the character of events which will occur around him.

The next important section of the film moves between a phone call the mother receives from her lover and Pikoo's visit to his sick grandfather. Cross-cutting between simultaneous actions is central to Ray's technique in the film. While the mother tells the lover that Pikoo is home but to come ahead anyway, Pikoo has a charming exchange with his "dadu." The grandfather is lying in bed recovering from his second heart attack. Pikoo flops down on the bed and they compare hands, Pikoo remarking how old and veiny his grandpa's hand is compared to his own. He then acts out his own imitation of his grandpa's attack while the grandpa laughs. It's clear that the two of them, the very young and the very old, have a love and ease of communication which contrasts sharply with problems between the middle-aged adults. It's also clear that Pikoo has no comprehension of death. The grandfather reinforces this by playfully telling him that the next time he has an attack he'll call Pikoo and he can bring his gun and shoot the boog-eyman dead. Pikoo then indirectly contributes to the grandpa's death by telling him a big secret about the fight he heard his mother and father having the night before in which they kept referring angrily to the "old man." Pikoo doesn't appear to be upset about the fight and certainly can't know how this information will affect his grandpa (nor, mercifully, will he experience any guilt after the death).

After Pikoo leaves his grandfather, our sense of the random nature of his day intensifies. He visits a servant who's eating, walks upstairs backwards counting backwards, and finally proceeds to dial a series of random telephone numbers (a beauty parlor, a bar, the telephone exchange), gaily informing each answerer that it is a wrong number. Ray shows us the beauty parlor, the bar, and the exchange—the only time the camera leaves Pikoo's house and grounds. The shot of the exchange is particularly telling for, like the shot of the street from the balcony when Pikoo waves good-bye to his dad, it emphasizes the chaotic, patternless character of much human experience. There's even a sense that Pikoo's calls are contributing to the confusion at the exchange. In the midst of this, there's a poignant shot of the grandfather lying alone, looking at a photograph of his wife on the wall and feeling that he doesn't have long to live. Beneath the random surface, events are building.

The lover's arrival is filled with unspoken tension and expectation. He wants to know what the wife has learned that morning from her husband and he wants to get in bed with her but Pikoo is in the way. Pikoo is sent out into the garden with a coloring set the lover has brought. In the bedroom the mother tells him of the husband's knowledge and then begins weeping. This sequence, like all of the film, is very subtle: the mother at first goes coolly about the room closing windows and pulling curtains while the lover sits uneasily on the bed digesting what she tells him; as she observes Pikoo in the garden she becomes upset, presumably from guilt, and the lover then becomes angry. Suddenly the whole business has become too complicated for him (he's a bit of a playboy).

The cinematic high point of the film now occurs with a series of relatively quick cross-cuts between Pikoo in the garden, the servants resting, the grandfather beginning to experience his last attack, and the lovers in the bedroom. The lovers are not actually shown, however. Instead Ray uses an effective low shot of the closed bedroom door with a cigarette smoldering in an ashtray in the foreground. Ray's use of the garden is also very artful here. It's an extensive place (the family is wealthy) and Ray shows Pikoo moving curiously into the hidden recesses of its paths and byways. It's a good visual embodiment of the complicated life he's soon to encounter. A cut back to the grandfather shows him in mid attack. A cut to the closed door of the bedroom reveals that the cigarette has gone out. At this point, Pikoo is standing near a wall on which a pot of white flowers rests. The weather has suddenly changed: the first drops of rain strike the lily pads in the pond; some of the white flowers seem to have just fallen onto the wall. The change in the light, the shot of the fallen flowers, the drops of rain—all of these suggest or foreshadow the changes which are about to happen around Pikoo. Or rather, they are the atmosphere, the dramatic environment within which this change is occurring. The shot of the fallen flowers, it could be said, contains the whole film. When Pikoo, through some instinctive sense of connection to his mother, cries out for her, we're given a shoulder-high shot of the lovers nude in bed. The lover is unsuccessfully attempting to prevent the wife from being distracted by Pikoo, who wants to know if he can use a black pencil instead of a white. When he receives no answer, he goes upstairs and overhears a fight between the lovers (she apologizing, he threatening not to come again). When Pikoo yells "Shut up!" (as he has earlier at a barking dog) they immediately fall silent. Pikoo then goes to visit his grandpa and discovers him dead. As Pikoo sits drying his tears in the hall, his mother comes out of the bedroom. The final shot of the film shows Pikoo resuming his drawing.

Many directors would have felt the need to explore the dramatic interest in Pikoo's informing his mother that the grandfather had gone away: how he would have said it and how she would have taken it, considering that her affair may just have broken up. But for Ray the film must end precisely at the moment when Pikoo picks up his coloring book again, resuming an old activity in a state of mind and spirit irrevocably altered.

28

SADGATI
(DELIVERANCE):
The Caste System at Its Worst

Ray's film production for 1981 involved two works in shorter forms, *Sadgati* and *Pikoo's Day*—both made for television. *Sadgati (Deliverance)* is, at 50 minutes, the longer of the two. It was made for Doordarshan, the Indian national television company. Based on the novel by Munshi Premchand, it examines the brutality of the caste system in a rural setting. The film has the simplicity and power of Tolstoy's last stories of peasant life.

The central character, Dukhi, is an untouchable who lives with his wife and daughter in a simple mud hut. He's recovering from a heavy fever but resolves that he must visit the Brahmin Ghashiram to persuade him to come to his house and find an auspicious date on which to marry off his daughter. Dukhi refuses his wife's offer of a morning meal and sets off empty-stomached and hollow-eyed. The Brahmin is irritated at the interruption of his morning rituals and makes Dukhi perform several chores while he eats and rests. The last of these chores involves chopping a large log with a dull axe the Brahmin provides. Dukhi becomes weaker and weaker as the Brahmin forces him to the task; finally he collapses and dies. A witness to this cruelty informs the villagers that it's the Brahmin's fault and that they shouldn't move the body or they'll be suspected by the police. The villagers inform the Brahmin that they won't use the local well until the body is moved from the main path to it. Finally the Brahmin himself drags the body away and attempts, at the end, to purify the ground on which it has lain by sprinkling holy water.

Out of this simple story Ray has constructed a powerful fable about the intimate linkage between the victim and the victimizer. In the first part of the film Dukhi is at the center and the Brahmin is off to one side—nearly a caricature of the evil master. Dukhi is a simple man; he doesn't expect much out of life. We see him sitting on his haunches cutting grass for the Brahmin (a gift to the master because in his poverty he can bring nothing else); we see him sweeping the Brahmin's terrace and carefully piling up the sweepings on top of the hand broom and dumping them; we see him scooping husks into large gunnysacks with his hands in a dimly lit storage room. In these sequences, and in the one when he tries to sharpen the dull axe on a wetted stone, Ray's deliberate pacing captures very well the low-liness and humbleness of Dukhi's way of life. He's one notch above a beast of burden, and he accepts his condition. When the Brahmin tells him to chop the log after he has carried the heavy sacks on his back, there's a flicker of resentment in his face as if to say, "This man is asking too much of me," but he goes on about his work and even apologizes to the Brahmin's wife while calling himself a fool at the same time. In the log-chopping sequence he pushes himself beyond the limit, goaded from within as well as by the Brahmin. This sequence, with all its fast cutting and its close-up shots, is the only shaky spot in the film. It's as if Ray is pulling out all the stops to manipulate the audience. We have close-ups of the shouting Brahmin, of Dukhi, and of the witnesses, the Brahmin's young son and a sympathetic neighbor. The timing of the cuts showing Dukhi's chopping becomes increasingly fast until there's an almost black-and-white silhouette shot of the axe in the log at the moment of his collapse. Ray's attempt here is to build a frenzied rhythm to accord with Dukhi's own frenzy, but it doesn't quite come off. Instead, it seems overstated, hortatory.

The last part of the film focuses mainly on the Brahmin's difficulties as well as the grieving of Dukhi's wife. At first, the presence of the body seems merely a minor complication but soon we begin to see that the Brahmin is being forced by circumstances, such as the villagers' refusal to move the body, to confront his own guilt. A shot of the Brahmin resting (he always seems to be either resting or eating) is followed by a shot of the body lying in the rain. But the body is not merely out there in the rain, it is increasingly in the Brahmin's head. A shot, a little bit earlier, of the body lying near the log, in which the camera moves up to show the Brahmin's house in the background, indicates for the first time how very close the body is to the house, perhaps 20 feet or so. Up to this point we can imagine that the body is at least a distance away, since the Brahmin can faintly hear the sound of chopping as he lies resting. It's as if Ray has artfully arranged the images so as to give the viewer a sense that the body is moving closer to the Brahmin. This sense is, of course, psychologically accurate. In a very nice sequence we see the body after the rain has passed; a forked stick is gingerly inserted under one leg and a rope noose placed about the foot. Only after these preliminary shots do we realize that the Brahmin himself is actually moving the body. It has begun to haunt him; he must remove it, no matter how repugnant the act is. We see him labor as he leans into the taut rope. He's no longer the superior man, so fastidious about his food and dress. In almost a direct quote from Bergman, Ray shows him in silhouette, laboring along the skyline. He shows, in a series of low shots, the heavy body dragging over dirt and rocks. Like Frost and Alma in Bergman's *Sawdust and Tinsel*, the Brahmin is at this point intimately connected to his victim. Ray even uses the tense rhythm of drums in this sequence as did Bergman. But of course Ray is a realist after all, and the Brahmin doesn't change that much. When he sprinkles holy water at the end we have the sense that the wished-for exorcism of Dukhi's spirit has mainly transpired for him. He won't order any more exhausted peasants to chop wood for him but he won't treat them much better, either.

For whom does deliverance occur? Not for Dukhi's wife, whose terrible grieving in the rain over the body and at the Brahmin's closed door is one of the film's powerful episodes. She's left a widow and an untouchable. Her first reactions, after the initial shock of sorrow at her husband's death, is to cry out at her own fate. The Brahmin isn't delivered either. As far as he's concerned (and this applies to his wife as well), he's already got one foot in heaven. Only Dukhi is delivered from a life of unremitting poverty and hard labor. Although the frenzy of his final actions doesn't suggest it, some part of him must welcome the deliverance.

29

GHARE-BAIRE (THE HOME AND THE WORLD): A Return to Tagore

At first glance, *The Home and the World* (1984) would appear to be a repetition of familiar material: Ray doing Tagore again—this time his novel of the same title—in a period setting just after the turn of the century. The film is a radical departure for Ray, however. This is a wide-screen production with an extraordinary number of close-ups and medium close-ups, lots of dialogue, and few silent passages. This may be due in part to Ray's desire to film a whole novel rather than a shorter form which gives him more space and which he usually prefers. Moreover, Tagore's *The Home and the World* is a dialectical novel; there's a lot being *said* in it. There are relatively few long shots and almost no use of deep focus images in which we enjoy the play of foreground and deep background. The camera moves relatively restrictively compared, say, to *Charulata*, the film with which *The Home and the World* is bound to invite comparison because of their similar subject matter, historical and physical settings, and character relationships. There's nothing like the marvelous opening seven minutes of *Charulata* in which, without dialogue, we observe Charu moving through the upstairs rooms of her house. Perhaps it's unfair to compare almost any film with *Charulata*, but, because *The Home and the World* invites it, one must say that it doesn't even come close to its great predecessor in quality. Visually it reminds one of Ray's comedy, *Hirok Rajar Deshe*, another film which is rhetorical and uses a great many close-ups in the first half. *The Home and the World* is, however, a film of much greater depth and shading than *Hirok*; it has real dimension and resonance. It's a good film but not one of Ray's best.

The first serious film script Ray ever wrote was based on Tagore's *The Home and the World*, in 1948, two years before he began a script for *Pather Panchali*. A producer was found and papers signed but that the project never came to fruition is probably a good thing. Ray has repeatedly said that his script for the film was poor, in a Hollywoodish way. His later script had some difficulty finding funding but was eventually produced by the National Film Development Corporation (as the title suggests, a federally funded organization) and the film has been a big moneymaker, confounding the opinion of at least one big producer who rejected it. Ray experienced severe heart problems at the very end of work on the film, but the film is his except for minor elements and bears his stamp.

As with *Charulata*, Ray is investigating the roots of modern India in the movement for independence from England. The historical background and basic story may be stated fairly briefly. In 1905, England under Lord Curzon decided to split Bengal into Hindu and Moslem areas. The artificial rift thus created between Hindus and Moslems would exacerbate already existing tensions and serve the colonial policy of "divide and rule." Widespread popular unrest is provoked by this act, spearheaded by the Swadeshi movement to boycott the importation of British goods. Against this background of political turbulence (baire, the world) Tagore and Ray choose to play out a domestic drama (ghare, the home) in which three major characters are involved. Bimala, the wife of the wealthy landowner Nikhil, is being educated by her husband to leave her traditional seclusion and enter the larger world. A liberal intellectual, Nikhil wants Bimala to meet other people and to make her own choices. The first person he introduces her to is his old college classmate, Sandip, a leader of the Swadeshi movement which he—Nikhil—personally opposes. Sandip is magnetic; he sweeps Bimala off her feet and gets her to give a large amount of money to the cause. Only gradually does Bimala come to see that Sandip is really an unscrupulous operator and that her kind, gentle husband is really the man she loves. Bimala's growth into understanding is both personal and political, for she comes to see the bankruptcy of the Swadeshi movement, at least as Sandip represents it. Nikhil gets what he wants; Bimala chooses him from her newfound freedom, but it's too late, for Nikhil dies attempting to calm the violent conflict between Hindus and Moslems which Sandip's actions have helped to unleash. Bimala is left a widow who will undoubtedly live the rest of her life dedicated to her husband's memory.

Like the Tagore novel, which uses letters and diaries, Ray divides the film into sections in which each character tells his or her story. Bimala begins and ends the film. Her story—the growth of a woman from the confines of convention into freedom and strength—is certainly timely today and may account in part (along with Ray's international reputation) for the film's popularity. It's not the most interesting aspect of the film, however. The viewer spots Sandip fairly early as a manipulator and wonders how long it will take Bimala to do the same. By comparison, the male characters, particularly Nikhil, are more interesting and the gradual revelation of their relationship is fascinating.

When Bimala opens the film, Nikhil has died. The fires of communal violence still burn (fire is the opening image of the film and remains a linking device throughout), but Bimala speaks of the fire within her which has burnt away all her old impurities, leaving her dedication to Nikhil. The film then shifts back in time to Bimala's early education at Nikhil's hands. She's a conventional young woman in an arranged marriage. She doesn't really want to come out into the world but does it to please her husband. Later on, when Sandip asks her why she emerged from traditional seclusion, she doesn't answer him; instead she hums the melody of the English song, "Long, Long Ago," which Nikhil and the British schoolteacher Miss

Gilby have taught her. Though she may not realize it, her humming is answer enough: She emerged because she had been taught to do so. Her jealous sister-in-law tells Nikhil that she's like a doll which he has created and dressed up (this isn't exactly fair, for Bimala's creativity is suggested when she designs some of her own clothes). Her early experience of freedom is artificially induced; it doesn't come from within her. Once she gets used to it, however, she develops a strong taste for it. She's a woman of strength and spirit. This is amply demonstrated in the scene in which she learns "Long, Long Ago." She's pleased to be learning the song with Miss Gilby until Nikhil walks in and with a rather patronizing manner asks how the student is progressing. Nikhil directs almost all his remarks to Miss Gilby in this scene, almost as if Bimala isn't there. She becomes more and more irritated; he has walked in on her private lesson and treats her nearly as if she's an object (the sister-in-law's remark about Bimala as a doll comes in the next scene). No wonder she's angry! Nikhil is very confident that his "program" for her is proceeding satisfactorily. It's in this state of incipient rebellion—very well hidden behind her calm exterior, both from us and from herself—that she meets Sandip and is swept away. Sandip's romanticism, his energy and flair, appeal deeply to her in contrast to her quiet husband. She's not out in the world enough to see the trouble he's causing, however. Nikhil has to inform her indirectly, when she witnesses a confrontation between them, in order for her to wake up and see Sandip for what he is. She's a tragic figure in her loss of Nikhil. The final images of the film consist of four slow dissolves of her grieving face. In the final dissolve, she's dressed in white like her sister-in-law, who's also a widow but an embittered one whose husband neglected her and killed himself with drink. The sister-in-law's vicious charge that Bimala has killed Nikhil through her hard-heartedness won't be able to damage her (the sister-in-law is strongly attracted to Nikhil). She's much stronger at the end than the sister-in-law.

Sandip occupies the second section of the film. (Each section is announced by a extreme close-up of the character speaking aloud a brief excerpt of one of his letters.) On the surface, Sandip is the character with the least depth, but Ray has managed, with the help of his mainstay Soumitra Chatterjee, a subtle and devastating portrait of a political radical. Bimala's first glimpse of Sandip from behind the pulled blinds of an upstairs window may be thrilling to her, but it isn't exactly for us. Sandip is carried into Nikhil's courtyard by his followers and makes a rousing speech. We see him partly from Bimala's point of view but mainly from a neutral position, and here Ray's usually superb sense of camera work momentarily deserts him. Sandip is framed symmetrically, standing under a central arch; he's making a speech full of formal, but impassioned, rhetoric and the camera's deliberate movement is symmetrical as well. Though Soumitra Chatterjee builds the speech well in vocal terms (and it's a real vocal workout), the camera movement is very frontal, stiff, and formal. The crowd's reaction is artificial as well. As a result, the scene doesn't do what it's intended to do: establish Sandip as a spellbinder.

In Sandip's first meeting with Bimala, Ray does much better with Sandip's second political speech to the small Moslem merchants. He's very smooth and seductive, telling her he can see she has a mind of her own and that she's not a pale copy of her husband. He half persuades her to join the Swadeshi movement even though he knows Nikhil, who is present, doesn't like it. He even sings a Swadeshi song to her in a charming, poetic way. She's bowled over by his gusto. She thinks he's mainly a talker, a persuader; she doesn't see until too late that he likes power and will do anything to get it, including causing bloodshed between the Hindus and Moslems. Nikhil points out to her that he's against the Swadeshi movement because it's hard on the poor Moslem traders who can't make any money if they're forced to sell inferior and more expensive Indian-produced goods. His point is supported by the failure of Sandip's second speech, in which the small traders say they won't join the cause. Sandip knows that violence will polarize the community and bring converts to him. He's less interested in the Swadeshi movement than in feathering his own nest. He's an adroit self-promoter, passionate, egocentric, and narcissistic. Ray uses a number of mirror shots when Sandip is wooing Bimala in Nikhil's drawing room. It's no surprise to us when he tells her that he once considered being a stage actor; "It's wonderful to hold an audience in the palm of your hand," he says. Behind his beguiling and flashy surface is an empty man. In one sense he's merely playacting as a leader of the movement and as a wooer of Bimala. But in a deeper sense he needs both desperately; they help to convince him that he's real, that his feelings have substance. When he tells Bimala that he needs to see her every day, there's a sense of desperation behind his urgency. His dependency is as extreme as his magnetism. Behind his joking references to Bimala as "Queen Bee," he's in dead earnest; he needs her as part of the mother cult which was so important a part of the Swadeshi movement. His love of her and the movement come to the same thing. They're a passionate and desperate attempt to create religious meaning from internal emptiness. Nikhil is wrong when he tells Bimala that as a Swadeshi Sandip's love for the country comes from an abstract belief in the mother goddess (Nikhil is the abstract one). Sandip's love is not abstract and philosophical, but troubled and anguished. Ray is implying, as others have before him, that political radicalism often has its origins in personal neurosis. When Sandip is really rejected by Bimala and then by his protege Amulya, his underlying desperation emerges fully. He has needed both of them in order to believe in himself. Nikhil is perceptive and compassionate when he says he feels pity rather than anger for Sandip at the end.

It's not hard to imagine Sandip finding another role, another platform, to use after his interest in the movement has waned. He's not a hypocrite, however. He really believes in the cause, but he also knows how to use it. His behavior in his final scene shows that his image of himself can keep him going where others, more humanly weak, might falter. Morally rejected by his two closest admirers, he behaves as if he is not shaken—and in a real sense he isn't. He comes into Nikhil's and Bimala's bedroom carrying the money and the jewel box he was about to make off with and makes a short speech in which he rationalizes his behavior by quoting some famous lines from the *Ramayana:* "My path is not the straight path." He ends by looking squarely at Bimala and voicing, without a trace of irony, the battle cry of his movement: "Hail Motherland." It's an awesome and cold performance.

All the major characters have a secondary character who helps define them; for Bimala it's the sister-in-law. Amulya's role is important in our gradual understanding of Sandip. At first he's the loyal follower, a bright student who has abandoned his studies in order to join the cause. The camera notices his uneasy reactions when Sandip and the old estate manager agree to sink a boat bringing in British manufactured goods and, later on, when Sandip threatens to burn the peasants' crops if they don't go along with the movement. It's Amulya who damages Sandip in Bimala's eyes, she never discovers these things for herself, when he tells her that a good part of her donation to the cause is going to support Sandip's high living ("He feels that a simple style of living damages a leader's strength," is how Amulya puts it). When Bimala decides to sell her jewels in order to pay back Nikhil for her rash gift to Sandip, Amulya robs the treasury of a nearby estate in order to give Sandip the money to pay her back, wounding a guard with his pistol in the process. He tells Sandip he's leaving him, and ends by saying "Hail Motherland" in a voice charged with irony ("Hail Motherland" is a kind of refrain, taking on greater and greater irony as the film goes along).

Much of the force of the film derives from the relationship between Sandip and Nikhil. They're opposites in the most basic sense and, though the film doesn't develop the full psychological ramifications of their opposition, there are enough tantalizing details to suggest it. They're old college classmates who evidently haven't seen each other in some time, because Nikhil only gradually becomes aware of the change in Sandip. He tells Bimala that, in college, they both agreed not to live according to outmoded conventions but that Sandip was a greater radical than he. There's an implication here that Nikhil looks up to Sandip as a more idealistic political activist than he's capable of being. He tells Bimala, early on, that it gives him pleasure to support his friend's "good works" (she's irritated, before she meets Sandip, that he has been taking advantage of her husband). In a more hidden way, Sandip looks up to Nikhil. Why else is he so interested, over the years, in Nikhil's descriptions of his marriage? His pursuit of Bimala is more than a power play; it's an attempt to become the other in the intimate manner of true opposition.

Nikhil is the most interesting character in the film, and his role is given a superb performance by Victor Banerjee. Even more than Bimala, he's in the central mediating position between her naivete and Sandip's cynicism. In a fine irony, we come to see him as a more courageous radical than Sandip; he's willing to risk his marriage so that his wife can have strength and freedom. But, of course, there's something basically naive and confused in Nikhil's principledness. He's also entirely human in his somewhat vain desire to bring Bimala into the world so he can show her off. Somehow, he's not aware, though, of the dangers of introducing her to Sandip. He may, subconsciously, even want her to be attracted to him. In a bedtime conversation they have after she's first met Sandip, Nikhil mentions and then withholds from Bimala a presumably highly complimentary remark Sandip has made about her, which of course only serves to inflame her imagination. He's trying not to be totally foolish at this point. His confusion is seen when he wants her to admire Sandip, but doesn't want her to become a convert to Sandip's kind of Swadeshi movement. He's principled, abstract, intellectual, and bookish, but he's also a realist. As a landowner he knows how hard the movement will be on the peasants and small traders. He's a Swadeshi in his own way. He has Bimala repeat the reasons behind the movement, which he has taught her, in an early scene. His friend the schoolmaster points out angrily to Sandip that Nikhil is a true Swadeshi, who has established local factories for the production of soap, cloth, and other items which are being imported.

The schoolmaster scene is a particularly interesting one, for directly after the schoolmaster attacks Sandip, Nikhil finally confronts his friend and warns him not to shove his Moslem tenants around. Nikhil's confrontation has been a long time in coming, considering the trouble Sandip has been stirring up in his home and on his land. Why has he waited so long? Bimala tells him he's too placid and too passive. When he remarks to her that he can say a lot more about her in complimentary terms than Sandip, she replies, "but you never do." There's an element of his personality which would wholeheartedly support Gandhi's later emphasis on nonviolent resistance. He has an innate abhorrence of violence and suffering, even for his enemy. He hates strong, chaotic emotions as well, though increasingly he's drawn toward an experience of them. The inexorableness of this process is beautifully characterized. The schoolmaster is a catalyst here. He's the articulating character for Nikhil. Evidently Nikhil needs him to propel himself into direct action, though he resists his suggestion in a later scene that he throw Sandip out. His quandary is more slowly and fully developed than that of Bimala, who comes to her awakening abruptly at the end. He knows that if he tells Sandip to leave he'll truncate Bimala's growth and leave her resentful. A part of him also doesn't want to face what has happened between her and Sandip. He's forced to see through the schoolmaster—and with his own eyes—when he enters the bedroom and finds a spilled container of Bimala's makeup. This is a very heavy-handed, even melodramatic shot, like the shot of the smoldering cigarette after she first meets Sandip and like the sequence when Nikhil takes off on horseback at the end. When he finally acts against Sandip, he does so with great force and vigor. He doesn't simplify his emotions the way Sandip does. He acts in full awareness of the complexity of the situation, and after he's sure Bimala has perceived Sandip. He's a much stronger man than Sandip, more scrupulous and secure and aware. The way Ray manipulates our developing knowledge of this strength is one of the film's finest achievements. The process is the reverse of our perception of Sandip, who at first appears so strong.

The condemnation of Sandip's form of political radicalism is not merely Tagore's but Ray's. Tagore wrote his novel in part to condemn a political movement which he saw as essentially middle class, unrelated to the interests of the poor, and deplorably saturated with violence. Ray's own prejudice against violent radicalism was first fully presented in *Pratidwandi* in the portrait of the Naxalite brother Tunu and in Siddhartha's refusal to engage in political activism. *The Home and the World* can be said to make a political statement about the present as well as recreating an era in the distant past.

The lack of visual play, as I've said, is the film's chief drawback. Most of the drama is rendered through dialogue and with the use of close-ups and medium close-ups. It's hard to think of a scene in which the purely visual is enjoyable for its own sake. One example is the lovely sequence when Bimala leaves the inner apartments for the first time. She walks over the threshold with Nikhil into a white corridor which has stained-glass windows and leads to the outer apartments. Ray takes a slow tracking shot and uses very subtle slow motion here. The sequence is beautiful and evocatively suggests the calm confidence in which Bimala, with Nikhil's help, is entering her new life. But there aren't many of such sequences. Ray's use of the four dissolves on Bimala's face at the end isn't as successful. It might be thought that these shots were added by Ray's son Sandip after the onset of his father's heart trouble, but they were not (Sandip made all the exterior shots in the film). In any case, it's doing an old thing in an old way, reminiscent of the dissolves on Apu's grieving face in *Apur Sansar* and the dissolves on the grieving Mrinmoyee in the *Samapti* section of *Two Daughters*. For the viewer who has seen *Apur Sansar* and *Samapti*, it's almost a cliché. The examination of the essential opposition between Sandip and Nikhil occurs largely in the dialogue. It isn't done visually in the way, for example, in which Bergman handles the same subject in *Persona* by using overlapping images of his protagonists' faces, and in other ways. *The Home and the World* makes its points more by what is said than what is shown.

CONCLUSION

Like many great artists, Ray created the bulk of his best work in the beginning. The Apu trilogy, *Jalsaghar*, *Postmaster*, and *Charulata* were made in the first ten years. Ray made no attempt to repeat these successes, instead launching into a career of astonishing variety. Not all his varied production was successful; some films were clinkers. *Abhijan* isn't very good and *Nayak* is downright bad in several important scenes. By all reports, *Chiriakhana* (*The Zoo*, 1967) is another bad film, which Ray disavows and I was unable to see. Nevertheless, the distinguishing marks of Ray's film career are its abundance, variety, and excellence over the long haul. *Pikoo's Day* and *Sadgati*, two shorter films made for television in 1981, show that, after nearly thirty years, Ray is still able to work at top form. *Pikoo's Day*, in particular, seems to me to have the same quality as Ray's mid-career masterpiece *Aranyer Din Ratri* (*Days and Nights in the Forest*). One might speculate why Ray hasn't made more contemporary films about the middle class, employing the superb, oblique style of *Days* and *Pikoo*. Still, not many major film directors have shown the same staying power.

Ray is probably the Indian film director most responsible for establishing a serious cinema in India which looks at life as it is. His realism is often distanced, however, by an examination of events set in the past. Saturated, as most of us are, by instant television images of "current events," his films seem at times to have an other-worldly character. They evoke the timeless rhythms which underlie our agitated dailiness. In addition, probably no modern filmmaker is as good at evoking the unsaid as Ray. We often know (or think we know) what one of his characters is thinking and feeling, without a single word of dialogue. Momentarily, we become a simple Bengali peasant, or a Calcutta business executive on holiday. This ability to create a sense of intimate connection between men and women of vastly different cultures is Ray's greatest achievement. More than any of his contemporaries in world cinema, he can create an awareness of universal man, and he doesn't do it in the abstract, but rather by using the simplest, most common and concrete details—a gesture, a glance, a sound of human effort. His realism is greater than his master De Sica's because it goes straight into the mythic while retaining its pungent surface detail.

Another reason Ray's best films speak to so many is that they employ, quite consciously, the rhythms of the universal language of music. Western musical forms (sonata, theme and variations) have often provided Ray with his basic structures. For instance, Ray has said that when he made *Days and Nights in the Forest* he had Mozart in mind. But which Mozart? Not the Mozart of the symphonies or the quartets and trios, I think, but the Mozart of *Don Giovanni*, *Cosi Fan Tutti*, and *The Marriage of Figaro*. In these operas the quicksilver movement between voices (different attitudes, ways of look-ing at the world) reaches the highest level of artistic play (*juego* in the Cer-vantes-like sense of inspired artistic freedom through invention). We have only to think of the musical rhythms of camera movement and cutting in the wonderful word game toward the end of *Days and Nights in the Forest*.

Such consummate artistry has been achieved under the most difficult cir-cumstances, for the best technology of film production has not always been available to Ray. Working under severe budgetary constraints, and with less than state-of-the-art technology, he has made masterpieces. Often, this has involved what he calls "editing in the camera," which I take to mean planning the shot very carefully in advance and then stopping the shot close to where the actual cut will be made in final editing. He's proud of saying that his ratio is 1 to 2 or 1 to 3, meaning that he usually needs three shots at the most to get the one he'll use in the final print.[1] His films aren't technically perfect (as are many North American films with their emphasis on technological invention) but they preserve an inner spirit.

The most common criticism of Ray one encounters, particularly in India, is the charge that he has failed to present urgent contemporary social and political issues. "Wherever Ray forays into contemporary urban life, he fal-ters. Whenever he tries to present his characters in the social context, the reality eludes him."[2] This comment, by the head of India's large and pow-erful government-funded film directorate, is only partially accurate as I've attempted to prove. It's the "company line" on Ray (or, as they say in sports in the U.S., it's the "book" on him). *Jana Aranya (The Middleman)* disproves it. The success of *Jana Aranya* was hard-earned. It took Ray three films in an urban setting (*Mahanagar [The Big City]*, *Pratidwandi [The Adver-sary]*, and *Seemabaddha [Company Limited]*) before he could demonstrate his skill in rendering an environment that was not his most congenial subject. But what about the more serious charge of Ray's calculated avoidance of political activism in his films? Ray has said that once a character commits himself to radical politics, he becomes less interesting (Siddhartha's brother Tunu in *Pratidwandi*, for example).[3] According to this logic, because a character decides to pursue radical politics, he is denied the complicated, subtle personal characteristics that we know don't disappear with political activity (the activity articulates them in a political context). Political activism is dismissed as a worthwhile, interesting area of human expression. Ray's urban films give, in detail, all the reasons for political action and yet fail to endorse that action, presumably because, in the long run, it won't really accomplish anything. Political activism is thus presented as an illusionary activity, an exercise in futility, or, as in the character of Sandip in *The Home and the World*, an act of unscrupulous self-aggrandizement. Perhaps this is the wisdom of Indian fatalism, but it doesn't go down very well for a Western viewer, or, for that matter, a fairly large number of articulate Indian viewers, to judge by the criticism Ray has received. Ray's Brahmo high-mindedness, which I discuss in the chapter on Tagore, may also be at work here. A Marxist could argue that he represents an essentially middle-class view. On the other hand, an argument of *perhaps* equal validity might stress that Ray gives us a break from politics; that he reminds us that man may be essentially nonpolitical. This attitude seems, however, to be increasingly untenable in a time when politics seems more and more to impinge on human conduct. To accuse Ray of lacking a social conscience, as some have done, is absurd. He simply believes that political advocacy damages his art.

Ray's greatest weakness seems to me to be the uncertain incorporation in his films of Marx (radical politics) and Freud (the unconscious), the two seminal thinkers of the early part of our century. His attempts to enter the unconscious life of his characters through dreams or nightmares (in *Nayak*, *Pratidwandi*, or *Seemabaddha*) is often wooden and schematic. It suggests an intelligence that can think through such presentations on a rational level but has difficulty bringing the subliminal, the subconscious into play. He's best, as I remarked in the chapter on *Pratidwandi*, when his investigation slides into the borderline area between full consciousness and sleep—in daydream or states of meditation.

Ray's distance from some of the problematic concerns of the twentieth century is also seen in his presentation of sex and violence. His presentation of sex has been circumscribed by the long-held tradition in Indian film that kissing (not to speak of other acts) cannot be presented on the screen. He's no prude, however. Perhaps the first direct kissing scene in Indian film is shown in *The Home and the World*. His presentation of violence is another matter. Unlike most directors today, he has a strong aversion to the direct presentation of violence. In *Pather Panchali*, his first film, little Apu witnesses a beating given to one of his schoolmates. As the beating begins, we have a shot of Apu's frightened but absorbed face and then a long shot of the schoolhouse from across the pond, the sound of the beating barely audible. There's no shot of the beating itself. When Marie Seton pointed out to Ray that the fight scene in *Abhijan* lacked realism, he gave her a characteristic reply: "Violence in the contemporary world is of a mean and petty variety compared to the heroic violence of the distant past."[4] Still, it's important to remember that Ray can present violence powerfully and directly, as in the scene in which the women attack and kill the rapist in *Distant Thunder*.

In an interview with Derek Malcolm, Ray offered an opinion which seems, at first, to contradict his words to Seton:

Somehow I feel that an ordinary person—the man in the street if you like—is a more challenging subject for exploration than people in the heroic mould. It is the half shades, the hardly audible notes that I want to capture and explore. There is also the fact that violence in our country somehow becomes debased. An element of pettiness, of crudity, creeps in. And that repels me. Of course, there's a kind of mystique of violence in the West. But we don't have that. I cannot imagine any Indian raising evil to the level of a work of art, like Bunuel. In any case, I am another kind of person, one who finds muted emotions more interesting and challenging.[5]

Ray's aversion to the rougher edges of contemporary life is palpable in these remarks. If there seems something vaguely patrician in his words, we must remember that nowhere in his films does he present peasants, laborers, or the unemployed with condescension. After all, I would argue that his presentation of reality is as valid as the visions, say, of two of his finest contemporaries in Indian film: Ritwik Ghatak and Mrinal Sen, both of them passionate believers in political activism. We in the West know now that Ray didn't "invent" serious Indian film, that Ghatak's *Ajantrik* (1958) and his unforgettable *Meghe Dhaka Tara* (1960) occurred at the same time as the Apu trilogy. Why should Ray be asked to speak in the same voice as Ghatak and Sen—particularly when he is so successful in evoking the shades and half-tones he prefers? As for his interest in the historical past, why, by the same reasoning, should he be criticized when he evokes the past so eloquently? After all, Kurosawa isn't criticized in Japan (which, admittedly, has a stronger social order) for his near obsession with dramas of medieval Japanese warlords.

Ray's strengths have given us eight masterpieces: the three films from the Apu trilogy, *Jalsaghar (The Music Room)*, *Postmaster*, *Charulata*, *Aranyer din Ratri (Days and Nights in the Forest)*, and *Pikoo's Day*. These films will live a long time. In their magnificent flow of images they evoke an attitude of acceptance and detachment which is profoundly Indian. This attitude depicts the nobility of man's struggle against a predetermined fate, since man cannot change the circumstances of his birth nor the surety of his death.

This struggle is portrayed with compassionate detachment and calmness—a serenity, a lack of restlessness, anxiety, and fear which we in the West would do well to attend to.

NOTES

1. Conversation between author and Satyajit Ray, Calcutta, July 10, 1985.

2. Raghunath Raina in the introduction to *The Cinema of Satyajit Ray* by Chidinanda Das Gupta (New Delhi: Vikas, 1980), p. iii.

3. See Udayan Gupta, "The Politics of Humanism," *Cineaste* 12 (1982): 24–29.

4. Quoted in Marie Seton's *Satyajit Ray* (Bloomington: Indiana University Press, 1971), p. 282.

5. Quoted in Derek Malcolm, "Satyajit Ray," *Sight and Sound* 51 (Spring 1982): 109.

FILMOGRAPHY

1955 *Pather Panchali (Song of the Little Road)*
   Produced by government of West Bengal; *Script and direction*, Satyajit Ray, based on the novel by Bibhuti Bhusan Bannerjee; *Photograpy*, Subrata Mitra; *Art direction*, Bansi Chandragupta; *Music*, Ravi Shankar; *Editing*, Dulal Dutta. *Main actors:* Kanu Bannerjee (Harihar Ray), Karuna Bannerjee (Sarbojaya), Subir Bannerjee (Apu), Runki Bannerjee (Durga at six years old), Uma Das Gupta (Durga at twelve years old), Chunibala Devi (Indir); 115 minutes, black and white; Best Human Document, Cannes, 1956; U.S. distributor as of 1987, Films Incorporated.

1956 *Aparajito (The Unvanquished)*
   Produced by Epic Films; *Script and direction*, Satyajit Ray, based on the novel by Bibhuti Bhusan Bannerjee; *Photography*, Subrata Mitra; *Art direction*, Bansi Chandragupta; *Music*, Ravi Shankar; *Editing*, Dulal Dutta. *Main actors:* Kanu Bannerjee (Harihar Ray), Karuna Bannerjee (Sarbojaya), Pinaki Sen Gupta (Apu as a child), Smaran Ghosal (Apu as an adolescent), Subodh Ganguly (school director), Charuprakash Ghosh (Nanda-babu), Kali Charan Ray (press owner), Ramani Sen Gupta (uncle); 113 minutes, black and white; Golden Lion, Venice, 1957; U.S. distributor as of 1987, Films Incorporated.

1957 *Parash Pather (The Philosopher's Stone)*
   Produced by L.B. Films International: *Script and direction*, Satyajit Ray, based on a short story by Parashuram; *Photography*, Subrata Mitra; *Art direction*, Bansi Chandragupta; *Music*, Ravi Shankar; *Editing*, Dulal Dutta. *Main actors:* Tulsi Chakravarty (Paresh Dutta), Ranibala Devi (Giribala Dutta), Kali Bannerjee (Priyatosh Biswas), Gangapada Basu (businessman), Haridhan Chatterjee (police inspector); 111 minutes, black and white.

1958 *Jalsaghar (The Music Room)*
   Produced by Satyajit Ray Productions; *Script and direction*, Satyajit Ray, based

on a short story by Tarashankar Bannerjee; *Photography*, Subrata Mitra; *Art direction*, Bansi Chandragupta; *Music*, Vilayat Khan and others; *Editing*, Dulal Dutta. *Main actors:* Chhabi Biswas (Biswambhar Roy), Padma Devi (Roy's wife), Gangapada Basu (Mahim Ganguli), Tulsi Lahiri (head servant), Kali Sarkar (servant), Begum Akhtar (singer), Ustad Wahid Khan (singer), Roshan Kumari (dancer); 100 minutes, black and white; U.S. distributor as of 1987, Films Incorporated.

1959 *Apur Sansar (The World of Apu)*

Produced by Satyajit Ray Productions; *Script and direction*, Satyajit Ray, based on the novel by Bibhuti Bhusan Bannerjee; *Photography*, Subrata Mitra; *Art direction*, Bansi Chandragupta; *Music*, Ravi Shankar; *Editing*, Dulal Dutta. *Main actors:* Soumitra Chatterjee (Apu), Sharmila Tagore (Aparna), Swapan Mukherjee (Pulu), Aloke Chakravarty (Kajal); 106 minutes, black and white; Best Original and Imaginative Film, London, 1960; U.S. distributor as of 1987, Films Incorporated.

1960 *Devi (The Goddess)*

Produced by Satyajit Ray Productions; *Script and direction*, Satyajit Ray, based on a story by Prabhat Mukherjee; *Photography*, Subrata Mitra; *Art direction*, Bansi Chandragupta; *Music*, Ravi Shankar; *Editing*, Dulal Dutta. *Main Actors:* Chhabi Biswas (Kalikinkar Roy), Soumitra Chatterjee (Umaprasad), Sharmilla Tagore (Doyamoyee), Karuna Banerjee (Harisundari), Purnendu Mukherjee (Tarapada); 93 minutes, black and white; U.S. distributor as of 1987, Films Incorporated.

1961 *Rabindranath Tagore* (Documentary)

Produced by Films Division, government of India; *Script direction and narration*, Satyajit Ray; *Photography*, Soumendu Roy; *Art direction*, Bansi Chandragupta; *Music*, Jyotirindra Moitra; *Editing*, Dulal Dutta. *Main actors:* Smaran Ghosal (Tagore as an adolescent), Raya Chatterjee, Shovanlal Gangopadhyaya, Purnendu Mukherjee, Kalol Bose; 54 minutes, black and white.

1961 *Teen Kanya (Three Daughters)*. Released internationally as *Two Daughters* with the omission of *Monihara*.

Produced by Satyajit Ray Productions; *Script, direction, and music*, Satyajit Ray, based on three stories by Rabindranath Tagore; *Photography*, Soumendu Roy; *Art direction*, Bansi Chandragupta; *Editing*, Dulal Dutta. *Main actors: Postmaster* section: Anil Chatterjee (Nandalal), Chandana Bannerjee (Ratan). *Monihara* section: Kali Bannerjee (Phanibhusan Shaha), Kanika Mazumdar (Monimalika), Kumar Roy (Madhusudan). *Samapti* section: Soumitra Chatterjee (Amulya), Aparna Das Gupta (Mrinmoyee); 171 minutes for *Three Daughters*; 114 minutes for *Two Daughters*, black and white; U.S. distributor as of 1987, Films Incorporated.

1962 *Kanchanjungha*

Produced by N.C.A. Productions; *Original script, direction, and music*, Satyajit Ray; *Photography*, Subrata Mitra; *Art direction*, Bansi Chandragupta; *Editing*, Dulal Dutta. *Main actors:* Chhabi Biswas (Indranath Choudhury), Karuna Bannerjee (Labanya), Anubha Gupta (Anima), Pahari Sanyal (Jagadish), Alakananda Roy (Monisha), Subrata Sen (Shankar), Arun Mukerjee (Ashok), Anil Chatterjee (Anil); 102 minutes, color; U.S. distributor as of 1987, Films Incorporated.

1962 *Abhijan (The Expedition)*
Produced by Abhijatrik; *Script, direction, and music*, Satyajit Ray, based on a novel by Tarashankar Bannerjee; *Photography*, Soumendu Roy; *Art direction*, Bansi Chandragupta; *Editing*, Dulal Dutta. *Main actors:* Soumitra Chatterjee (Narsingh), Waheeda Rehman (Gulabi), Robi Ghosh (Rama), Ruma Guha Thakurta (Mary Neelima), Gyanesh Mukherjee (Joseph), Charuprakash Ghosh (Sukhanram); 150 minutes, black and white.

1963 *Mahanagar (The Big City)*
Produced by R. D. Bansal; *Script, direction, and music*, Satyajit Ray, based on a novel by Narendranath Mitra; *Photography*, Subrata Mitra; *Art direction*, Bansi Chandragupta; *Editing*, Dulal Dutta. *Main actors:* Madhabi Mukherjee (Arati Mazumdar), Anil Chatterjee (Subrata), Haren Chatterjee (Priyogopal), Haradhan Bannerjee (Mr. Mukherjee), Vicky Redwood (Edith), Jaya Bhaduri (Bani); 122 minutes, black and white; U.S. distributor as of 1987, Films Incorporated.

1964 *Charulata*
Produced by R. D. Bansal; *Script, direction, and music*, Satyajit Ray, based on a short story by Rabindranath Tagore; *Photography*, Subrata Mitra; *Art direction*, Bansi Chandragupta; *Editing*, Dulal Dutta. *Main actors:* Madhabi Mukherjee (Charulata), Soumitra Chatterjee (Amal), Sailen Mukherjee (Bhupati), Shyamal Ghosal (Umapada), Geetali Roy (Mandakini); 117 minutes, black and white; Best Direction, Berlin, 1965; U.S. distributor as of 1987, Trans-World Films.

1964 *Two* (Also known as *The Parable of Two*)
Produced by Esso; *Original script, direction, and music*, Satyajit Ray; *Photography*, Soumendu Roy; *Editing*, Dulal Dutta; *Main actor*, Rabi Kiron; 13 minutes, black and white; U.S. distributor as of 1987, Kit Parker Films.

1965 *Kapurush-o-Mahapurush (The Coward and the Holy Man)*
Produced by R. D. Bansal; *Script, direction, and music*, Satyajit Ray based on two stories by Premendra Mitra and Parashuram; *Photography*, Soumendu Roy; *Art direction*, Bansi Chandragupta; *Editing*, Dulal Dutta. *Main actors:* In *Kapurush:* Madhabi Mukherjee (Karuna), Soumitra Chatterjee (Amitabha Roy), Haradhan Bannerjee (Bimal Gupta). In *The Holy Man:* Charuprakash Ghosh (Birinchi), Robi Ghosh (the assistant); 139 minutes, black and white.

1966 *Nayak (The Hero)*
Produced by R. D. Bansal; *Original script, direction, and music*, Satyajit Ray; *Photography*, Subrata Mitra; *Art direction*, Bansi Chandragupta; *Editing*, Dulal Dutta; *Main actors:* Uttam Kumar (Arindam Mukherjee), Sharmila Tagore (Aditi), Sumita Sanyal (Promilla Chatterjee), Bharati Devi (Manorama Bose), Ranjit Sen (Haren Bose), Kanu Mukherjee (Pritish Sakar), Bimal Ghosh (Jyoti); 120 minutes, black and white; U.S. distributor as of 1987, Trans-World Films.

1967 *Chiriakhana (The Zoo)*
Produced by Star Productions; *Script, direction, and music*, Satyajit Ray based on a novel by Saradindu Bannerjee; *Photography*, Soumendu Roy; *Art direction*, Bansi Chandragupta; *Editing*, Dulal Dutta; *Main actors:* Uttam Kumar (Byomkesh Bakshi), Sailen Mukherjee, Sushil Mazumdar.

1968 *Goopy Gyne Bagha Byne (The Adventures of Goopy and Bagha)*
Produced by Purmina Pictures; *Script, direction, and music*, Satyajit Ray based

on a story by Upendrakishore Raychowdhury; *Photography*, Soumendu Roy; *Art direction*, Bansi Chandragupta; *Editing*, Dulal Dutta; *Main actors:* Tapen Chatterjee (Goopy), Robi Ghosh (Bagha), Santosh Dutta (King of Shundi, King of Halla), Jahar Roy (prime minister), Harindranath Chatterjee (the magician); 132 minutes, black and white, color; Best film, Melbourne, 1970.

1970 *Aranyer Din Ratri (Days and Nights in the Forest)*
Produced by Priya films; *Script, direction, and music*, Satyajit Ray based on a story by Sunil Ganguly; *Photography*, Soumendu Roy; *Art direction*, Bansi Chandragupta; *Editing*, Dulal Dutta; *Main actors:* Soumitra Chatterjee (Ashim), Sharmila Tagore (Aparna), Shubhendu Chatterjee (Sanjoy), Robi Ghosh (Shekar), Samit Bhanja (Hari), Simi Garewal (Duli), Pahari Sanyal (Sadasiv Tripathi), Kaberi Bose (Jaya), Aparna Sen (Hari's former lover); 115 minutes, black and white; U.S. distributor as of 1987, Corinth Films.

1970 *Pratidwandi (The Adversary)*
Produced by Priya films; *Script, direction, and music*, Satyajit Ray based on a novel by Sunil Ganguly; *Photography*, Soumendu Roy; *Art direction*, Bansi Chandragupta; *Editing*, Dulal Dutta; *Main actors:* Dhritiman Chatterjee (Siddhartha), Debraj Roy (Tunu), Krishna Bose (Sutapha), Jayashree Roy (Keya); 110 minutes, black and white; U.S. distributor as of 1987, Films Incorporated.

1971 *Sikkim* (documentary, out of distribution)
Produced by government of Sikkim; *Script, direction, music, and narration*, Satyajit Ray; *Photography*, Soumendu Roy; *Editing*, Dulal Dutta; 50 minutes (approx.), color.

1971 *Seemabaddha (Company Limited)*
Produced by Chitranjali; *Script, direction, and music*, Satyajit Ray based on a novel by Shankar; *Photography*, Soumendu Roy; *Art direction*, Ashoke Bose; *Editing*, Dulal Dutta; *Main actors:* Barun Chanda (Shyamalendu Chatterjee), Sharmila Tagore (Tutul), Paramita Chowdhury (Dolan); 112 minutes, black and white; U.S. distributor as of 1987, Films Incorporated.

1972 *The Inner Eye* (documentary)
Produced by Films division, government of India; *Script, direction, music, and narration*, Satyajit Ray; *Photography*, Soumendu Roy; *Editing*, Dulal Dutta; 20 minutes, color.

1973 *Ashani Sanket (Distant Thunder)*
Produced by Sarbani Bhattacharya; *Script, direction, and music*, Satyajit Ray based on a novel by Bibhuti Bhusan Bannerjee; *Photography*, Soumendu Roy; *Art direction*, Ashoke Bose; *Editing*, Dulal Dutta; *Main actors:* Soumitra Chatterjee (Gangacharan), Babita (Ananga), Sandhya Roy (Chhutki), Ramesh Mukherjee (Biswas), Chitra Bannerjee (Moti); 101 minutes, color; Golden Bear, Berlin, 1974; U.S. distributor as of 1987, Cinema Five.

1974 *Sonar Kella (The Golden Fortress)*
Produced by Ministry of Information, government of Bengal; *Original script, direction, and music*, Satyajit Ray; *Photography*, Soumendu Roy; *Art direction*, Ashoke Bose; *Editing*, Dulal Dutta; *Main actors:* Soumitra Chatterjee (Felu), Santosh Dutta (Lalmohan Ganguly), Kushal Chakravarty (Mukul), Kamu Mukherjee (Mandar Bose), Ajoy Bannerjee (Barman); 120 minutes, color.

1975 *Jana Aranya (The Middleman)*

Produced by Indus Films; *Script, direction, and music,* Satyajit Ray based on a novel by Shankar; *Photography,* Soumendu Roy; *Art direction,* Ashoke Bose; *Editing,* Dulal Dutta; *Main actors:* Pradip Mukherjee (Somnath), Satya Bandopadhyaya (his father), Lili Chakravarty (Kamala), Utpal Dutt (Bishuda), Robi Ghosh (Mitter), Soven Lahiri (Goenka); 131 minutes, black and white.

1976 *Bala* (documentary on dance)

Produced by National Center for Performing Arts and government of Tamil Nadu; *Script, direction, and. narration,* Satyajit Ray; *Photography,* Soumendu Roy; *Editing,* Dulal Dutta; 29 minutes, color.

1977 *Shatranj Ke Khilari (The Chess Players)*

Produced by Devki Chitra Productions; *Script, direction, and music,* Satyajit Ray based on a short story by Munshi Premchand; *Photography,* Soumendu Roy; *Art direction,* Bansi Chandragupta; *Editing,* Dulal Dutta; *Songs,* Reba Muhuri, Birjir Maharaj; *Choreography,* Birjir Maharaj; *Main actors:* Amjad Khan (Wajid Ali Shah), Sanjeev Kumar (Mirza), Saeed Jaffrey (Mir), Richard Attenborough (General Outram), Shabana Azmi (Mirza's wife), Farida Jalal (Mir's wife), Victor Bannerjee (prime minister), Tom Alter (Outram's aide de camp); 113 minutes, color; U.S. distributor as of 1987, Films Incorporated.

1979 *Joi Baba Felunath (The Elephant God)*

Produced by R. D. Bansal; *Original script, direction, and music,* Satyajit Ray; *Photography,* Soumendu Roy; *Art direction,* Ashoke Bose; *Editing,* Dulal Dutta; *Main actors:* Soumitra Chatterjee (Felu), Santosh Dutta (Lalmohan Ganguly), Siddhartha Chatterjee (Tapesh), Utpal Dutt (Maganlal), Jit Bose (Ruku), Manu Mukherjee (Machhli Baba); 112 minutes, color.

1980 *Hirok Rajar Deshe (The Kingdom of Diamonds)*

Produced by Ministry of Information, government of Bengal; *Original script, direction, and music,* Satyajit Ray; *Photography,* Soumendu Roy; *Art direction,* Ashoke Bose; *Editing,* Dulal Dutta; *Main actors:* Soumitra Chatterjee (Udayan), Utpal Dutta (king of Hirok), Robi Ghosh (Bagha), Tapen Chatterjee (Goopy), Santosh Dutta (scientist); 118 minutes, color.

1981 *Pikoo's Day*

Produced by Henri Fraise for French television; *Original script, direction, and music,* Satyajit Ray; *Photography,* Soumendu Roy; *Editing,* Dulal Dutta; *Main actors:* Arjun Guha-Thakurta (Pikoo), Aparn Sen (his mother), Victor Bannerjee (the lover), Soven Lahiri (the grandfather); 23 minutes, color.

1981 *Sadgati (Deliverance)*

Produced by Doodarshan Television; *Script, direction, and music,* Satyajit Ray based on a short story by Munshi Premchand; *Photography,* Soumendu Roy; *Editing,* Dulal Dutta; *Main actors:* Om Puri (Dukhi), Smita Patil (his wife), Mohan Agashe (Ghasiram); 50 minutes, color.

1984 *Ghare-Baire (The Home and the World)*

Produced by National Film Development Corporation of India; *Script, direction, and music,* Satyajit Ray based on a novel by Rabindranath Tagore; *Photography,* Soumendu Roy; *Art direction,* Ashoke Bose; *Editing,* Dulal Dutta; *Main actors:* Soumitra Chatterjee (Sandip), Victor Bannerjee (Nikhil), Swatilekha Chatterjee (Bimala), Gopa Aich (the sister-in-law), Manoj Mitra (the headmaster), Indrapramit Roy (Amulya), Jennifer Kapoor (Miss Gilby); 123 minutes, color.

BIBLIOGRAPHY

ON RAY

Books

Bahadur, Satish. *Satyajit Ray's Pather Panchali: Screenplay and Analytical Notes*. Privately printed at National Film Archives, Pune, 1981.

Barnouw, Erik, and S. Krishnaswamy. *Indian Film*. New York: Oxford University Press, 1980.

Burra, Rani, ed. *Looking Back, 1896–1960* [India's Early Cinema]. New Delhi: Directorate of Film Festivals, 1981.

Cowie, Peter, ed. *Fifty Major Filmmakers*. South Brunswick, N.J.: A. S. Barnes, 1975.

Da Cunha, Uma, ed. *The New Generation, 1960–1980* [India's New Cinema]. New Delhi: Directorate of Film Festivals, 1981.

Das Gupta, Chidananda. *The Cinema of Satyajit Ray*. New Delhi: Vikas, 1980.

————. *Satyajit Ray, An Anthology of Statements on Ray and by Ray*. New Delhi: Directorate of Film Festivals, 1981.

————. *Talking about Films*. Calcutta: Orient Longman, 1981.

Geduld, Harry M., ed. *Film Makers on Filmmaking*. Bloomington: Indiana University Press, 1967.

Houston, Penelope. *The Contemporary Cinema*. London: Penguin, 1963.

Kael, Pauline. *I Lost It at the Movies*. Boston: Little, Brown, 1965.

————. *Kiss, Kiss, Bang, Bang*. Boston: Little, Brown, 1965.

————. *Reeling*. Boston: Little, Brown, 1972.

————. *When the Lights Go Down*. New York: Holt, Rinehart and Winston, 1980.

Kaufmann, Stanley. *A World on Film*. New York: Delta, 1966.

Micciollo, Henri. *Satyajit Ray*. Lausanne: Editions l'Age d'Homme, 1981.

Rangoonwalla, Firoze. *Satyajit Ray*. New Delhi: Clarion, 1980.
Ray, Satyajit. *The Apu Trilogy*. Calcutta: Seagull Books, 1985.
———. "On Charulata." Unpublished essay written in Bengali and translated into English by Kiron Raha.
———. *Our Films, Their Films*. Calcutta: Orient Longman, 1976.
———. *Stories*. Calcutta: Seagull Books, 1987.
Rhode, Eric. *Tower of Babel*. London: Weidenfield and Nicholson, 1966.
Sarris, Andrew. *Interviews with Film Directors*. New York: Avon, 1969.
Sen, Mrinal. *Views on Cinema*. Calcutta: Ishan, 1977.
Seton, Marie. *Satyajit Ray: Portrait of a Director*. Bloomington: Indiana University Press, 1971.
Taylor, John Russell. *Directors and Directions*. New York: Hill and Wang, 1975.
Tyler, Parker. *Classics of the Foreign Film*. New York: Citadel, 1967.
Wood, Robin. *The Apu Trilogy*. New York: Praeger, 1971.

Articles

Allen, W., and R. Spikes. "Satyajit Ray." *Stills* 1 (Autumn 1981): 40–48.
Armes, Roy. "Satyajit Ray: Astride Two Cultures." *Films and Filming* (August 1982): 6–11.
Buruma, Ian. "The Last Bengali Renaissance Man." *New York Review of Books* 38 (November 19, 1987): 12–16.
Bosson, R. "Satyajit Ray: Cineaste des Contrastes." *Revue de Cinema* (May 1982): 71–84.
Blue, James. "Satyajit Ray." *Film Comment* 4 (Summer 1968): 4–17.
Ciment, M., ed. Special sections of *Positif* devoted to Ray (May/June 1979).
Croce, Arlene. "'Pather Panchali' and 'Aparajito'." *Film Culture* 19 (April 1959): 44–50.
———. "'The World of Apu'." *Film Culture* 21 (n.d.): 62–65.
Das Gupta, C., and A. Robinson. "A Passage to India." *American Film* 11 (October 1985): 32–38.
Das Gupta, C. "Ray and Tagore." *Sight and Sound* 36 (Winter 1966–67): 30–34.
Decaux, E. "Entretien avec Satyajit Ray." *Cinematographe* (June 1985): 56–58.
Dutta, K. "Cinema in India: An Interview with Satyajit Ray's Cinematographers." *Filmmaker's Newsletter* 8 (January 1975): 32–33.
Glushanok, Paul. "On Ray." *Cineaste* 1 (Summer 1967): 3–6.
Gray, Hugh. "Satyajit Ray." *Film Quarterly* 12 (Winter 1958): 4–7.
Gupta, U. "The Politics of Humanism." *Cineaste* 12 (1982): 24–29.
Houston, Penelope. "Ray's *Charulata*." *Sight and Sound* 35 (Winter 1965–66): 31–33.
Isaksson, Folke. "Conversation with Satyajit Ray." *Sight and Sound* 30 (Summer 1961): 133–36.
Kael, Pauline. "Current Cinema." *New Yorker* 49 (March 17, 1973): 121–26.
Malcolm, D. "Satyajit Ray." *Sight and Sound* 51 (Spring 1982): 106–9.
Micciollo, H. "*Pather Panchali*." *Avant Scène du Cinema*, February 1, 1980, pp. 3, 5–20, 33–47.
Micciollo, H., J. Magny, and C. McMullin. "La Longue Patience du Regard dans l'Oeuvre de Satyajit Ray." *Cinema* (March 1981): 38–63.
Montage. Special issue (July 1966).

Ray, B. "Ray Off the Set." *Sight and Sound* 53 (Winter 1983–84): 52–55.

Ray, Satyajit. "Calm Without, Fire Within." *Show* 4 (April 1964): 86–87.

———. "Dialogue on Film." *American Film* 3 (July-August 1978): 39–50.

———. "From Film to Film." *Cahiers du Cinema in English* (1966): 12–19.

———. "A Long Time on the Little Road." *Sight and Sound* 26 (Spring 1957): 203–5.

———. "Renoir in Calcutta." *Sequence* (1950): 146–50.

Rhode, Eric. "Satyajit Ray." *Sight and Sound* 30 (Summer 1961): 133–36.

Robinson, Andrew. "Bombay, Columbo, Calcutta." *Sight and Sound* 54 (Summer 1975): 182–86.

———. "A Conversation with Satyajit Ray." *Films and Filming* (August 1982): 12–22.

———. "The Inner Eye: Aspects of Satyajit Ray." *Illustrated London Magazine* 22 (October 1982): 885–92.

Roy, Karuna Shankar. "The Artist in Politics: From an Interview with Satyajit Ray in *Kolkata*, May, 1970." *Drama Review* 15 (Spring 1971): 310.

Seton, Marie. "Satyajit Ray at Work on his Film *Kanchanjunga*." *Sight and Sound* 31 (Spring 1962): 73–75.

Stanbrook, Alan. "The World of Ray." *Films and Filming* 12 (November 1965): 54–58.

Thomsen, Christian Braad. "Ray's New Trilogy." *Sight and Sound* 42 (Winter 1972–73): 31–33.

Films

Benegal, Shyam. *Satyajit Ray*. 1973.

Garga, B. D. *Satyajit Ray*. (n.d.)

General

Bhushan, Bibhuti. *Pather Panchali*. Bloomington: Indiana University Press, 1968.

Bose, Nemai Sadhan. *The Indian Awakening and Bengal*. Calcutta: K. L. Mukhopadhyay, 1969.

Chatterji, Bankim Chandra. *Rajmohan's Wife*. Calcutta: R. Chatterjee, 1935.

———. *Renaissance and Reaction in Nineteenth Century Bengal*. Columbia, Mo.: South Asia Books, 1977.

Furrell, James W. *The Tagore Family*. Calcutta: Thacker, Spink, 1892.

Kopf, David. *The Brahmo Samaj and the Shaping of the Modern Indian Mind*. Princeton: Princeton University Press, 1979.

Khanolkar, G. D. *The Lute and the Plow: A Life of Rabindranath Tagore*. Bombay: Book Center, 1963.

Kripalani, Krishna. *Rabindranath Tagore*. New York: Grove, 1962.

Lago, Mary M. *Rabindranath Tagore*. Boston: Twayne, 1976.

Ray, Niharranjan. *An Artist in Life: A Commentary on the Life and Works of Rabindranath Tagore*. Trivandrum: Kerala University Press, 1967.

Rhys, Ernest. *Rabindranath Tagore*. New York: Macmillan, 1970.

Roy, Samaren. *The Roots of Bengali Culture*. Calcutta: Eureka, 1966.

Sarkar, Sumit. *The Swadeshi Movement in Bengal*. New Delhi: People's, 1973.

Sarkar, Susobhan Chandra. *Bengal Renaissance and Other Essays*. New Delhi: People's, 1970.

Tagore, Rabindranath. *The Broken Nest*. Columbia, Mo.: University of Missouri Press, 1971.

———. *Gitanjali*. New York: Macmillan, 1971.

———. *Gora*. London: Macmillan, 1924.

———. *The Religion of Man*. London: Allen, Unwin, 1963.

———. *A Tagore Reader*. Boston: Beacon, 1961.

INDEX

ABOUT THE AUTHOR

BEN NYCE graduated from Princeton in 1954 and took his Ph.D. at Claremont Graduate School in 1967. He has been Fulbright Professor of American Literature at Rabat, Morocco and Nairobi, Kenya. He has published articles on literature and film in such journals as *Modern Language Quarterly* and *New Orleans Review*. Currently he is professor of literature and film at the University of San Diego.